Your Everlasting Life

Who Will You Be in Paradise?

DAVID CHARLES CRALEY

LifeRich Publishing is a registered trademark of The Reader's Digest Association, Inc.

LifeRich Publishing books may be ordered through booksellers or by contacting:

LifeRich Publishing
1663 Liberty Drive
Bloomington, IN 47403
www.liferichpublishing.com
844-686-9607

Because of the dynamic nature of the Internet, any web addresses or links contained in this book may have changed since publication and may no longer be valid. The views expressed in this work are solely those of the author and do not necessarily reflect the views of the publisher, and the publisher hereby disclaims any responsibility for them.

ISBN: 978-1-4897-4081-6 (sc)
ISBN: 978-1-4897-4082-3 (e)

Print information available on the last page.

LifeRich Publishing rev. date: 03/23/2022

"For the gifts and the calling of God
are irrevocable."

–Romans 11:29 (REV)

CONTENTS

INTRODUCTION

The Hope of Glory...an Anchor of the Soul

Years ago when I was a member of the staff of a vibrant biblical research and teaching center in the Midwest, while soaking up the great principles and truths of biblical accuracy and integrity in class after class, as well as during Sunday night teaching sessions, in our worship services we loved to raise our voices as one in singing some of the great old gospel hymns. One of our favorites spoke of this world not being our home, but that we are merely passing through. Alas, I learned years later from Bible teachers a lot smarter than I that not all of the song lyrics we used to sing in church were biblically accurate.

The Bible clearly informs us that believers in Jesus Christ will spend some amount of time in heaven—the spiritual abode of God—and that we will participate in the awesome events described by Paul as "the Judgement Seat of Christ"—a time of glorious thanksgiving and rejoicing for most—because it is "Christ in you, the hope of glory." However, the Apostle Paul's prophecy of "the hope of glory" holds promise far beyond the Christian believer's short adventure in heaven, as the chapters of this biblical research study propose.

Indeed, "Christ in you, the hope of glory"--the phenomenal truth revealed by Paul in Colossians 1:27 and 28 (REV)--should be an anchor of the soul for every Christian believer: "God wanted to make known to them [His "holy ones"-- the "saints"] what is the riches of the glory of this Sacred Secret among the Gentiles, which is Christ in you, the hope of glory. We proclaim him, admonishing everyone and teaching everyone, with all wisdom, so that we can present everyone mature in Christ." And in Hebrews 6:18 and 19 (REV) Paul states: "...so that by two unchangeable things, in *each of* which it is impossible for God to lie, we have strong encouragement, we who have found refuge in laying hold of the hope set before us. We have this *hope* as an anchor for the soul, both sure and steadfast, and extending into the inner part of the veil, where, as a forerunner, Jesus entered for us...."

In the Bible God uses the concept of "hope" to refer to the things He has promised His people but which are not yet available. In the Greek text of the New Testament, the word for "hope" is *elpis,* meaning a "joyful and confident expectation of eternal salvation," according to Strong's Lexicon. The word "hope" is never used in the Bible in the secular sense of "wish" or that something has a reasonable chance of coming to pass. It is used only in the sense that which God promises will *absolutely* come to pass in His timing. For example, Titus 1:1,2 (REV) begins: "Paul, a servant of God and an apostle of Jesus Christ, for the sake of the trust of God's chosen and their knowledge of the truth that leads to godliness, in hope of life *in the Age to come,* which God, who never lies, promised long ages ago...."

The Bible has much to say about God's promises of everlasting life for those who believe-- about Israel's hope of "inheriting the land," about the Rapture of the Christian Church, about the second coming of Jesus Christ to the earth, about the Judgment Seat of Christ, about the fabulous spiritual "gifts of grace" Christ gives to His people in this life, about the Millennial Kingdom to come, and about Paradise restored to the earth. In His Word God presents and enlarges upon these wonderful promises in order that His people, both Christians and Jews, might have hope—a "joyful and confident expectation"—a veritable "anchor of the soul"—an anchor that inspires vision, conviction, and steadfast faithfulness to Him. Having hope as an anchor of the soul energizes and strengthens God's people to endure pressures and hardships in this life. People who have no hope for the future tend to become defeated, unable to cope with adversity. Hopeless people give up. To remain faithful to the Lord, to love Him, to serve Him, and to love and serve fellow believers day in and day out—with "the hope of glory" set before us—requires an enduring hope that anchors one's soul.

Sadly, many Christians do not realize that a vital aspect of "the hope of glory" is the promise of spiritual rewards for one's service and faithfulness in this life to be given by the Lord Jesus Christ Himself at the Judgment Seat of Christ. The Scriptures reveal in detail that Christ enables each of His followers with specific spiritual gifts in order to guide and help them to serve effectively in the building up and strengthening of the Church in love. How well a believer learns to function in his or her spiritual gifts in this life will greatly affect his identity, his function in the Millennial Kingdom, and his reign with Christ in his everlasting life in both the Millennial and Everlasting Kingdoms to come.

Israel's Hope

The Old Testament informs us that the "hope" of the historical Children of Israel was God's promise that they would "inherit the land." Their hope was never for eternity in heaven, and God never promised them heaven. In fact, the prophet Ezekiel makes it clear that faithful believers in God in Old Testament times will be resurrected in God's timing and go directly into "the land"—in the Millennial Kingdom. No prophecy or scripture whatsoever suggests that the Children of Israel will spend any time in heaven. "Therefore prophesy and say to them, 'Thus says the Lord God: 'Behold, O My people, I will open your graves and cause you to come up from your graves, and bring you into the land of Israel'" [Ezekiel 37:12 NKJV]. Psalm 37:9-11(NKJV) states: "For evildoers shall be cut off; but those who wait on the Lord, they shall inherit the earth. For yet a little while and the wicked shall be no more; indeed, you will look carefully for his place, but it shall be no more. But the meek shall inherit the earth, and shall delight themselves in the abundance of peace." And Isaiah 57:13b (NKJV): "...he who puts his trust in Me shall possess the land, and shall inherit My holy mountain." And Revelation 5:9 and 10 (REV): "And they were singing a new song, saying: 'Worthy are you to take the scroll and to open its seals, for you were slain, and purchased for God with your blood *people* of every tribe, and tongue, and people, and nation, and made *to be* a kingdom and priests to our God, and they will reign on the earth."

God promised Abraham and his descendants that they would inherit the land forever: "...for all the land which you [Abraham] see I give you and your descendants forever" [Genesis 13:15 NKJV]. "On the same day the Lord made a covenant with Abram, saying: 'To your descendants I have given this land, from the river of Egypt to the great river, the River Euphrates" [Genesis 15:18 NKJV]. Israel's hope has forever been to inherit the land promised to them by God.

The Christian's Hope

In contrast to Israel, Christians living or "asleep in Christ" will be "caught up together"—"raptured" (from the Latin Vulgate *rapturo*)—"in the clouds for a meeting with the Lord in the air, and in this manner, we will always be with the Lord" [1 Thessalonians 4:17 REV]. The question is: If Christians will "always be with the Lord," where will the Lord be? A number of prophesies inform us that Jesus Christ will return to the earth in God's timing and reign in His Millennial Kingdom for 1000 years. And Paul tells us in 1 Thessalonians 3:13 (NKJV) that when Christ comes back to the earth, He comes with "all His saints," which means all Christians, along with His holy angels: "Behold, the Lord comes with ten thousands of His saints" [*hagios*—"most holy thing"--Jude 14 NKJV]. And 2 Thessalonians 1:7 (REV): "...and to give relief to you who are being afflicted, as well as to us, when the Lord Jesus is revealed from heaven with his powerful angels" [*aggelon*—"angelic messenger"]. And also Matthew 25:31 (REV): "But when the Son of Man comes in his glory, and all the angels with him, then he will sit on his glorious throne" [in the new temple in Jerusalem].

The Christian's hope is to be transformed into the likeness of Christ's glorious body [Philippians 3:21 REV], to be rewarded for faithfulness at the Judgment Seat of Christ [2 Corinthians 5:10 REV], and ultimately to reign with Christ in everlasting life beginning in the Millennial Kingdom: for you "have purchased for God with your blood *people* of every tribe, and tongue, and people, and nation, and have made them *to be* a kingdom and priests to our God; and they will reign on the earth" [Revelation 5:9,10 REV].

Thus the abundant biblical evidence is clear: Both Christians and Old Testament believers ultimately share a common destiny--Paradise *restored* to the earth where we will enjoy everlasting life together.

"My people are destroyed for lack of knowledge."

-Hosea 4:6 (NKJV)

In his day the Prophet Hosea cried out to the Children of Israel: "My people are destroyed for lack of knowledge." Sadly, this is also true of many of God's people today. Although many Christians believe that they will spend their everlasting lives in heaven with God, the angels, and all of their loved ones, clearly this is not what the Bible teaches. The old gospel hymn we used to sing in church about this world not being our home may have been a nice sentiment for those weary of this present world of trouble, toil, and heartache, but the world to come— Paradise restored--*is* our promised destiny for both Jews and Christians in companionship with the Lord Christ Himself.

As well, Christians need to understand that, as members of the spiritual Body of Christ—the true Church--how well we learn to function in our specific gifts in the Church and in our lives will absolutely affect the quality of our destiny in the Millennial Kingdom to come. Because "the gifts and the calling of God are irrevocable" [Romans 11:29 REV]. They are a part of us and will go with us and will characterize our identity forever.

In the chapters that follow, the reader will discover that God has never given up on His original plan for humanity—Paradise on earth. As well, you will learn to recognize your own spiritual gifts and how to function in them effectively in your life, providing you with remarkable insight into *who you will be* and *what you will be doing* in Paradise. Because the Christian's "hope of glory" is for everlasting life beginning in the Millennial Kingdom where we will reign with the Lord Jesus Christ in a fabulous Paradise restored to the earth.

ONE

Your Everlasting Life

"Truly, truly, I say to you, whoever
believes *has life in the Age to come.*"
-John 6:47(REV)

"For God so loved the world," Jesus says in John 3:16 (REV), "that he gave his
only begotten Son, so that whoever believes in him will not perish but have
everlasting life." And in Galatians 6:7 and 8 (REV), the Apostle Paul states:
"Do not be deceived, God is not mocked; for whatever a person sows, that
he will also reap. For the one who sows to his own flesh will from the flesh
reap corruption; but whoever sows to the spirit will of the spirit reap life in
the Age to come."

In this opening chapter, I present the following essential biblical
propositions regarding "everlasting life:"

★One: God has promised everlasting life to all who believe in His Son,
Jesus Christ. Jesus says: "Truly, truly, I say to you, whoever believes has life
in the Age to come" [John 6:47 REV].

★Two: Old Testament believers in God and in His promise of the Messiah,
and all Christians who have died, are not now alive in heaven. Solomon says:
"For the living know that they will die; but the dead know nothing, and they
have no more reward..." [Ecclesiastes 9:5 NKJV].

★Three: Old Testament believers in God and in His promise of the
Messiah, along with all Christians who have died, will be made alive at the
second coming of Jesus Christ. Jesus says: "Do not be amazed at this; for the

hour is coming for which all who are in the tombs will hear his voice and will come out…" [John 5:28,29 REV].

    ★ Four: Old Testament believers in God and in His promise of the Messiah, along with all Christians, will enjoy everlasting life on the earth in Paradise restored at the second coming of Jesus Christ. Consider "Israel's Hope" and "The Christian's Hope" in the Introduction.

A RECORD IN JOHN CHAPTER 4 regarding Jesus' discussion with the woman at Jacob's well arrests our attention. "So He came to a city of Samaria which is called Sychar, near the plot of ground that Jacob gave to his son Joseph. Now Jacob's well was there. Jesus therefore, being wearied from *His* journey, sat thus by the well. It was about the sixth hour. A woman of Samaria came to draw water. Jesus said to her, 'Give Me a drink.' For His disciples had gone away into the city to buy food. Then the woman of Samaria said to Him, 'How is it that You, being a Jew, ask a drink from me, a Samaritan woman?' For Jews have no dealings with Samaritans. Jesus answered and said to her, 'If you knew the gift of God, and who it is that says to you, 'Give Me a drink,' you would have asked Him, and He would have given you living water.' The woman said to Him, 'Sir, You have nothing to draw with, and the well is deep. Where then do You get that living water? Are You greater than our father Jacob, who gave us the well, and drank from it himself, as well as his sons and his livestock?' Jesus answered and said to her, 'Whoever drinks of this water will thirst again, but whoever drinks of the water that I shall give him will never thirst. But the water that I shall give him will become in him a fountain of water spring up into everlasting life'" [verses 5-14 NKJV].

    For our understanding, John 7:37-39 (NKJV) clarifies the Lord's strange statement to the woman at the well: "On the last day, that great *day* of the feast [Feast of Tabernacles], Jesus stood and cried out, saying, 'If anyone thirsts, let him come to Me and drink, He who believes in Me, as the Scripture has said, out of his heart will flow rivers of living water' [some versions read: "out of his belly," "innermost being," "from within him"]. But this He spoke concerning the Spirit, whom those believing in Him would receive; for the Holy Spirit was not yet *given*, because Jesus was not yet glorified." Here is the Lord's great prophecy of the outpouring of the gift of holy spirit, which occurred first to the apostles on the Day of Pentecost. Perhaps...just perhaps... the woman of Samaria to whom Jesus spoke at Jacob's well was alive following the Day of Pentecost and was one of the many referred to in Acts 2:47(REV): "...praising God, and having favor with all the people. And day after day the Lord was adding to them [the congregation] those who were being saved" (during the early growth of the First Century Church).

In John 6:40 (REV) Jesus says to the people in Capernaum: "For this is the will of my Father who sent me, that everyone who sees the Son and believes in him will have life *in the* Age *to come*; and I will raise him up at the last day." For the Children of Israel, their "last day" commencing everlasting life ["last day" is used idiomatically for the onset of the age to come] begins at the "resurrection of life" promised by Jesus in John 5:29 (NKJV). For the saints of the Church of the Body of Christ, their "last day" commencing everlasting life begins at the Rapture of the Church [1 Thessalonians 4:17 REV].

Everlasting life in the Age to come is a fundamental theme of everything Jesus teaches in the Four Gospels and everything we read in the Church Epistles of Paul, Peter and John. In Romans 6:22 (REV), Paul says to the Church: "But now that you have been set free from sin, and have become slaves to God, the fruit you get results in holiness and in the end, life *in the* Age *to come*." In his first letter to the Church, John writes: "And this is the testimony: that God gave to us life *in the* Age *to come*, and this life is in his Son. Whoever has the Son has life; whoever does not have the Son of God does not have life. I have written these things to you who believe in the name of the Son of God so that you can know that you have life *in the* Age" [1 John 5:11-13 REV]. And Peter exhorts believers: "Therefore, brothers, be all the more diligent to be sure of your calling and choice, for if you do these things [listed in verses 5-7] you will absolutely not stumble; for in this way entrance into the kingdom of our Lord and Savior Jesus Christ will be richly provided to you in the Age *to come*" [2 Peter 1:10,11 REV].

"We shall not all sleep, but we shall all be changed..."
-1 Corinthians 15:51 (REV)

Many people believe that when you die you go to heaven and live forever in glory. But that's not what the Bible says. Paul states in 1 Corinthians 15:51-54 (REV): "Look!, I tell you a sacred secret: we will not all sleep [euphemism for "die"], but we will all be changed. In a moment, in the blink of an eye, at the last trumpet, for the trumpet will sound, and the dead will be raised incorruptible, and we will be changed. For this corruptible [mortal] must put on incorruption [spiritual], and this mortal must put on immortality. But when this corruptible puts on incorruption, and this mortal puts on immortality, then the word that has been written will be brought to pass: 'Death is swallowed up in victory.'" And Paul enlarges on this theme in 1 Thessalonians 4:16-18 (REV): "For the Lord himself will descend from heaven with a loud command, with the voice of the archangel, and with the sound of the trumpet of God, and the dead in Christ will rise first. Then we who are alive, who are left, will be *suddenly* caught up together with them in the clouds for a meeting with the Lord in the air, and in this manner we will always be with the Lord. So then, encourage one another with these words." As well, Jesus Himself provides the believer with great encouragement by His promise in John 14:3 (REV): "And if I go and prepare a place for you, I will come again and will receive you to myself so that where I am you will be also."

In the Bible a few verses speak of Christians who are "sleeping in Christ." For example, 1 Corinthians 15:6 (REV) says "some [Christians] have fallen asleep;" and 1 Corinthians 11:30 (REV) says "For this reason [not discerning the Lord's body] many are weak and sick among you, and many sleep in death." This simply means that some believers have died. 1 Thessalonians 4:13-16 (REV), quoted above, explains it clearly: "But I do not want you to be ignorant, brethren, concerning those who have fallen asleep...even so God will bring with Him those who sleep in Jesus. For this we say to you by the word of the Lord, that we who are alive *and* remain until the coming of the Lord will by no means precede those who are asleep....And the dead in Christ—those who 'sleep in Jesus'--will rise first." Where are those who "sleep in Jesus"? They are dead, in the grave, awaiting the Rapture of the Church. And so "asleep in Christ" is merely a softened expression referring to those Christians who have died.

"...in a moment, in the blink of an eye, at the last trumpet."

-1 Corinthians 15:52 (REV)

1 Corinthians 15:52 (REV) states: "at the last trumpet" and "the trumpet will sound...." And 1 Thessalonians 4:16 (REV) also says: "and with the trumpet of God." The trumpet is a symbol of extraordinary consequence in both Old and New Testament prophecies. Joel 2:1 (NKJV): "Blow the trumpet in Zion, and sound an alarm in My holy mountain! Let all the inhabitants of the land tremble; for the day of the Lord is coming." And Zechariah 9:14-16 (NKJV): "Then the Lord will be seen over them [the nations], and His arrow will go forth like lightning. The Lord God will blow the trumpet, and go with whirlwinds from the south." These end times prophecies inform us that a trumpet, in effect, announces "the Day of the Lord," which is a process beginning with the Rapture of the Christian Church and ending with the actual return of Christ to the earth to fight the battle of Armageddon, subdue the rebellious nations, and establish His Millennial Kingdom.

In Matthew 24:29-31 (REV) Jesus prophesies: "Immediately after the tribulation of those days, the sun will be darkened and the moon will not give its light; and the stars will fall from heaven, and the powers of the heavens will be shaken, and then the sign of the Son of Man will appear in heaven, and then all the tribes of the earth will mourn, and they will see the Son of Man coming on the clouds of heaven with power and great glory. And He will send out His angels with a loud trumpet blast, and they will gather together His chosen *ones* from the four winds, from the one end of heaven to the other end of it." This describes Jesus Christ's second coming to the earth. In correspondence with this prophecy, John writes in Revelation 8:2 and 6 (REV): "And I saw the seven angels that stand before God, and seven trumpets were given to them....And the seven angels that had the seven trumpets prepared themselves to blow them." And in Revelation 11:15 (REV): "And the seventh angel blew his trumpet, and there were great voices in heaven *saying*, 'The kingdom of the world has become *the kingdom* of our Lord, and of his Christ, and he will reign forever and ever.'"

And so, the Rapture of the Church, which begins the process of "the Day of the Lord," is also preceded by a mighty trumpet blast. The fact that God inspires Paul to prophesy about the Rapture of the Church with the sound of the trumpet is significant, not only regarding the event itself, but also in light of the awesome events to follow. "For the trumpet will sound, and the dead will be raised incorruptible, and we shall be changed." How shall we be "changed"? Philippians 3:20, 21 (REV): "For our citizenship is in heaven, from which we also wait for a Savior, the Lord Jesus Christ, who will transform our lowly body so it will be like his glorious body, by the exertion of the power that he has, even to subject all things to himself." And in 1 Thessalonians 4:16,17 (REV) Paul reiterates that the dead in Christ [Christian believers only, not Old Testament believers] will rise from the dead first. Then we [Christians only] "who are alive and remain shall be *caught up together* with them in the clouds to a meeting with the Lord in the air. And in this manner we shall always be with the Lord." Christ does not return to the earth at this time. His second coming, prophesied in Matthew 24, is when Christ actually returns to the earth to establish His kingdom. However, the Rapture of the Church is when all Christians "meet the Lord in the air" prior to the events of the Judgment Seat of Christ, which will take place in heaven during the seven years of tribulation on the earth. Beginning with the Rapture, all Christians "shall always be with the Lord." The question arises: If Christians will always be with the Lord from this time forward, where will the Lord actually be?

"...caught up together with them in the clouds"
1 Thessalonians 4:17 (REV)

The word "rapture" does not appear in any English versions of the Bible. The New King James Version reads "caught up together." Other versions of the Bible say "taken up together" or "snatched (up) together." In the Greek text the single word for "caught up" is *harpazo* which means "catch up," "taken by force," "catch away," "pluck," or "pull." In the Latin Sacra (Vulgate), the phrase "caught up together" is *simul rapiemur. Rapiemur* is a conjugation of *rapio* from which has come the popular term "rapture." There is no suggestion in the text that the "Rapture" of the Church will indeed be rapturous, but it's a good bet. So because Christians "will always be with the Lord," it's important to understand where the Lord will be. Because wherever the Lord will be, all Christians will be with Him forever.

"...and the dead in Christ will rise first."
-1 Thessalonians 4:16b (REV)

As we have noted, few readers of the Bible understand that in 1 Corinthians 15 and 1 Thessalonians 4 the phrase "dead in Christ" does not mean "alive in glory in heaven," as many people believe. "Dead" in the Bible means *dead*—without life, without consciousness. Orthodox Christianity has for centuries taught that after death, the Lord designates a temporary place of repose for the soul—either heaven or hell. But that's not what the Scriptures tell us. Psalm 6:5 (NKJV): "For in death there is no remembrance of You; In the grave who will give You thanks?" Psalm 115:17 (NKJV): "The dead do not praise the Lord, nor any who go down into silence." Ecclesiastes 9:5 (NKJV): "For the living know that they will die; But the dead know nothing." Does that mean that even righteous King David, "a man after God's own heart," is dead? "Men *and* brothers, let me speak freely to you of the patriarch David, that he is both dead and buried, and his tomb is with us to this day" [Acts 2:29 REV]. But what about the "mighty cloud of witnesses" spoken of in Hebrews 11 and 12—Abel, Enoch, Noah, Abraham, Sarah, Isaac, Jacob, Joseph, Moses, Joshua, Rahab, Gideon, Samson, David, Samuel, and all the prophets—who many people believe are up in heaven cheering us on? Hebrews 11:13 (NKJV) says: "These all died in faith, not having received the promises...." Not having received *what* promises?—the promises of the resurrection from the dead and everlasting life in Paradise restored to the earth. "These all died in faith, not having received the promises, but having seen them afar off were assured of them, embraced them and confessed that they were strangers and pilgrims on the earth. For those who say such things declare plainly that they seek a homeland. And truly if they had called to mind that country from which they had come out, they would have had opportunity to return. But now they desire a better, that is, a heavenly country. Therefore God is not ashamed to be called their God, for He has prepared a city for them" [Hebrews 11:13-16 NKJV]. What promises did these faithful men and women embrace, what homeland, what heavenly country, what city? They longed for the fulfillment of God's promise to Abraham that Israel would "inherit the land"—the "new heaven and a new earth" and "the holy city, New Jerusalem" [Revelation 21:2 REV] which will all come to pass in the future in God's timing.

"...Elijah went up by a whirlwind into heaven."
2 Kings 2:11 (NKJV)

2 Kings 2:11 (NKJV) states that "Elijah went up by a whirlwind into heaven." Many Christians assume that this statement means that the Prophet Elijah was taken up by God to be with God, the angels, and the "mighty cloud of witnesses" in heaven. But that's not what Elijah's contemporaries believed. In fact 2 Kings 2:15 and 16 (NKJV) inform us that they believed that if they searched far and wide, they would find Elijah: "Now when the sons of the prophets who were from Jericho saw him [Elisha], they said, 'The spirit of Elijah rests on Elisha.' So they came to meet him and bowed to the ground before him. Then they said to him, 'Look now, there are fifty strong men with your servants. Please let them go and search for your master, lest perhaps the spirit of the Lord has taken him up and cast him upon some mountain or in some valley.'"

In the Bible "heaven" often refers to places other than the heavenly abode of God. Sometimes it refers to a place where birds fly or where rain and snow originate. Genesis 7:23 (NKJV) speaks of "the rain from heaven;" and 1 Kings 18:45 (NKJV) mentions "the clouds in heaven." Elijah's contemporaries knew that he was taken up into the air in a whirlwind but believed that he would eventually be set down somewhere. They believed that if they searched for him, they would find him. The truth of the matter is that God had told Elijah to anoint Elisha to succeed him as the prophet [1 Kings 19:6 NKJV]. Yet

Elisha could not assume leadership of the prophets as long as Elijah was still present. Therefore God graciously moved Elijah by means of a whirlwind to another location. Elijah was not taken up by God to be in the heavenly abode of God. Rather, he was taken up into the air and set down in another location to live out his days elsewhere. Elijah could not have gone into heaven to be with God because he lived before the time of Christ the Redeemer. The shed blood of Christ is the propitiation—payment in full—for every person's sin, including Elijah's. If Elijah was taken up into heaven to be with God, what need would there have been for the birth, ministry, crucifixion, death, and resurrection of the Son of God, Jesus Christ, in order to redeem mankind from their sins? Indeed, Hebrews 11 informs us that the faithful believers who are of the "mighty cloud of witnesses" *all died in faith*, not having received the promises of God that they would "inherit the land." And in John 3:13 (REV) Jesus says: "No one has gone up to heaven, but he who came down from heaven, the Son of Man, who is in heaven."

"...out of the body...at home with the Lord"
-2 Corinthians 5:8 (REV)

Some Bible scholars have assumed that Paul's declaration in 2 Corinthians 5:8: "We are of good courage, I say, and would prefer to be away from *this* home, out of the body, and to be at home with the Lord," means that when a Christian believer dies, he is therefore "out of the body" but immediately "present with the Lord" in heaven. Moreover, Paul says in Philippians 1:21 (REV): "For to me to live is Christ, and to die is gain." Thus some assume that Paul meant that this "gain" is to immediately be with Christ when a person dies. However, Paul says in verse 23: "Now I am hard pressed from the two *directions*, (having the intense desire for the return and to be with Christ, for it is very far better....)" Perhaps Paul was even thinking here of his revelation of the Church being "caught up [*harpazo*] together...to a meeting with the Lord in the air," which he presents in 1 Thessalonians 4:17 (REV). Here he is saying that it was his *desire* to depart his mortal body and to be with the Lord, but he was not making the case for death as a quick ticket to heaven to be with the Lord. If this were so, it would contradict the many Scriptures that inform us that "dead" in the Bible simply means "dead" and not alive in glory.

"Lazarus in Abraham's bosom"
-Luke 16 (REV)

Much confusion has arisen from a misinterpretation of Jesus' parable of "Lazarus in Abraham's bosom" from Luke 16 (REV). It has been suggested by some commentators that the point of this parable is that even after they die, people are still alive and immediately face the judgment of God. We must understand, however, that Jesus is simply telling a story—a parable, a figure of speech—and that he is specifically addressing the Pharisees who believed in rewards and punishments immediately upon death. Many people believe the same today. The point of Jesus' parable was to condemn the Pharisees by catching them in their erroneous beliefs. Thus this parable of the Lord must be interpreted in the light of the many Scriptures which teach us that in the Bible "dead" does not mean "alive" and awaiting the judgment of God. Misunderstanding arises when people try to take this teaching of the Lord literally. Verse 23 says: "And in the grave he lifted up his eyes, being in torment, and sees Abraham afar off, and Lazarus in his bosom." The people in Jesus' parable--Abraham, Lazarus, the rich man, and the beggar--were characters in a story and not literally alive in the grave or—as the NKJV reads "in Hades"-- and experiencing judgment. Jesus used these characters figuratively to make an impact on the Pharisees.

"Lazarus, come forth!"
-John 11:43 (REV)

John chapter 11(REV) begins: "Now a certain man was sick, Lazarus of Bethany, the village of Mary and her sister Martha. (And it was this Mary who anointed the Lord with perfume and wiped his feet with her hair, whose brother Lazarus was sick). Therefore the sisters sent to him, saying, "Lord, Look! he who is your friend is sick." As this true story, not a parable, unfolds, Jesus raises His friend Lazarus from the dead.

Verse 39 (REV): "Jesus says, 'Take away the stone.' Martha, the sister of the deceased, says to Him, 'Lord, by this time there will be a bad odor, for he has been *dead* four days.'" The fact that Jesus waited four days before going to Bethany to see Lazarus begs the question: *Why four days?* It is important to understand that according to the Jewish Kabbalah, which translated means "that which is received" based on mysticism and tradition passed down among Jewish mystics and rabbis for centuries, it was believed that when a person died, through the third day the spirit remained with the body so that there was still hope of resuscitation to life. This is why Jesus waited four full days to raise Lazarus from the dead—so that there could be absolutely no question that Lazarus was dead. One might wonder if Jesus' raising Lazarus from the dead after four days foretold the fact that Jesus Himself would be dead and buried for "three days and three nights," not only to fulfill His own prophecy [Matthew 12:40 REV], but also to satisfy Kabbalah tradition regarding the dead. One might also wonder—if Lazarus, loved by Jesus but dead and in the tomb four days—ascended to heaven immediately upon dying, as some people believe, and was up in glory with God and the angels—why in the name of God would Jesus pull him out of glorious heaven and bring him back to this veil of tears of a fallen world in order for him to have to die all over again? It would have been a ludicrous situation. Lazarus never ascended to heaven following his death. He was dead and in the grave four days. "I am the resurrection, and the life," Jesus assured Martha. "Whoever believes in me will live even if he dies, and whoever lives and believes in me will not ever die in the Age *to come*" [John 11:25 REV]. When will Lazarus live again? If Lazarus died the second time *prior* to the Day of Pentecost with the outpouring of the gift of holy spirit, he will be in "the resurrection of life" [John 5:28,29] awaiting all Jewish faithful. However, a good possibility is that after Jesus' resurrection, Lazarus may have been one of the "more than 500 brothers" [1 Corinthians 15:6 REV] to whom Jesus appeared, and it is possible that he was among the "about three thousand souls" who were baptized and became Christians as the result of Peter's sermon on the Day of Pentecost [Acts 2 REV]. If so, Lazarus—now "asleep in Christ"--will participate in the Rapture of the Church at the end of this age.

Sheol, Hades and Gehenna

It's an important fact of ancient history that after Alexander the Great conquered Palestine, now Israel, in 332 BC, within about 100 years most Jews were speaking and communicating in Greek and no longer speaking Hebrew. Thus it became necessary to develop a Greek translation of the twenty four books of the Hebrew Bible. This translation is known as the Septuagint because of the seventy scholars who did the work. Significantly, the translators chose the Greek word *hades* for *sheol* in many instances in the Hebrew text. Everywhere in the Hebrew text *sheol* meant "grave" or "gravedom," referring to the state or condition of the dead. However, the souls in Hades, according to Homer and ancient Greek myth and religion, are all alive. Thus, as the result of a mistranslation, dead souls in *hades* in the Septuagint were *made alive* in torment by imparting the imagery of the nether world of Greek mythology. Thus great confusion has persisted to this day in understanding the actual disposition of the dead. When the Greek texts of New Testament writings were translated into English in the late fourteenth century, the word Hades was used in ten instances. For example, Matthew 16:18 (NKJV): "And I also say to you that you are Peter, and on this rock I will build My church, and the gates of Hades shall not prevail against it." And Acts 2:27 (NKJV): "For David says concerning Him: 'I forsaw the Lord always before my face, for He is at my right hand, that I may not be shaken. Therefore my heart rejoiced, and my tongue was glad; Moreover my flesh shall also rest in hope. For You will not leave my soul in Hades.'" And Revelation 20:14 (NKJV): "Then Death and Hades were cast into the lake of fire." As the result of these mistranslations and misinterpretations, the word *sheol* from the Hebrew Old Testament, as well as Hades and also *gehenna,* which replaced *sheol* in the Greek translations of the Four Gospels in the first and early second centuries, were translated "hell" in most English versions of the Bible. Therefore in Western cultures today, it is believed that "hell" is a place where unrighteous souls of those who have died are yet alive and conscious and experiencing continuous torment now and forever. Many Bible scholars have found these mistranslations and misinterpretations as problematic because they contradict the meaning of *sheol* in the early Hebrew Old Testament writings.

The Greek word *gehenna,* translated "hell" throughout English versions of the Four Gospels, refers to a location outside the city walls of Jerusalem. The term *gehenna* was formed from the Hebrew for "Valley of Hinnom" which means "place of fire." In the times of the kings of Judah and Israel, it was a place where human sacrifice occurred. 2 Kings 23:10 (NKJV) tells how King Josiah, in his campaign of reformation, "defiled Topheth, which *is* in the Valley of the Son of Hinnom, that no man might make his son or his daughter pass through the fire to Molech." Years later in a prophecy citing the abominations of Israel, Jeremiah exclaims: "And they have built the high places of Tophet, which *is* in the Valley of the Son of Hinnom, to burn their sons and their daughters in the fire…" [Jeremiah 7:31 NKJV]. Essentially it became the city dump, an area where many fires burned intermittently. In Luke 12:5 Jesus says: "But I will show you whom you should fear: fear Him who, after He has killed, has power to cast into hell" [*gehenna*]. And Matthew 5:22 (NKJV): "…whoever says, 'You fool!' shall be in danger of hell fire" [*gehenna*]. And Mark 9:47 (NKJV): "And if your foot causes you to sin, cut it off. It is better for you to enter life lame, rather than having two feet, to be cast into hell [*gehenna*], into the fire that shall never be quenched—where 'Their worm does not die, and the fire is not quenched.'" From this passage and others, *gehenna,* translated "hell" or "hell fire," came to be believed over time as a figure for the final punishment of the wicked, and that in "hell" the fire burns continuously. But in *gehenna* in the Valley of Hinnom, the city dump, the fires were intermittent—many fires burning out and others starting at various times. As well, Revelation 20:14 (NKJV) informs us that at the Great White Throne Judgment, which Jesus prophesied as the "resurrection to condemnation" [John 5:29], whoever was not found written in the Book of Life was cast into the lake of fire—which will be an instantaneous incineration—"the second death." Revelation 20:10 (NKJV) states that "The devil, who deceived them, was cast into the lake of fire and brimstone where the beast [Antichrist] and the false prophet [the second beast of Revelation 14:11 NKJV] *are.* And they will be tormented day and night forever and ever." The fact that they will be "tormented day and night forever and ever" has, perhaps, encouraged the false notions that 1) the Devil reigns in "hell," and 2) all God-rejecters burn in "hell" forever. These notions are not biblical, as we have seen. The Antichrist and the false prophet will be charismatic men possessed and controlled by major satanic spirits at the Devil's bidding. When they are cast into the lake of fire, their bodies will be incinerated instantly—the "second death." However, the spirits possessing them will be "tormented day and night forever and ever" because all spirit life is eternal life.

"...like angels of God in heaven."
-Matthew 22:30 (REV)

Matthew 22 (REV) records a discussion between Jesus and the Sadducees, who did not believe in the resurrection of the dead. They asked the Lord what would happen to a woman who had seven husbands in her lifetime—whose wife would she be in the resurrection? Jesus replies that "in the resurrection they neither marry, nor are given in marriage, but are like angels in heaven" [verse 30]. In His reply Jesus was not suggesting that in the resurrection people will live in heaven like the angels. He simply pointed out to the Sadducees that angels do not marry and have spouses in heaven, and that in the resurrection people will not marry and have spouses. Thus, in that sense, the saved will be like the angels.

"My kingdom is not of this world."
-John 18:36 (REV)

In John 18:36 (REV), Jesus, standing before Pontius Pilate in the Praetorium, says: "My kingdom is not of this world. If my kingdom were of this world, then my servants would be fighting." Some commentators have speculated that if Christ's kingdom "is not of this world," then it must be in heaven. However, in stating that His kingdom was not of "this world," Jesus was referring to the world as it is now—in a fallen state and under the influence of the evil that so characterizes our world today. Jesus was not indicating that His future kingdom—in context, the Millennial Kingdom—would not be on the earth. Indeed, the prophets and apostles inform us in many sections of the Scriptures that Christ's kingdom will be on the earth as Paradise restored.

"Flesh and blood cannot inherit the kingdom of God;"
-1 Corinthians 15:50 (REV)

Paul writes in 1 Corinthians 15:50 (REV) that "flesh and blood is not able to inherit the Kingdom of God." Some commentators suggest that this statement means that Christians, in their new and immortal bodies, will be spirit beings in heaven without flesh and blood. Philippians 3:20 and 21(NKJV) inform us that Jesus Christ will "transform our lowly body that it may be conformed to His glorious body, according to the working by which He is able even to subdue all things to Himself." After His resurrection from the dead, Jesus was still "flesh and bone." He says to His disciples, "Look at my hands and my feet, that it is I Myself. Handle me, and see, for a spirit does not have flesh and bones, as you see I have" [Luke 24:39 REV]. If the resurrected Christ had "flesh and bones," then flesh and bones can certainly enter the kingdom of God.

The phrase "flesh and blood" that Paul uses occurs several times in the Bible and simply indicates natural, unsaved people in a general sense. For example, Ephesians 6:12 (REV): "For we [Christians] do not wrestle against flesh and blood [people], but against the rulers, against, authorities, against the world-rulers of this *present* darkness...." Thus 1 Corinthians 15:50 means that "natural, unsaved" people of "flesh and blood"--but without the gift of the holy spirit of God--cannot enter the kingdom of God because they don't have everlasting life. Their bodies are "corruptible" and must become "incorruptible" and immortal like Christ's body to enter the kingdom of God.

"...in the heavenly *places*"
-Ephesians 2:6 (REV)

Ephesians 2:6 (REV) informs Christian believers that "God raised us up with him (Christ), and seated us with him (Christ) in the heavenly *places*, in Christ Jesus...." Paul's statement here is a figure of speech called the "prophetic perfect." The "prophetic perfect" is an idiom known to Bible scholars as the concept of "here, now, but not yet." It uses the past tense when speaking of a future event that is certain to occur. In the judgment of God, Christians have already been raised from the dead and given honor and authority "in the heavenly places in Christ Jesus." We might consider three phases of the fulfillment of this amazing prophecy: One: Christians here and now in this mortal life have authority to use the name of Jesus Christ in prayer for good; Two: At the Rapture of the Church Christians will be "caught up together" to be with Christ in the heavenly realms and to receive honor and rewards at The Judgment Seat of Christ; and Three: Christians will enjoy honor and authority in Christ in our everlasting lives in the Millennial and Everlasting Kingdoms. This is a promise so certain to come to pass in God's timing that in Ephesians 2:6 it is spoken of as having already occurred. It does not mean, however, that Christians will live in heaven forever.

"...they desire a better *land*...a heavenly one."
-Hebrews 11:16 (REV)

Hebrews 11:16 (REV) speaks of "a heavenly land" for which the Old Testament faithful believers longed. As well, Hebrews 13:14 (REV) tells of "the city that is to come." There is no suggestion that this "heavenly land" and "the city that is to come" will be in heaven. The Scriptures inform us that there will be "new heavens and a new earth in which dwells righteousness" [2 Peter 3:13 REV], and that there will be "the holy city Jerusalem, coming down out of heaven from God, having the glory of God" [Revelation 21:10,11 REV]. This event ushers in the Everlasting Kingdom at the conclusion of the Millennial Kingdom during which Jesus Christ will reign along with resurrected Old Testament believers and the raptured saints of the spiritual Body of Christ. The "heavenly country" and the "enduring city" for which the Old Testament faithful longed will be the "new heavens and a new earth," and the holy city will be New Jerusalem, which will be the capitol of all the earth during the

Millennial Kingdom as well as throughout the Everlasting Kingdom, as Jeremiah 3:17 (NKJV) prophesies: "At that time Jerusalem shall be called The Throne of the Lord, and all the nations shall be gathered to it, to the name of the Lord, to Jerusalem." Believers in God do not go to "the new heavens and a new earth" or to the New Jerusalem when they die. Hebrews 13:13 and 14 (REV) exhort us: "Therefore, let us go to him [Christ] outside the camp, bearing the reproach he endured. For we do not have a permanent city here, but we are seeking *the city* that is to come."

Moreover, some commentators claim that the faithful saints of this "mighty cloud of witnesses" spoken of in Hebrews 11and 12 are now alive and up in heaven "cheering us on." However, "These all died," Hebrews 11:13 (NKJV) informs us, "not having received the promises, but having seen them afar off were assured of them, embraced them and confessed that they were strangers and pilgrims on the earth." If these pilgrims in the "mighty cloud" are, indeed, alive in glorious heaven, then one has to wonder: What did they need a Redeemer for if they went to heaven before the coming of Christ? What, then, was the purpose of the life and ministry of Jesus Christ—His crucifixion, death on the cross, resurrection to life—and Christ's promise of the resurrection of life [John 5:29 NKJV] for the Old Testament faithful, as well as everlasting life for Christians? The very idea that these Old Testament faithful believers went to heaven without the need of the Redeemer is wholly unfounded biblically.

"...a house...eternal in the heavens."
-2 Corinthians 5:1(REV)

Paul writes in 2 Corinthians 5:1: "For we know that if our house here on earth, our tent, is destroyed, we have a building from God, a house not made with hands, everlasting in the heavens" (REV). This verse seems to indicate that the saved will live in heaven forever. However, the word "everlasting" describes the word "house," not the phrase "in heaven." The verse does not say that the Christian will have a house eternally in heaven. Rather, it is our "house"—our new body like Christ's glorious body—that will be eternal. But what does it mean

17

that the Christian's "house" is in heaven? 1 Corinthians 15:51 and 52 inform us that the Christian's mortal body will be "changed" into an immortal body. Just as we understand the use of the figure of speech the "prophetic perfect" in Ephesians 2:6, when God reserves something for the future that is not presently available, it is said to be "reserved in heaven" and is certain to come to pass in God's timing. At the Rapture of the Church, Christ will "transform our lowly body so it will be like His glorious body…" [Philippians 3:21 REV]. Thus this promise of God for our future is said to be "reserved in heaven."

"In My Father's house are many mansions;"
-John 14:2 (NKJV)

"Do not let your heart be troubled;" Jesus assures His disciples in John 14:1-3 (REV), "Continue to trust in God and continue to trust in Me. In My Father's house are many places to live. If it were not so I would have told you, for I go to prepare a place for you. And if I go and prepare a place for you, I will come again and will receive you to myself so that where I am you may be also." This promise of the Lord has been used to teach that Christians will spend eternity in heaven. However, the "house" of the Lord's Father is a figure of speech to represent the kingdom of God. There is no reason that the word "house" must be taken literally. The Bible never speaks of God living in His "house" in heaven as if He lives in a spiritual castle or temple. In many places in the Bible the word "house" is used to represent a kingdom such as "the house of Israel" or when Jesus said, "Every kingdom divided against itself is brought to desolation, and a house *divided* against a house falls" [Luke 11:17 REV]. As well, this verse does not say that believers will all live in separate "mansions," as the NKJV states, either in the kingdom of God or in the Millennial Kingdom on the earth. Here the word "mansions" (NKJV) in the Greek text is *mone* which simply means "abiding place," "abode," "dwelling." In the future kingdom of heaven which Jesus preached early in His ministry, Christians will actually be living all over the world. Indeed there will be many places to stay in the Millennial Kingdom. When Jesus promised His disciples that He would "come again and receive you to Myself, that where I am you may be also," He was talking about His return to the earth to establish His kingdom. He was not suggesting, contrary to erroneous teachings, that each time a Christian dies, Jesus would come to receive him and take the believer to heaven so that he would live in a "mansion" in God's "house."

We must understand that in His earthly ministry Jesus had no knowledge of the Church of the Body of Christ. This was a "mystery"—a Sacred Secret--revealed for the first time to the Apostle Paul [Romans 16:25]. Therefore it must be understood that in these verses in John 14, Jesus could not have been prophesying about the Rapture of the Church. Rather, He was talking about His return to the earth to establish His kingdom. However, it can be said with assurance that at the Rapture of the Church, Christians will be "caught up together...in the clouds to meet the Lord in the air" [1 Thessalonians 4:17 REV]. Christ will not return to the earth at that time. He will receive believers "in the air" and take them to heaven. How long Christians will spend with the Lord and with God and the angels in heaven no one knows. However, we know that at this time tribulation is beginning on the earth. According to Daniel's prophesies and corresponding prophesies in the Book of Revelation, the tribulation will have two phases—3 ½ years and 3 ½ years. Jesus calls the second 3 ½ years "great tribulation" in Matthew 24:21. Then Christ returns to the earth "with ten thousands of His holy ones" [Jude 14 REV]. Thus it is possible that Christians will spend seven years in heaven with the Lord—or perhaps less time if one accepts the possibility of a "mid-tribulation" Rapture. In any event, while all Christians are in heaven with the Lord, the events of the Judgment Seat of Christ will progress, during which time believers will be rewarded for their faithful service to the Lord in our mortal lives. These "rewards" will include glorious "crowns" representing spiritual authority and functions for Christians in our everlasting lives in the Millennial Kingdom.

"There is one body and one Spirit:"
-Ephesians 4:4 (REV)

19

In Paul's letter to the Ephesians, we learn that all Christians are members of the spiritual Body of Christ: "And He [God] put all things in subjection under his [Christ's] feet, and appointed him *to be* head over all things for the congregation, which is his body, the fullness of the *one* filling all things in all" [Ephesians 1:22,23 REV]. Then in Ephesians 4 (REV): "*There is* one body and one spirit, even as also you were called in one hope of your calling [verse 4]....Instead, speaking the truth in love, let us grow up in every way into *union with* him who is the head, *into* Christ, from whom the whole body, being fitted together and united through that which every joint supplies, by the working of each individual part, in *its* proper measure, produces the growth of the body for the building up of itself in love" [verses 15,16]. And in 1 Corinthians 12 (NKJV) Paul explains: "For as the [human] body is one and has many members of the one body, but all the members of the one body, being many, are one body, so is Christ. For by one Spirit we were all baptized into one body—whether Jews or Greeks, whether slaves or free—and have all been made to drink into one Spirit...Now you are the body of Christ, and members individually" [verses 12,13,27].

The Scriptures tell us that Jesus Christ will physically return to the earth in God's timing. Acts 1:10 and 11 (REV): "And while they [the apostles] were looking into heaven as he was going, Look! two men stood by them in white apparel, who said, 'Men of Galilee, why do you stand looking into heaven? This Jesus, who was taken up from you into heaven, will come in the same way as you saw him going into heaven.'" In Matthew 24 (REV), Jesus prophesied regarding His return: "For as the lightning goes out from the east and shines even to the west, so will be the coming of the Son of Man...But immediately after the tribulation of those days the sun will be darkened, and the moon will not give its light, and the stars will fall from heaven, and the powers of heaven will be shaken, and then the sign of the Son of Man will appear in heaven, and then all the tribes of the earth will mourn, and they will see the Son of Man coming on the clouds of heaven with power and great glory" [verses 27, 29-31 REV]. And Revelation 1:7 (REV) declares: "Look!, he is coming with the clouds, and every eye will see him, even those who pierced him, and all the tribes of the earth will mourn because of him. So will it be. Amen."

The Church of the Body of Christ has little or no part in the "tribulation of those days." 1 Thessalonians 1:10 (REV) assures Christians that we "wait for his Son from heaven, whom he raised out from the dead, *that is,* Jesus, our Deliverer from the coming wrath." And 1 Thessalonians 5:9 (REV) tells us: "For God did not appoint us to wrath, but to obtain salvation through our Lord Jesus Christ." As one studies the Book of Revelation, it appears that the great intensity of the wrath of God begins in chapter 6 with the introduction of the symbolism of the "white horse" who goes out "conquering and to conquer;" then the "red horse" who goes out "to take peace from the earth, and that people should kill one another;" then the "black horse" who causes great famine; and finally the "pale horse" so that "power was given to him over a fourth of the earth, to kill with sword, with hunger, with death, and by the beasts of the earth." Surely if the Church of the Body of Christ has been delivered "from the coming wrath," the Rapture will certainly occur prior to the onset of these terrible events. Students of the Bible have forever speculated and debated regarding the timing of the Rapture. Some argue for a pre-tribulation Rapture, some for mid-tribulation, some for post-tribulation at the Return of Christ. One thing is for certain—the Scriptures assure us that "God did not appoint us to wrath" and that we have been "delivered from the coming wrath." Hallelujah!

At the conclusion of the seven years of tribulation of those days [the seventy weeks of Daniel's prophecy equal to seven years—[Daniel 9:24-27], Christ returns to the earth to destroy the armies of the rebellious nations in the battle of Armageddon and to establish His Millennial Kingdom. At that time all members of the Church of the Body of Christ return with Him. 1 Thessalonians 3:13 (NKJV) confirms this: "...so that He may establish your hearts blameless in holiness before our God and Father at the coming of our Lord Jesus Christ with all His saints [*hagion*]." And consider Jude 14b (NKJV): "Behold, the Lord comes with ten thousands of His holy ones [*hagias*]." "Holy ones," in the Bible, are the angels as well as God's elect—"saints." Consider Romans 1:7: (REV) "To all who are in Rome, beloved of God, called holy *ones* [*hagiois*]." And 1 Corinthians 1:2: (NKJV) "To the church of God which is at Corinth, to those who are sanctified in Christ Jesus, called *to be* saints

21

[*hagias*]." Also Ephesians 1:1 and Colossians 1:2. When Christ returns to the earth, all Christians—those raised from the dead and those alive at the Rapture of the Church—will return with Him, because where the head of the spiritual Body of Christ will be, all members of His spiritual body will be with Him. Thus, beginning with the Rapture of the Church, "we will always be with the Lord" [1Thessalonians 4:17b REV]. This is an important truth that many Christians simply do not realize.

"...treasures in heaven"
-Matthew 6:20 (REV)

Some theologians argue that the phrase "treasures in heaven" suggests that Christians will spend their everlasting lives in heaven. They point to several verses. In Matthew 6:19 and 20 (REV), Jesus says: "Do not store up for yourselves treasures on the earth...but store up for yourselves treasures in heaven...for where your treasure is, there your heart will be also." And Colossians 1:5 (REV): "...because of the hope which is being stored up for you in heaven;" and also 1 Peter 1:4 (REV): "...to an inheritance incorruptible and undefiled and unfading, kept in heaven for you." These verses may seem convincing to some, but they do not state that Christians will spend their everlasting lives in heaven. Rather, the concept is that God, who is in heaven, is "reserving"—keeping--our rewards or maintaining a record of them on our behalf. The actual receipt of our spiritual rewards will occur in the future, beginning with our appearance at the Judgment Seat of Christ and thereafter on the earth in the Millennial Kingdom.

Your Everlasting Life

In summation, the Scriptures inform us in many places that God has promised everlasting life both to His original chosen people—the Children of Israel—and to all who confess Jesus Christ as Lord and believe in their hearts that God has raised Him from the dead. The latter are the members of the spiritual Body of Christ, some of whom have died and are referred to as "asleep in Christ." Jesus assures us that "the hour is coming in which all who are in the grave will hear His voice and come forth—those who have done good [Old Testament faithful] to the resurrection of life, and those who have done evil [all unbelievers and God-rejecters] to the resurrection of condemnation" [John 5:28,29 REV]. Unspoken in His prophecy is any reference to the Rapture of the Church simply because Jesus knew nothing of the Great Mystery, first revealed to the Apostle Paul, that both Jews and Gentiles who would become Christians after the Day of Pentecost would constitute the spiritual Body of Christ with Christ as the Head of the Body. These all—both Jews and Christians alive and dead—are awaiting the second coming of Jesus Christ to the earth and everlasting life—not up in heaven as many people erroneously believe, but in the Millennial and Everlasting Kingdoms to come. The Children of Israel will "inherit the land" and will serve the Lord throughout Israel and in the "Holy City" Jerusalem. All Christians, as members of Christ's spiritual Body, will reign with Christ in "judging the world" [1 Corinthians 6:2], for where the Head of the Body is, there the members of His Body will be also. These are the wonderful promises of God to those who have "an ear to hear." And so God's ultimate plan for humanity will finally come full circle in *Paradise restored.*

Note: Words in italics in quoted verses are words or phrases not in the Greek or Hebrew text but were added to the English by the translators. However, some words or phrases in italics are used by this author for emphasis. As a note of clarification, in the New King James Version of the Bible (NKJV) the words "Holy Spirit" and "Spirit" are capitalized when referring to God, to Jesus Christ, and also to God's gift of the spirit. This can only be confusing to the reader. In the Revised English Version (REV), the pronouns he and him, referring to Christ, are not capitalized. For the purpose of this study, in order to differentiate between God and the gift of holy spirit, Holy Spirit and Spirit are capitalized in the discussion when referring both to God and to Christ, but in lower case when referring to God's gift of holy spirit. As well, readers will notice the intermittent use of both the NKJV and REV versions of scripture. This was necessitated by the limitations of the total number of verses permitted to be quoted by the publishers of those versions. However, in no way is the point of view of the text compromised; indeed, it is enhanced.

TWO

"The Lord God planted a garden eastward in Eden..."

-Genesis 2:8 (NKJV)

Paradise! The very idea evokes visions of pristine grandeur—vibrant images of primordial gardens or sunwashed beaches, visions of enchanting delight. The legends of many ancient cultures include tales of fabulous gardens or magical domains dating back to the founding of human civilization on the earth.

*According to translations of ancient Mesopotamian writings, Nibiru was the extraterrestrial land of the Anunnaki, early Sumerian-Babylonian gods who genetically manipulated mankind, resulting in the creation of the Nephilim. As well, the legend is associated with the Babylonian creation epic "Enuma Elish," which some historians say predates the creation account in the Book of Genesis.

*Islam's Paradise, described in the Quran [Surat number 52, verse 17]: "Verily, the pious [good Muslims] will be in gardens of the Muslims, and the delight, enjoying in that which their lord has bestowed on them....They would recline on beds, arranged in ranks, and we shall marry them to fair women with wide, lovely eyes."

*Shangri-La, according to ancient Buddhist lore, was a mystical harmonious valley enclosed in the western end of the Kunlun Mountains on the northern edge of the Tibetan Plateau. It was a mythical Himalayan utopia, a permanently happy land isolated from the world.

*Valhalla, in Norse mythology, was a majestic, enormous hall, ruled over by the god Odin, and the destiny of all those who die in combat.

*Atlantis was Plato's legendary lost continent, which supposedly sank into the Atlantic Ocean. The allegorical aspect of Atlantis was taken up in utopian works of certain Renaissance writers, such as Francis Bacon's "New Atlantis" and Thomas Moore's "Utopia." Atlantis has become a byword for any supposed advanced prehistoric civilization.

*In Greek mythology, the Elysian Fields were the final resting place of the heroic and the virtuous. As well, the Garden of the Hesperides was Hera's sacred garden from where the gods got their immortality. And Mount Olympus was referred to as "home of the gods."

*Aaru was the "other world" which the Egyptians believed was the reed fields of ideal hunting and fishing grounds where the virtuous dead lived after judgment.

*For the Celts, it was the Fortunate Isle of Mag Mell, a pleasurable paradise thought of as either an island far to the west of Ireland or somewhere beneath the ocean.

*The Vedic Indians, whose religion evolved into ancient Hinduism and Brahmanism, held that when the physical body was destroyed, it was recreated and reunited in the Third Heaven in a state of bliss.

*Hawaiki was the mythological ancestral island of the Polynesians, particularly the Maori of New Zealand.

*Avalon was a legendary island where Excalibur, King Arthur's sword, was forged, and was believed by some to be Arthur's final resting place.

S UFFICE IT TO SAY THAT these listings are but a few of the many idyllic tales passed down through the rise and fall of diverse human societies. In a cosmological context, "paradise," for these ancient cultures, simply describes the world before it was tainted by evil.

"All Scripture *is* God-breathed..."
2 Timothy 3:16 (REV)

The story of the garden of Eden or the garden of God in Genesis is, in the view of many Bible historians, the archetypical source and foundation for the paradisiacal tales of many ancient cultures. Some historians suggest that the garden of Eden story is a Hebrew recast of Mesopotamian myth which explains how mankind came to be created. This myth is referred to as the Babylonian Genesis because of obvious parallels to the account in the Bible. Historians consider it to be hundreds of years older than the earliest manuscripts of the Bible. However, such stories were handed down from generation to generation and culture to culture in the ancient Near East. Some scholars agree that the Babylonian and Assyrian tales which bear a resemblance to the biblical account of creation antedate Moses, but that merely tends to confirm rather than invalidate the God-given inspiration of Moses' account in Genesis. Indeed, Moses' creation account does not date it to his time or even to the earliest Hebrew writings; rather, Moses was writing by inspiration from God about an antediluvian time pre-dating the earliest civilizations of humanity and prior to the formation of the mystical legends of creation of the earliest cultures. Certainly some ancient traditions of creation would inevitably be handed down from earliest generations. Following the order of most traditions, these ancient accounts would take on incongruous and mythological features, as they do in the Babylonian records. Therefore, the task of an inspired account of creation could be to supplant the absurd and mythological tradition with a revelation of the truth. This is precisely what we find in Moses' Pentateuch [circa 1450-1410 BC], which presents us with a true and logical introduction to the entire Bible.

2 Peter 1:20 and 21 (REV) tell us how the Bible came to us: "Knowing this first, that no prophecy of Scripture is of private interpretation. For no prophecy ever came by human will, but people spoke from God, being moved by holy spirit." The word prophecy, as it is used in the Bible, means either "forth-telling" or "foretelling." Most of the Bible is simply "forth-telling"—"to tell forth, to publish." Very little of the biblical record is "foretelling"—"predicting, forecasting." Peter is informing us that the "forth-telling" and the "foretelling" of the biblical record did not come to us because certain individuals decided of their own volition to write the book of Genesis or Leviticus or the Gospel of John or the book of Romans; rather, certain men chosen by God "spoke" *as they were* "moved"—inspired and taught—by the Holy Spirit. As well, Paul states in 2 Timothy 3:16 (REV): "All Scripture [the Bible] *is* God-breathed and is profitable for teaching, for reproof, for correction, for instruction in righteousness...." In the Greek text the word for "Scripture" is *graphe*. It means "a writing, thing written, document, holy writ." And the phrase "given by inspiration of God"

in the NKJV is one word in the Greek--*theopneustos*—which means "divinely breathed" or "God-breathed," a figure of speech for emphasis. The Bible states emphatically that this is how it came to be, and this is the theological position of our study.

Indeed, either Moses, Jesus, Peter, Paul and other holy men of God who spoke and taught and prophesied were telling the truth, or they were greatly mistaken. What we believe about the Bible will determine our attitude toward it, toward God, toward Jesus Christ, and toward the "precious and exceedingly great promises, so that by them you become partakers of the divine nature" [2 Peter 1:4 REV].

Can we trust the Bible?

People have many misconceptions about the Bible. A common misconception is that it was passed down by word of mouth from generation to generation, so that it is unreliable. However, there are more ancient manuscripts and pieces of manuscripts of the Bible in existence today than of any other document from the ancient world. In fact there are more than 5,500 Greek manuscripts and more than 10,000 in Latin available for scholars to study. As well, the New Testament was translated very early in many other languages including Aramaic, Ethiopic, and Armenian, so that we have today more than 24,000 ancient handwritten manuscripts of the New Testament plus more than 36,000 patristic citations such as quotations or other records from the early Church Fathers that scholars use in helping to determine the original "God-breathed" text. Generations of Bible scholars have carefully studied these texts over and over in order to arrive at a basis for the original text. Indeed, eminent scholars testify that the Bible we read today is more than 99.5% pure in relation to the original writings of Matthew, Mark, Luke, John, Paul, Peter, and other "holy men" of God.

Doubters are plenty. Some say that the Bible is only a collection of folklore passed down through the ages, or that it is full of contradictions, or that even if God spoke to men, men make mistakes, or that the Bible has been copied and translated so many times that it is unreliable. The actual evidence is wholly to the contrary. Over the centuries as the individual books of the Bible were assembled as one book, they had been preserved, studied, and recognized by generations of scholars as truly being the word of God. In contrast, non-canonical books were recognized as not being "God-breathed." Paul says in Hebrews 4:12 (REV): "For the word of God *is* living and active, and sharper than any two-edged sword, even piercing as far as the dividing of soul and spirit, of both joints and marrow, and is able to judge the considerations and intentions of the heart." In a variety of verses, God inspired the psalmist to write: "Your word *is* a lamp to my feet and a light to my path" [Psalm 119:105 NKJV]; and "The entrance of Your words gives light; It gives understanding to the simple" [119:130 NKJV]; and "The entirety of Your word is truth" [Psalm 119:160 NKJV]; and "I rejoice at Your word as one who finds great treasure" [Psalm 119:162 NKJV]; and "I will worship toward Your holy temple, and praise Your name for Your lovingkindness and Your truth; For You have magnified Your word above all Your name" [Psalm 138:2 NKJV]. Moreover, when Jesus was tempted by the devil in the wilderness, He replied: "It is written, *Man does not live by bread alone, but by every word that proceeds out of the mouth of God*'" [Matthew 4:4 REV]. And in John 6:63b (REV) Jesus says: "The words that I have spoken to you are spirit, and are life." The fact is, the Bible was not written for the doubter, the sceptic, the unbeliever. It was written for those who have longed to know "the way, and the truth, and the life" that leads to salvation and to everlasting life.

Another common misconception about the Bible is that it is incomplete—that some books are missing. The 66 books that comprise the Bible today are known as the "canon," which simply means the books officially accepted as Holy Scripture. The Church hierarchy did not "create" the canon of the Bible, as some critics assert. Rather, they *recognized* it over the centuries. There is good reason why scholars do not include the so-called "lost books"—such as "The Infancy Gospel of Thomas," "The Gospel of Judas," "The Gospel of Nicodemus," "The Gospel of Barnabas," "The Epistles of Ignatius," "The Fourth Book of Maccabees," and others—in the canon of the Bible. It is because they were not "God-breathed." They are full of historical inaccuracies, falsehoods, and contradictions with the actual canon—fatal flaws that reveal that they are not the word of God.

Dispensationalism vs. Covenant Theology

Dispensationalism and Covenant Theology are the two most widely held systems or frameworks for understanding the Bible. Dispensationalism is the primary view held by most Baptist, Pentecostal, and Charismatic churches, and by other "Bible" churches which emphasize Scripture over tradition. Covenant Theology, also known as Reformed Theology because it embraces the teachings of John Calvin, is the view of most of the mainline Protestant denominations, as well as Roman Catholicism and many "holiness" groups. In my view, adherence to Covenant Theology is a key reason that much of denominational Christianity today is apostate—having fallen away from the "upward call of God in Christ Jesus," and having disaffiliated themselves from the steadfast message of the "God-breathed" Scriptures. Indeed, the esteemed editors of The Scofield Study Bible, New King James Version, state that a rejection of the dispensational message of the Scriptures does "violence" to the accuracy and integrity of the word of God. Jesus warned His followers of the coming spiritual deception in Matthew 24 (REV): "And as he was sitting on the Mount of Olives, the disciples came to him privately, saying. 'Tell us, when will these things be, and what *will be* the sign of your coming and end of the age?' [verse 3]. Jesus expounds many of the signs that will occur toward the "end of the age," and concludes: "And then will many fall away, and will hand over one another and will hate one another. And many false prophets will arise, and will mislead many" [verses 10 and 11]. Likewise Paul warns the Church about apostasy in 1 Timothy 4:1 and 2 (REV): "But the Spirit says expressly that in later times some will fall away from the Faith, paying attention to seducing spirits and things taught by demons, *which come* through the hypocrisy of liars, who have their own consciences seared with a hot iron...." It's been more than 2,000 years since Paul prophesied. The "later times" revealed by the Spirit are here.

Doubtless it was obvious early on to many readers of this biblical study that it adheres to the dispensational point of view of the Bible. Dispensationalism is a theological system that recognizes certain ages ordained by God to order the affairs of humanity and the world. Dispensationalists believe that the Bible presents us with five to seven dispensations (*oikonomia*-"administrations, management, stewardship"), beginning, for example, with Innocence (Paradise), and including the Law of Moses, this present Age of Grace, and concluding with the Millennial Kingdom. Some theologians also include the dispensations of Conscience, Human Government, and Promise following original Paradise and prior to the giving of the Law. The dispensations present a recognizable pattern of how God worked with, and continues to work with, people living during that time including responsibility, failure and judgment, and grace. For example, in Romans 10:4 (REV) Paul declares: "For Christ is the fulfillment of the law, with the result that *now* there is righteousness for everyone who believes." Paul is stating unequivocally that *the rules have changed* and that the legal requirements presented by God in the dispensation of the Law of Moses are *fulfilled* in Christ and that a new dispensation has begun. He describes this new dispensation in Ephesians 3:2 (REV): "surely you have heard of the administration [*oikonomia*] of the grace of God that was given to me for you...." In fact Paul actually announces this new administration in 1 Corinthians 9:17 (REV) where he says: "For if I do this willingly [preach the gospel], I have a reward, but if unwillingly, I *still* have an administration" [*oikonomia*-"dispensation, administration, management"] entrusted to me."

Dispensationalism has two primary distinctions: 1) a consistently literal interpretation of Scripture, and 2) a view of the uniqueness of Israel as separate from the Church in God's plans. In holding to the literal interpretation of Scripture, Dispensationalism gives each word the literal meaning it would have in everyday usage while taking into account the more than 200 figures of speech at use in the Bible. Even so, figures of speech have literal meanings behind them. Language was given by God for the purpose of being able to communicate. Words are vessels of meaning. Suffice it to say that every Old Testament prophecy regarding the first coming of Jesus Christ was fulfilled literally. The prophecies were literal. The prophecies of Christ's second coming to the earth are meant to be literal. If a literal interpretation is not used in studying the Scriptures, there is no objective standard by which to interpret and understand the Bible. Each reader would be able to interpret the Bible as he sees fit. In contradiction to this point of view, 2 Peter 1:20 and 21(NKJV) says "Knowing this first, that no prophecy (forthtelling or foretelling) of Scripture is of any private (*idias*- "their own,") interpretation, for prophecy never came by the will of man, but holy men of God spoke as they were moved by the Holy Spirit." If each person chooses to interpret the Bible as he sees fit, biblical interpretation would devolve into "what this word or passage says to me" instead of what God intended it to say. Sadly, this is a key flaw of Covenant Theology. Indeed, God has intended His word to be interpreted literally *where it is meant to be literal* and to be understood figuratively *where it is meant to be understood figuratively*. How does a student of the Bible know the difference? 2 Timothy 2:15 (REV): "Make a diligent effort (*spoudason*- "make every effort," "study") to present yourself approved before God, a workman who does not need to be ashamed, rightly handling the word of truth."

Dispensationalism teaches us that there are two distinct peoples in God's eternal planning: Israel and the Church, that the Church has not replaced Israel in God's planning, and that God's promises to Israel for the future have not been transferred to the Church, as Covenant Theology asserts. Indeed, Dispensationalism teaches that God's promises to Israel in the Old Testament will ultimately be fulfilled in the Lord's Millennial Kingdom. As well, it assures us that just as God in this present "dispensation (*oikonomia*)) of the grace of God" [Ephesians 3:2 NKJV] is allowing His attention to be focused on the affairs of the Church through His Son Jesus Christ, He will again in the future focus His attention on Israel in the new dispensation of the Millennial Kingdom.

Covenant Theology's basic premise is that in eternity past, the three persons of the Trinity covenanted with each other to accomplish salvation by grace, and that all of history would be governed on the basis of three covenants—the covenant of works, redemption, and grace. Thus it is a system of theology that views God's dealing with man in respect of covenants rather than dispensations. A major flaw of Covenant Theology, in my view, is the idea that following Christ's crucifixion, God replaced Israel entirely in His prophetic plan, and that the promises He made to Israel in the Abrahamic Covenant, for example, have been transferred to the Church. Some Covenant theologians contend, however, that God has not disavowed His promises to Israel entirely but that all of Old Testament Israel since the time of Abraham have become members of the Church by grace. The Apostle Paul contradicts this theology in his discourse in Ephesians 2 (REV): "Therefore, remember that at one time you, the Gentiles in the flesh, who are called 'uncircumcision' by those who are called 'uncircumcision' (which is done in the flesh by *human* hands); that at that time you were without Christ, excluded from the citizenship of Israel, and estranged from the covenants based on the promise, having no hope and without God in the world. But now in Christ Jesus you who were formerly far off have been brought near by the blood of the Christ. For he is our peace who made both *groups* [Jew and Gentile] *into* one, and broke down the middle wall of partition (that is the enmity), by having made the law of no effect (that is to say, commandments expressed in regulations) by means of his flesh, so that in himself he could create the two *groups* into one new man, *thus* making peace, and could reconcile them both to God in one body by means of the cross, having slain the enmity by it, and when he came he told the Good News—peace to those far off [Gentiles], and peace to those near [Israel], because through him we both have access by one spirit [the gift of holy spirit] to the Father" [Ephesians 2: 11-18 REV]. Covenant Theology maintains that Paul's declaration of the "one body" in Christ of Jew and Gentile is *retroactive* to the time of Abraham, thus making all of Israel since the time of Abraham members of the Church. But what Paul is declaring in Ephesians is that the Church—the Body of Christ—is the result of the baptism in holy spirit which God first made available to both Jew and Gentile on the day of Pentecost.

God promises in the Bible that He will bring to pass "new heavens and a new earth in which dwells righteousness" [2 Peter 3:13 REV]. Covenant Theology has no explanation for this promise that God will restore the heavens and the earth to its pre-fallen condition. In fact Covenant Theology redefines God's promise of the Millennial Kingdom from a literal 1000-year future period on earth to the current Church Age, a belief referred to as Amillenialism. This philosophy maintains that Christ's earthly kingdom is spiritual rather than physical and in the future. According to this view, ever since His death and resurrection, Christ has been reigning from heaven and that His followers are steadfastly in the process of bringing the world under His complete dominion, which will be realized prior to His return, to take

His true believers into the eternal kingdom in heaven. This point of view has become known as Dominion Theology and is embraced by some holiness churches and groups. The idea that the earth is becoming a better place and that Christianity will somehow bring to pass complete dominion over the earth in order to facilitate Christ's return is in clear contradiction to what the Bible actually says: "But know this, that in the last days difficult times will come. For people will be lovers of themselves, lovers of money, boasters, arrogant, blasphemers, disobedient to parents, ungrateful, unholy, without family affection, unwilling to be reconciled to others, slanderers, without self-control, brutal, not lovers of good, treacherous, reckless, conceited, friends of pleasure rather than friends of God, having a form of godliness but having denied its power. Turn away from such *people*" [2 Timothy 3:1-5 REV].

As well, Covenant Theology has no answer for the Apostle John's declaration in 1 John 5:19 (REV) that "the whole world lies in *the power of* the Wicked One." The Bible says that Satan—"the god of this world" [2 Corinthians 4:4 REV]—has legal rights over the whole world: "And the Slanderer said to him [Jesus], 'To you I will give all this authority, and their glory; for it has been delivered to me, and to whomever I want I give it'"[Luke 4:6 REV]. If Christianity is bringing the whole world under Christ's complete dominion in order to facilitate His return, as Dominion Theology asserts, it has no explanation as to how "the whole world" will remain "in the power of the Wicked One," as John prophesies, until the advent of the Millennial Kingdom on the earth and Satan's ultimate dethroning by God toward its conclusion [Revelation 20:7].

Essentially, Covenant Theology is a humanistic-centered system. Man is the god of humanism which maintains the belief that, ultimately, all answers lie in Man and that the glory of God is consummated only in the redemption of man. It does not include God's plan for the redemption of all creation. Sadly, Covenant Theology is a hermeneutic that spiritualizes the words of Scripture—in direct contradiction to Peter's explicit warning: *"Knowing this first, that no prophecy of Scripture is of private interpretation"*—reinterpreting the literal "God-breathed" word into something figurative, thus creating a platform for humanism.

The fact is, the Bible states that God has exalted and honored His word above all else. He intends it to be understood literally where it is meant to be literal and figuratively where it is meant to be figurative. The psalmist declares: "I will worship toward Your holy temple, And praise Your name for Your lovingkindness and Your truth; For You have magnified Your word above all Your name" [Psalm 138:2 NKJV]. The word "magnified" in the Hebrew is *higdalta,* meaning "exalted, increased." Proverbs 30:5 and 6 (NKJV) say: "Every word of God is pure; He *is* a shield to those who put their trust in Him. Do not add to His words, lest He rebuke you and you be found a liar." The word "pure" in the Hebrew is *tsaraph,* meaning "refined," "reduced to a pure state." In other words, as 2 Timothy 3:16 (REV) states: "All Scripture is God-breathed [*theopneustos*], and is profitable for teaching, for reproof, for correction, for instruction in righteousness...."

The Bible and Science

Some critics contend that the Bible and science contradict each other. But God never intended the Bible to be a science book. Yet it contains physical knowledge about the world that was not known when the writers recorded the words of God. God created the heavens and the earth, and He often informed His prophets about the nature of the earth and the heavens. For example, Solomon writes in Ecclesiastes 1:6 (NKJV): "The wind goes toward the south, and turns around to the north; The wind whirls about continually, and comes again on its circuit." Scientists today are aware of the circular patterns of the winds, but ancient man was not. Also, Job 26:7 (NKJV): "He stretches out the north over empty space, and hangs the earth on nothing." Ancient man taught that the earth was being held on the shoulders of Atlas, a titan in Greek mythology; others believed it was held on the backs of elephants. God revealed to Job that the earth is simply suspended in space.

Some critics scoff at the Bible's contention that God created the earth, the heavens, plant life, animal life, and mankind in six days and then rested on the seventh. But it has come to light through recent biblical research that there may in fact be no conflict between what the Genesis story of creation actually teaches us and science's contention that the earth is about 4 ½ billion years old. An esteemed Bible scholar, Arthur C. Custance, published a book in 1970 entitled *Without Form and Void.* The title is taken from the Hebrew text in Genesis 1:2 (NKJV): "and the earth was without form, and void" [*tohuw bohuw*], meaning "emptiness, confusion, wasted, ruined." Dr. Custance contends that in verse two the Hebrew word *hayah,* translated "was" in our English Bibles, could, because of the context, more accurately be translated "became," as it is in other places in the Old Testament. In other words, Genesis 1:1 and 1:2 (NKJV) could read: "In the beginning God created the heavens and the earth. The earth *became* without form and void...." Dr. Custance's research contributes to the highly debated "gap theory" of creation, indicating a mysterious "gap" between verses 1 and 2. This "gap theory" was not the brainchild of Dr. Custance, however. Early fundamentalist preachers and writers like Thomas Chalmers (1814) and G. H. Pember in his book *Earth's Earliest Ages* (1876) postulated the theory. Dr. Custance merely revived and enlarged upon it. Briefly, the "gap theory" attempts to resolve the apparent conflict between the Scriptures and modern geology by suggesting a gap of unknown eons in order to explain geological eras. It presumes that "In the beginning God created the heavens and the earth" *pristine.* Then, as verse 2 states, that the world "became without form and void" suggests that something cataclysmic happened to the earth and the heavens in the period between Genesis 1:1 and Genesis 1:2 so that the earth and the heavens, as originally created, were corrupted and destroyed. Some scholars suggest this occurred when God ejected Lucifer and millions of fallen angels out of heaven and to the earth. This is described in Isaiah 14:12-16 and Ezekiel 28:13-17, but more dramatically in Revelation 12:7-9 (REV): "And there was war in heaven. Michael and his angels *went* to fight with the dragon, and the dragon fought (and his angels), and they were not strong enough, nor was a place found for them in heaven any more. And the great dragon was thrown down, the old serpent, he who is called the Slanderer and the Adversary, the deceiver of the whole inhabited world, he was thrown down to the earth [the NKJV reads "cast out"], and his angels were thrown down ["cast out"] with him." In the Greek text, the phrase "thrown down" [or "was cast out"] and the word "cast" used three times, is the word *ballo,* which means "thrust or scatter or pour out with violent intensity." Could it be that this is what caused the earth and the heavens above the earth to *become* "without form and void"--so that the earth was wasted--in complete ruin--and needed to be restored and refurbished?

In Genesis 1:1 (NKJV), the word "created"—"God created the heavens and the earth"—is the word *bara* in the Hebrew. It means "to shape or fashion of new conditions or circumstances." In other words, something "brand new." However, in Genesis 1:7, which reads: "Then God made the firmament [heaven]...," the word for "made" in the Hebrew is *asah,* which means "to dress, fashion, accomplish, restore, appoint, to act with effect." The same in verse 16: "Then God made [*asah*] two great lights...." And in verse 25: "And God made [*asah*] the beast of the earth...." And in verse 26: "Then God said, 'Let us make [*asah*] man in our image....'" And in verse 31: "Then God saw everything that He had made [*asah*], and indeed it was very good." It's interesting that verse 21 says: "So God created great sea creatures and every living thing that moves, with which the waters abounded...." Here the word "created" in the Hebrew is *bara,* indicating that the creation of "great sea creatures" and "every living thing" in the seas was something brand new. Certainly God could create something new in harmony with His restoration of the heavens and the earth.

What most of these verses in Genesis 1 are suggesting to us is that "in the beginning" God created [*bara*] the heavens and the earth pristine, but it *became* corrupted and wasted from the cataclysm which occurred in the period of time between verses 1 and 2. Thus it was necessary for God to "dress, fashion, restore, appoint" new features for the heavens and the earth—to refurbish the earth, the plant life, the animal life, even the moon and the stars—in preparation for the creation of Adam and Eve in Eden. This took time.

Now we consider the use of the word "day" in Genesis chapter 1 (NKJV). Verse 5b: "So the evening and the morning were the first day." Verse 8: "So the evening and the morning were the second day." Verse 13: "third day." Verse 19: "fourth day." Verse 23: "fifth day." Verse 31: "sixth day." The use of "the evening and the morning" in 1:5 is held by some scholars to limit "day" to the solar day, but others suggest that it simply means that each creative day was a period of time marked off by a beginning and ending, such as in Psalm 90:6: "In the morning they [humans] are like grass which grows up; In the evening it is cut down and withers." Scholars have suggested that the word "day" is used in Scripture in four ways: 1) that part of the solar day of twenty-four hours which is light [reference Genesis 1:5, 14; John 11:9]; 2) a period of twenty-four hours [Matthew 17:1, Luke 24:21; 3); a time set apart for some distinctive purpose such as "Day of Atonement" [Leviticus 23:27]; 4) a longer duration during which the purposes of God were, or are to be, accomplished. For example, 2 Peter 3:10 (REV) says that "the Day of the Lord will come as a thief, in which the heavens will pass away with a great noise, and the elements will be dissolved with fervent heat, and the earth and the works that are in it will be burned up." In each case, the word for "day" in the Hebrew text is *youm*. It is translated "day" more than 2,000 times in our English Old Testaments. But the same word is translated 64 times in the sense of a division of time—"lifetime" or "time" or "days," even "chronicles." For example, Genesis 4:3 (NKJV): "And in process of time [*yowm*], it came to pass that Cain brought of the fruit of the ground an offering to the Lord." Numbers 20:15 (NKJV): "How our fathers went down to Egypt, and we have dwelt in Egypt a long time" [*youm*]. 1 Samuel 7:2 (NKJV): "And it came to pass, while the ark abode in Kirjathjearim, that the time [*youm*] was long; for it was twenty years, and all the house of Israel lamented after the Lord." 2 Samuel 2:11 (NKJV): "And the time [*youm*] that David was king in Hebron over the house of Judah was seven years and six months." 1 Kings 22:45 (NKJV): "Now the rest of the acts of Jehoshaphat, and his might that he showed, are they not written in the book of the chronicles [*yowm*] of the kings of Judah."

Could it be that the Genesis story of creation is actually a record of how God fashioned and restored the heavens and the earth after it had been wasted and corrupted from its original pristine condition, and that He did not accomplish it all in seven days of 24 hours each, but rather over *epochs of time*, just as science asserts. This would certainly account for the millions of years on science's geologic scale—the Precambrian, Phanerozoic, Paleozoic, Mesozoic, Cenozoic, and other epochs of the earth's formation represented, in a figure, by the seven "days" of God's work. We are reminded that 2 Peter 3:8 (REV) tells us: "But do not forget this one thing, beloved, that with the Lord one day is as 1,000 years, and 1,000 years are as one day." The reality is, distinctions of time mean little in God's reckoning. God is infinite, and His work and the duration of His work are infinity. God has always had an abundance of time to accomplish His designs. We should realize that it makes little difference to Him whether they are accomplished in one day of 24 hours or extended to a thousand years—or even a million years.

On the other hand, the traditional view of "day" in Genesis 1 and 2 as being a period of 24 hours is supported in Exodus 31(NKJV) where God tells Moses to "speak to the children of Israel, saying: 'Work shall be done for six days, but the seventh is the Sabbath of rest, holy to the Lord. Whoever does any work on the Sabbath day, he shall surely be put to death. Therefore the children of Israel shall keep the Sabbath, to observe the Sabbath throughout their generations as a perpetual covenant. It is a sign between Me and the children of Israel forever; for in six days the Lord made [*asah:* "fashioned," "refurbished"] the heavens and the earth, and on the seventh day He rested and was refreshed'" [verses13a,15–17]. Still, it remains likely that the "gap" of time between Genesis 1:1 and 1:2 could have allowed for the many epochs of millions of years on the scientific geologic scale, including millions of years of evolution within species, before God determined to prepare the world—in six days?-- for the advent of humanity.

Finally, let it be said that the Bible is the only religious treatise with historically verifiable prophesies that have faithfully been fulfilled. In Genesis 12:2 God promised Abraham that He would make him a great nation. Today the people of three major religions—Judaism, Christianity, and Islam—all honor Abraham. Isaiah 44 records that prophet foretelling that Jerusalem would be rebuilt at the command of Cyrus. It came to pass more than 150 years later. Indeed, the Old Testament contains a multitude of prophecies concerning the Messiah hundreds of years before Jesus was born. 2 Samuel 7 says the Messiah would be a descendent of David. Micah 5:2 says He would be born in Bethlehem. Zechariah 9:9 says He would ride into Jerusalem on a donkey. Psalm 22:16 says He would have His hands and his feet pierced when, at that time, there was no known practice of crucifixion. Psalm

22:18 says people would gamble for His clothing. Psalm 16:10 says He would not decay in the grave. Psalm 16 and Isaiah 53 prophesy He would be raised from the dead. Psalm 110 and Daniel 7 both state that He would ascend to heaven. And Acts 1(REV) says He will return to the earth "in the same way as you saw him going into heaven." In the Garden of Gethsemane, prior to His capture, trial, and crucifixion, Jesus prayed to the Father for His friends. He said: "I have given them your word….Make them holy by the truth; your word is truth" [John 17:14a,17 REV]. Either the Bible reveals the truth, and is reliable, and can be trusted, as Jesus and all the prophets testify, or they were all greatly mistaken. People need to decide for themselves.

Where was the garden of Eden?

Moses writes: "The Lord God planted a garden eastward in Eden, and there He put the man who He had formed. And out of the ground the Lord God made every tree grow that is pleasant to the sight and good for food. The tree of life *was* also in the midst of the garden, and the tree of the knowledge of good and evil. Now a river went out of Eden to water the garden, and from there it parted and became four riverheads. The name of the first *is* Pishon; it *is* the one that skirts the whole land of Havilah, where there *is* gold. And the gold of that land *is* good. Bdellium and the onyx stone *are* there. The name of the second river *is* Gihon; it *is* the one that goes around the whole land of Cush. The name of the third river *is* Hiddekel; it *is* the one that goes around the east of Assyria. The fourth river *is* the Euphrates. Then the Lord God took the man and put him in the garden of Eden to tend and keep it" [Genesis 2:8-15 NKJV].

Although some scholars consider the garden of Eden to be mythological, those who consider it to have been real proffer several theories for its location. "Now a river went out of Eden to water the garden, and from there it parted and became four riverheads" [verse 10]. Two of the four rivers are the Tigris (ancient Hiddekel) and the Euphrates. Therefore some scholars have suggested that Eden was in Babylonia or southern Mesopotamia [Iraq] where the rivers flow into the Persian Gulf. Ancient Sumerian legend places a similar garden here. Over the millennia deposits of silt have radically altered the configuration of lower Babylonia, and the Tigris and Euphrates have shifted their river beds several times through history. Archeological studies have indicated that around 4000 BC a river of southern Iraq "braided" or divided into several separate streams—possibly the four riverheads of Genesis 2. Other suggested locations for the garden have included Armenia near the headwaters of the Tigris and Euphrates or even Bahrain, an island in the Persian Gulf. However, southern Babylonia remains the generally accepted locale. If true, then Genesis places the beginning of mankind in the very region that archeology has shown to be the "cradle of civilization," the original home of the races of man.

Numerous fascinating books and videos chronicling the search for the lost garden of Eden have been produced over the years, and yet they all miss the point of Genesis 3:22-24 (NKJV): "Then the Lord God said, 'Behold, the man has become like one of Us, to know good and evil. And now, lest he put out his hand and take also of the tree of life, and eat, and live forever'—therefore the Lord God sent him out of the garden of Eden to till the ground from which he was taken. So He drove out the man, and He placed cherubim at the east of the garden of Eden, and a flaming sword which turned every way, to guard the way to the tree of life."

Adam and Eve, the record states, ate of the tree of the knowledge of good and evil, which God had forbidden. As the result of their disobedience, God expelled them from the garden to prevent them from eating of the tree of life and thus be condemned to live forever in the fallen condition of sin. God placed cherubim—winged angelic beings—at the eastern entrance to the garden, as well as "a flaming sword which turned every way to guard the way to the tree of life." In other words, God spiritually, and in some physical manner, shuttered the entrance to the garden until such time as He removes the blockage. Search as they may, explorers absolutely cannot find the garden of Eden today.

Paradise

In the Hebrew Bible, which is also called Tanakh or Mikra, as well as the Masoretic Text, the word *pardes* or *pardec,* that is, paradise, meaning a forest or orchard, appears three times: In the NKJV, Nehemiah 2:8: "…a letter to Asaph the keeper of the king's forest" [pardes]; Ecclesiastes 2:5: "I made myself gardens and orchards" [pardec]; and Song of Solomon 4:14: "Your plants are an orchard [pardec] of pomegranates." The Septuagint, which is the Greek translation of the Hebrew Old Testament, uses the word for paradise around thirty times as well as the word *eden* meaning "pleasure," in Genesis 2 and Ezekiel 28, and in Ezekiel 36 as Eden restored. In the New Testament, the word "Paradise" [paradeisos in the Greek text] appears three times: Luke 23:43 (NKJV): "And Jesus said to him, 'Assuredly, I say to you, today you will be with Me in Paradise;" 2 Corinthians 12:3 and 4 (REV): "And I [Paul] know such a man (whether in the body or apart from the body, I do not know, God knows), that he was taken into Paradise and heard unspeakable words, which it is not permitted for a person to speak;" and Revelation 2:7b (REV): "To him who overcomes, to him I will give to eat of the tree of life, which is in the Paradise of God." In each case, the word *paradeisos* means "a garden," "pleasure ground," "grove," or a "park," especially an "Eden" meaning "pleasure."

Some students of the Bible have thought of "Paradise" and "heaven" as having interchangeable meanings, but that is not at all the case. In the Hebrew Old Testament, "heaven" appears more than 420 times as *shamayim,* meaning "sky," "above the stars," or "abode of God." For example, Ecclesiastes 5:2 (NKJV): "For God is in heaven [shamayim] and you on earth." Daniel 2:38 (NKJV) reads: "…and wherever the children of men dwell, or the beasts of the field or the birds of heaven" [shamayim]; Isaiah 66:1 (NKJV): "Heaven [Shamayim] is My throne, and earth is My footstool;" and Genesis 1:8 (NKJV): "And God called the firmament [raqiya, meaning "expanse or arch of the sky"] Heaven" [Shamayim].

In the New Testament Greek, the word for "heaven" or "heavens" is invariably *ouranos* and appears more than 280 times. It means "vaulted expanse," "the universe," "sky," and by implication, "the seat or order of things." Throughout the Bible in Hebrew, Greek, or Aramaic, "heaven" refers to "vaulted expanse, sky, or the heavenly abode of God." In contrast, "Paradise" invariable refers to a place on earth—a "garden, orchard, or an Eden (pleasure ground)." The two meanings are not interchangeable and must not be confused.

Confusion sometimes results in a reading of Luke 23:42 and 43 (NKJV). One of the criminals crucified with Jesus asks a favor of Him: "Lord, remember me when You come into your kingdom." Jesus replies, "Assuredly, I say to you, today you will be with me in Paradise." Here we have a problem. We know from the Scriptures that Jesus did not go to Paradise that day, nor did He go to heaven. In fact, He died and was buried in the garden tomb for three days and three nights. 1 Peter 3:19 (REV) suggests that "he went and heralded *his victory* to the spirits in prison" while His body was in the grave, but this verse does not appear in most biblical texts prior to 650 AD. As well, the New International Version (NIV) reads: "He was put to death in the body but made alive by the Spirit through whom he went and preached to the spirits in prison," suggesting that His preaching to the spirits in prison was a resurrection appearance. Even after He was raised from the dead, He appeared to more than 500 witnesses [1 Corinthians 15:6] on the earth over a period of 40 days [Acts 1:3] before He ascended to the Father in heaven. Jesus never went to Paradise! Confusion arises from the misplacement of a simple comma in the verse. Two early Syriac texts of Luke 23:43 translate the verse differently than what we find in our English bibles. They read: "Today I tell you that you will be with Me in Paradise." We know that the words and sentences of the earliest portions of biblical manuscripts extant—the uncials (capital letters) and the cursives (lower case) run together and contain no punctuation or paragraphs. Punctuation and paragraphs were supplied to modern texts by translators to the best of their understanding. Sometimes they were wrong, which can influence the reader's understanding of the text. Jesus did not say to the criminal "today you will be with Me in Paradise," as the NKJV reads. He said: "Truly I say to you today, you will be with me in Paradise," as the REV correctly reads. When will the believing criminal be with the Lord in Paradise?—when Paradise is restored in Christ's Millennial Kingdom following His return to the earth. God gave the Prophet Isaiah visions of such a time: "The wilderness and the wasteland shall be glad for them, and the desert shall rejoice and blossom as the rose; it shall blossom abundantly and rejoice, even with joy and singing..." [Isaiah 35:1,2 (NKJV)]; "The wolf also shall dwell with the lamb, the leopard shall lie down with the young goat, the calf and the young lion and the fatling together, and a little child shall lead them. The cow and the bear shall graze; their young ones shall lie down together; and the lion shall eat straw like the ox. The nursing child shall play by the cobra's hole, and the weaned child shall put his hand in the viper's den. They shall not hurt nor destroy in all My holy mountain, for the earth shall be full of the knowledge of the Lord as the waters cover the sea. And in that day there shall be a Root of Jesse, who shall stand as a banner to the people; for the Gentiles shall seek Him, and His resting place shall be glorious" [Isaiah 11:6-10 NKJV]. This will be Paradise restored.

Visions of Paradise

Paul writes in 2 Corinthians 12:1-4 (REV): "I must go on boasting. Though it is not profitable, I will move on to visions and revelations of the Lord. I know a man in Christ [speaking of himself] who fourteen years ago was taken to the third heaven (whether in the body I do not know, or whether out of the body I do not know, God knows). And I know such a man (whether in the body, or apart from the body, I do not know, God knows), that he was taken into Paradise [*paradeisos*] and heard unspeakable words, which it is not permitted for a person to speak."

Throughout the Bible the word "heaven" invariably is either *shamayim* [Hebrew Old Testament] or *ouranos* [Greek New Testament], but it has three different meanings according to context. It may refer to the "first heaven," which is simply the atmosphere above the earth: Genesis 1:26: "…the birds of the air" [*shamayim*]; or Genesis 8:2: "…the rain from heaven" [*shamayim*]. Or it may refer to the "second heaven"—the universe or the stars: Genesis 22:17: "I will surely multiply your offspring as the stars of heaven" [*shamayim*]. The "third heaven"—which is used only in Paul's declaration in 2 Corinthians 12—refers to the abode of God which is "outside" the first and second heavens. Paul is pointing out that the "visions and revelations" of the Lord came to him while he was "taken" to the third heaven [*ouranos*], the abode of God. Paul states that spiritually he was in the presence of God in a future time as he received "visions and revelations" of Paradise—a future place on earth, and that he was not merely in the clouds or among the stars. In stating that he did not know whether he was "in the body" or "out of the body," it's likely that Paul experienced a form of "astral projection" or "astral travel" by means of the holy spirit born in him. This is a form of "out-of-body" experience denoting a visionary conscious awareness of one's presence leaving the physical body behind and "traveling" to a higher realm—in Paul's case into the very presence of God. Paul's experience of "visions and revelations" might be compared with the revelations experienced by John as recorded in Revelation. It's clear that the Lord gave Paul these "unspeakable" visions and revelations in order to inspire and encourage him in his ministry of taking the gospel of Jesus Christ to the nations.

The third and final use of *paradeisos* in the New Testament is in Revelation 2:7 (REV): "Anyone who has an ear had better listen to what the Spirit says to the congregations. To him who overcomes, to him I will give to eat of the tree of life, which is in the midst of the Paradise of God." In original Eden, "the Lord God commanded the man, saying, 'Of every tree of the garden you may freely eat, but of the tree of the knowledge of good and evil you shall not eat, for in the day that you eat of it you shall surely die'" [Genesis 2:15-17 NKJV]. As it turned out, Adam and Eve disobeyed God and eventually ate of the tree of the knowledge of good and evil. "Then the Lord God said, 'Behold, the man has become like one of Us, to know good and evil. And now, lest he put out his hand and take also of the tree of life, and eat, and live forever'—therefore the Lord God sent him out of the garden of Eden to till the ground from which he was taken" [Genesis 3:22,23 NKJV]. In Eden Adam and Eve were able to eat freely from the tree of life. If they had taken and eaten of the tree of life *after* their disobedience to God, they would have been condemned to live forever in their wretched fallen state—"Cursed is the ground for your sake; in toil you shall eat of it all the days of your life. Both thorns and thistles it shall bring forth for you, and you shall eat the herb of the field. In the sweat of your face you shall eat bread..." [Genesis 3:17b-19a NKJV]. In Paradise restored, the tree of life is for "the healing of the nations" [Revelation 22:1,2 REV]: "And he showed me a pure river of water of life, clear as crystal, proceeding from the throne of God and of the Lamb. In the midst of its street, and on either side of the river, was the tree of life, which bore twelve fruits, each tree yielding its fruit every month. The leaves of the tree were for the healing of the nations." The "nations" referred to in this verse will be the many tribes and races of natural men and women who will have survived the Great Tribulation of the wrath of God or who will be born into families throughout the years of the Millennial Kingdom. The leaves of the tree of life are not for those who will participate in the first resurrection—the resurrection of the just--early in the Millennial Kingdom or for the members of the Church—Christ's Body—who will already have everlasting life.

The Paradise of God spoken of in Revelation 2:7 is the new Eden—Paradise restored to the earth. It is the fulfillment of Paul's great prophecy to the Church in Colossians 1:26 and 27 REV: "...the Sacred Secret, which has been hidden for ages and generations, but now has been revealed to His holy ones. God wanted to make known to them what is the riches of the glory of this Sacred Secret among the Gentiles, which is Christ in you, the hope of glory." This hope of glory for which every born-again believer yearns, is to have this "lowly body" "transformed," "so it will be like his glorious body" [Philippians 3:2 REV], and to enjoy everlasting life in the Paradise of God in the Millennial Kingdom--and thereafter in the Everlasting Kingdom of the "new heaven and a new earth in which righteousness dwells" [2 Peter 3:13 REV].

God's perfect habitat for man

The original garden of Eden was God's design for a perfect habitat for humanity. "And out of the ground the Lord God made every tree grow that is pleasant to the sight and good for food...and a mist went up from the earth and watered the whole face of the ground" [Genesis 2:6,9 NKJV] Eden was a place of happiness and delight, a place of contentment and fulfillment. As Adam and Eve looked after the garden, they learned how to "tend it and keep it" [Genesis 2:15].

"Out of the ground the Lord God formed every beast of the field and every bird of the air, and brought them to Adam to see what he would call them. And whatever Adam called each living creature, that was its name. So Adam gave names to all cattle, to the birds of the air, and to every beast of the field" [Genesis 2:19,20 NKJV].

Day by day Adam and Eve not only enjoyed a loving relationship with one another, they also enjoyed a loving relationship with the Lord God. "So God created man in His own image, in the image of God He created him; male and female He created them. Then God blessed them and God said to them, 'Be fruitful and multiply; fill the earth and subdue it; have dominion over the fish of the sea, over the birds of the air, and over every living thing that moves on the earth. And God said, 'See, I have given you every herb which yields seed which is on the face of the earth, and every tree whose fruit yields seed; to you it shall be for food. Also, to every beast of the earth, to every bird of the air, and to everything that creeps on the earth, in which there is life, I have given every green herb for food; and it was so. Then God saw everything that He had made, and indeed it was very good" [Genesis 1:27-31 NKJV].

The question arises: What was "the image of God" which God created in the first man? Theologians and philosophers have forever debated the meaning of the phrase. Some have suggested that it simply means that man was uniquely gifted intellectually and ethically so that he could relate to God as a steward of the garden. In the Hebrew text the phrase "in His own image" is one word—*tselem*, meaning "likeness," "resemblance." Jesus informs us in John 4:24 (REV) that "God is Spirit, and those who worship him must worship in spirit and truth." It may be true that "the image of God" means that man was uniquely gifted intellectually and ethically so that he was made a rational and moral being. As well, "God is Spirit," and in creating the first man "in the image of God," God made Adam a three-part being of body, soul, and spirit. I Peter 1:15 and 16 state: "...but as the one who called you is holy, be holy yourselves in all your manner of life, because it is written, 'Be holy, for I am holy.'" God is Spirit and God is holy—He is *the* Holy Spirit. So then, Isaiah 43:7 (NKJV) explains the three-fold nature which God created in the first man: "Everyone who is called by My name, whom I have created [*bara*, meaning "something brand new" which was the spirit of God on Adam], for My glory; I have formed him [*yatsar*, meaning "framed," "fashioned" from "the dust of the ground"—Genesis 2:7 NKJV], yes, I have made him [*asah*, meaning "to prepare," "accomplish"—"the breath of life" in Adam]." Genesis 1:27 (NKJV): "So God created man [*bara,* something brand new] in His own image [spirit]...." Genesis 2:7 (NKJV): And the Lord God formed man [*yatsar*] of the dust of the ground, and breathed into his nostrils the breath of life; and man became a living being" [Isaiah 43:7 NKJV: "I have made him—*asah,* "prepared" for life].

God, by means of "holy spirit" given to Adam, was Adam's supreme teacher. "Out of the ground the Lord God formed every beast of the field and every bird of the air, and brought them to Adam to see what he would call them. And whatever Adam called each living creature, that was its name. So Adam gave names to all cattle, to the birds of the air, and to every beast of the field" [Genesis 2:19,20 NKJV]. God *taught* Adam about every living creature in the garden and *instructed* him what to name them—by means of the spirit that God had created [*bara,* something brand new] in Adam. God, who is the Holy Spirit, communicated to Adam's spirit, and Adam's spirit revealed the information to his understanding. Some commentators have suggested that Genesis 2:19, in stating that God brought "every beast of the field and every bird of the air...to Adam to see what he would call them," was a trial of the wisdom of man—so that Adam might give proof of his knowledge. I find this to be unfathomable. It suggests that Adam had somehow acquired such perfect intellectual knowledge of each living creature in the garden that he could name every one of them with perfect insight. A more likely scenario is that as God brought and presented each creature to Adam, He taught Adam all about each one so that Adam was able to give each creature an appropriate name.

As well, God commanded Adam: "Of every tree of the garden you may freely eat; but of the tree of the knowledge of good and evil you shall not eat, for in the day you eat of it you shall surely die" [Genesis 2:16,17 NKJV]. Why, then, did Adam *not* die as God had warned? Genesis 3:6 and 7 (NKJV) tell us: "So when the woman saw that the tree was good for food, that it was pleasant to the eyes, and a tree desirable to make one wise, she took of its fruit and ate. She also gave to her husband with her, and he ate. Then the eyes of both of them were opened, and they knew that they were naked, and they sewed fig leaves together and made themselves coverings." When Adam and Eve ate of the forbidden fruit, "the eyes of both of them were opened, and they knew that they were naked…." In other words, in a proverbial sense, they "fell" from the grace of God. More precisely, the *spiritual dimension of the presence of God* which Adam and Eve were enjoying in Paradise *changed*. In that hour of their disobedience, God took His spirit from them—"Then the eyes of both of them were opened"—a figure of speech indicating that their *perception* and *consciousness* of being in the presence of God changed. "They knew that they *were* naked"—they perceived the loss of innocence, resulting in their consciousness of sin [Gen 3:7 NKJV]. At that time they become merely natural man and woman of body and soul. They *forfeited* the spirit which God had placed on them and which had enabled them to communicate freely with Him and to enjoy everlasting life in Paradise in conscious *fellowship* with their Creator. This is the profound reality of what Adam and Eve lost, this is what died on that fateful day in Eden—the spirit of God on them—when they were deceived into disobeying God.

Moreover, the ramifications of what Adam and Eve forfeited on that fateful day in Paradise echoed far beyond their personal crises: "Cursed is the ground for your sake; In toil you shall eat *of* it all the days of your life;…In the sweat of your face you shall eat bread till you return to the ground (death), for out of it you were taken; For dust you are, and to dust you shall return" [Genesis 3:17,19 NKJV]. In Genesis 1:28 (NKJV), God had blessed Adam and Eve and said to them: "Be fruitful and multiply, fill the earth and subdue it; have dominion over the fish of the sea, over the birds of the air, and over every living thing that moves on the earth." When Adam and Eve lost the spirit that God had placed on them, they *forfeited dominion* "over every living thing that moves on the earth." In a larger sense, they actually *transferred* their dominion over the earth to the devil, the enemy of God. How do we know this to be true? Luke 4:5 and 6 (REV) inform us that when Jesus was tempted by the devil for forty days in the wilderness: "Then the devil, taking Him up on a high mountain, showed Him all the kingdoms of the world in a moment of time. And the devil said to Him, 'All this authority I will give You, and their glory, for *this* has been delivered to me, and I give it to whomever I wish.'" The dominion, the authority over "all the kingdoms of the world" was delivered to the devil as the result of

Adam and Eve's disobedience to God in the garden of Eden. At that time the devil actually became, legally and practically, "the god of this world" [*aionos* – "age," "world;" [2 Corinthians 4:4 REV]; and "the ruler of the authority of the air, the spirit who is working in those who are disobedient" [Ephesians 2:2 REV]. And 1 John 5:19 (REV) informs us that "the whole world [*kosmos* – "ordered system"] lies in *the power of the Wicked One.*"

"For I know *that* my Redeemer lives..."
-Job 19:25 (NKJV)

In Genesis 3:15 (NKJV) God says to the deceiver, the serpent: "And I will put enmity between you and the woman, between your seed [demon spirits] and her seed [ultimately Christ]. He shall bruise your head [ultimate destruction] and you shall bruise His heel [crucifixion]. Throughout the generations that followed Adam's disobedience in the garden, mankind has *longed* for a fulfillment of God's prophecy, for redemption and a return to Eden and to the delight and fulfillment of the soul in fellowship with their Creator. Mankind has longed for a Redeemer, a holy one who would free us from the curse, from the spiritual and ultimate physical death that befell every soul born into a world fallen from grace—fallen from the *conscious perception and dimension of the presence of God* in Paradise to the dimension of a cursed world in which humanity now lives. In a moment of inspired utterance, Job cries out: "For I know that my Redeemer lives, and He shall stand at last on the earth; and after my skin is destroyed, this I know, that in my flesh I shall see God" [Job 19:25 NKJV]. Jesus Christ is that Redeemer that Job foresaw—the Son of God, the "seed" of the woman prophesied by God who was "bruised" in death and crucifixion but raised to newness of life by God. Galatians 3:13 (REV): "Christ redeemed us from the curse of the law, having become a curse instead of us (for it is written, 'Cursed is everyone who is hung on a tree'), so that in Christ Jesus the blessing of Abraham could come to the Gentiles, *and* so that through trust we could receive the [holy] spirit that was promised."

Acts 2:1 (REV) tells of the momentous hour when Christ the Redeemer poured out the gift of holy spirit on His disciples—the holy spirit *lost* to mankind for ages and for generations since Adam and Eve's transgression. "And when the Day of Pentecost arrived, they [the apostles] were all together in one place. And suddenly a sound came from heaven like a strong rushing wind, and it filled the whole house where they were sitting. And there appeared to them tongues as if as of fire, which spreading out, came to rest upon each one of them. And they were all filled with holy spirit, and began to speak in other tongues, as the Spirit was giving to them utterance." Thus, in one momentous hour of redemption for mankind, the fulfillment of Christ's prophecy in Luke 24:49 (REV) came to pass: "And look! I am sending the promise of my Father upon you...," and in Acts 1:8 (REV): "But you will receive power when the holy spirit has come upon you, and you will be witnesses both in Jerusalem, and in all Judea and Samaria, and to the uttermost part of the earth."

Today this wonderful gift of holy spirit is available to every person who receives Jesus Christ as his Lord and Savior: "For the promise is to you, and to your children, and to all who are afar off, even to as many as the Lord our God will call" [Acts 2:39 REV]. And every person who has taken Jesus Christ at His word is waiting for "the blessed hope and appearing of our great God and Savior's glory--Jesus Christ, who gave himself in our stead, in order to redeem us from all lawlessness and to cleanse for himself a people for his own possession, zealous for good works" [Titus 2:13,14 REV].

"Do not take Your Holy Spirit from me."
-Psalm 51:11 (NKJV)

Beginning with the Abrahamic Covenant and throughout the years of God's personal dealings with His chosen nation of Israel, and up until the Day of Pentecost, God apportioned holy spirit upon selected individuals in order to teach and guide them directly. The Prophet Isaiah writes: "Then He remembered the days of old, Moses and his people, saying: 'Where is He who brought them up out of the sea with the shepherd of His flock? Where is He who put His Holy Spirit within them, who led them by the right hand of Moses, with His glorious arm?" [Isaiah 63:11,12 NKJV]. 2 Kings 2:9 (NKJV) speaks of the prophets Elijah and Elisha: "And so it was, when they had crossed over, that Elijah said to Elisha, 'Ask! What may I do for you?' Elisha said, 'Please let a double portion of your spirit be upon me.'" Judges 14:6 (NKJV) tells us that Samson had holy spirit upon him: "And the Spirit of the Lord came mightily upon him, and he tore the lion apart as one would have torn apart a young goat...." King David also enjoyed holy spirit in instructing his son Solomon in the building of a house for the Lord: "Then David gave his son Solomon the plans for the vestibule, its houses, its treasuries, its upper chambers, its inner chambers, and the place of the mercy seat; and the plans that all that he had by the Spirit" [1 Chronicles 28:12 NKJV]. Other faithful Old Testament (NKJV) men and women who enjoyed a portion of holy spirit included Gideon [Judges 6:34]; Joseph [Genesis 41]; Bezalel [Exodus 31:3]; Saul [1 Samuel 10:6]; Daniel chapter 8 and ff., Deborah [Judges 4], and all the Old Testaments prophets. However, the portion of holy spirit remained upon these chosen individuals only while they remained faithful to the Lord God and followed His leading. We understand this because David, in meditating upon the ramifications of his sin with Bathsheba and Uriah, cries out to the Lord: "Create in me a clean heart, O God, and renew a steadfast spirit within me. Do not cast me away from Your presence, and do not take Your Holy Spirit from me" [Psalm 51:10,11 NKJV]. David understood that he could forfeit the holy spirit upon him as the result of sinful unfaithfulness to God (just as Adam and Eve forfeited the spirit of God that was upon them in Paradise).

In every case, these men and women of old enjoyed the holy spirit *upon* them for the purposes of God and for a period of time. Since the Day of Pentecost, however, God' people today are *born* of the spirit. In His ministry of announcing the Kingdom of God to the nation of Israel, Jesus tells Nicodemus: "Most assuredly, I say to you, unless one is born again [*gennao anothen,* meaning "begat," "engendered from above"], he cannot see the kingdom of God." 1 Peter 1:22 and 23 (REV) tell us: "Having purified your souls by your obedience to the truth so that you have sincere brotherly affection, love one another fervently from a clean heart, for you have been born again [*anagennao,* "born anew"], not of corruptible seed, but incorruptible, through the living and enduring word of God." And the Apostle John writes: "Beloved, let us love one another, since love is of God; and everyone who loves is born of God and knows [*ginosko,* "come to know," "perceive"] God." One can only truly "perceive" and "come to know" God by being "born again" of His spirit. As well, John says: "Everyone who believes that Jesus is the Christ has been born of God, and everyone loving the one who gave birth also loves the one who has been born of him" [1 John 4:7 and 5:1 REV]. In Old Testament times certain men and women enjoyed the spirit of God upon them under conditions. Since the Day of Pentecost, believers in Jesus Christ are *engendered—born from above.* This is permanent salvation and the assurance of Jesus Christ's promise in John 3:16 of "everlasting life." This is the grace and the love of God to all and for all who call upon His name.

THREE

Gifts and Callings

"But since we have gifts that differ according to the grace that was given to us, *let us use them accordingly.*"
-Romans 12:6 (REV)

THE APOSTLE PAUL'S DECLARATION TO the Church in Romans 10:9-13 (REV) is foundational to the Christian doctrine of salvation in Christ: "…because if you confess with your mouth, 'Jesus is Lord,' and believe in your heart that God raised him out from among *the* dead, you will be saved. For with the heart a person believes, resulting in righteousness, and with the mouth confession is made, resulting in salvation. For the Scripture says, 'Whoever believes in him will not be put to shame.' For there is no distinction between Jew and Greek, for the same *Lord* is Lord of all, enriching all who call on him; 'for everyone who calls on the name of the Lord will be saved.'"

In the Greek text the word for "saved" in verses 9 and 13 is *sozo*. It means "kept safe and sound," "rescued," "made whole." What exactly does it mean to be "rescued" and to be "made whole"? Colossians 1:13 and 14 (REV) tell us that "He [God in Christ] rescued us out of the authority of darkness and transferred us into the kingdom of his beloved Son." Christ has rescued believers from Adam's curse and from the power of satanic darkness over this fallen world, and He has conveyed us out from the curse of eternal death unto everlasting life in the kingdom of His Son. Moreover, He has "saved" us—made us "whole" now and forever. To be "made whole" is to become a three-part being of body, soul, and holy spirit, as we discussed in the last chapter. 1 Corinthians 2:14 (REV) tells us that "the soul-oriented person [that is, the man of body and soul only; the NKJV reads "the natural man"] does not receive the things of the spirit of God, for they are foolishness to him, and he is not able to know them because they are spiritually judged." The Bible clearly distinguishes between a man of body and soul but without the spirit of God—the "soul-oriented person"—and the person who has confessed Jesus Christ as his Lord and Savior and thus has been "saved"—"made whole"—as a complete person of body, soul, and holy spirit. Such a person is able to receive and understand the deep spiritual truths of the Bible which the "natural man" cannot receive nor discern. Jesus says in Luke 19:10 (REV): "For the Son of Man came to seek and to save that which was lost." We know that what Adam lost as the result of His transgression was the "spirit" that God had placed upon him. Jesus Christ came to make the spirit of God available once again to whosoever believes in Him. "Whoever believes and is baptized will be saved [*sozo*—"made whole"], but whoever does not believe will be condemned" [Mark 16:16 REV].

"...the spirit of truth"
-John 14:17 (REV)

Toward the end of His earthly ministry, Jesus promised His disciples: "I will ask the Father, and he will give you another helper, which will be with you forever. *This helper is* the spirit of truth, which the world is not able to receive, because it does not see it, neither knows it. You know it, for it is present with you, and will be in you" [John 14:16,17 REV]. The Lord's promise to His disciples was fulfilled on the Day of Pentecost with the outpouring of the gift of holy spirit. This indescribable gift of holy spirit—"Christ in you, the hope of glory"—indwells the believer forever. This is the promise of "everlasting life" of John 3:16. Paul explains further in Ephesians 1:13 (REV): "...in whom [Christ] you also trusted, when you heard the word of truth, the Good News of your salvation, and when you believed in him, you were sealed with the promised holy spirit." When a person confesses Jesus Christ as his Lord and believes in his heart that God has raised Him from the dead, he is "saved"—"rescued" from the curse of Adam, "made whole" as a complete being, "sealed" with the holy spirit of promise. This is what it means to be "born again, not of corruptible seed, but of incorruptible, through the living and enduring word of God" [1 Peter 1:23 REV]. "For by grace you have been saved through trust, and this is not of yourselves, *it is* the gift [*doron*—"a gift of honor"] of God, not as a result of works, so that no one can boast" [Ephesians 2:8 REV]. This gift of God that makes a believer "whole" also makes the believer "complete in Him:" "For in him [Christ] dwells, in a bodily manner, all the fullness of what God is, and you have been given that fullness *by being* in *union with* him, the one who is the head of all rule and authority" [Colossians 2:9,10 REV]. The NKJV reads: "and you are complete in Him." The word "complete" in the Greek text is the word *pleroo* which means "liberally supplied so that nothing is wanting," "a full measure," "rendered perfect." To be "complete" is what Colossians 1:27 says is "Christ in you, the hope of glory."

Not only does the gift of holy spirit in a believer inspire *hope* for the future at the Judgment Seat of Christ and everlasting life in the Millennial Kingdom, the gift of holy spirit is an outstanding *enabler* in the believer's present mortal life. In John 14 (REV) Jesus promises His disciples: "I will ask the Father, and he will give you another helper, which will be with you forever...I will not leave you as orphans; I am coming to you....In that day you will know that I am in *union with* my Father, and you are in *union with* me, and I am in *union with* you....These things I have spoken to you *while I am* still with you. But the helper, the holy spirit, which the Father will send in my name, it will teach you all things, and bring to your remembrance all that I said to you" [verses 15-20,25,26]. Some of these outstanding enablements of the gift of holy spirit are summarized in Paul's first letter to the Corinthian Church: "Now to each one the manifestation [evidence] of the spirit is given for common good. For to one is given through the spirit a message of wisdom, and to another a message of knowledge by means of the same spirit, to a different one trust [faith] by the same spirit, and to another gifts of healings by the one spirit, and to another energizing of miracles, to another prophecy, to another discerning of spirits, to a different one *various* kinds of tongues, and to another the interpretation of tongues. Now all these are energized by the one and the same spirit, distributing to each one individually just as he purposes [1 Corinthians 12:7-11 REV].

As well, it is the "helper"—the gift of holy spirit born in each believer—which enables him to become more and more like Christ in this present mortal life, which most definitely will affect who he will be in terms of spiritual quality of life, spiritual authority, and missions in his everlasting life in the Millennial Kingdom. Paul tells us that the "fruit"—the evidence of the gift of holy spirit at work in a believer's mortal life—is "love [*agape*—Godly love, benevolence], joy [*chara*—gladness], peace [*eirene*—rest to one's soul], longsuffering [*makrothymia*—endurance], kindness [*chrestotes*—gentleness], goodness [*agathosyne*—uprightness], faithfulness [*pistis*—believing assurance], meekness [*praotes*—humility], self-control [*egkrateia*—temperance]. There is no law against such things" [Galatians 5:22,23 REV].

"I am the way, and the truth, and the life."
-John 14:6 (REV)

Some people believe that all faiths lead to God in one way or another. But that's not what the Bible says, and it is the position and purpose of this study that the Bible is "the word of God" and can be believed and trusted. In His agony in the Garden of Gethsemane, Jesus prayed to His Heavenly Father: "Make them [those who believe in Me] holy by the truth; your word is truth" [John 17:16b REV]. As well, Peter, soon after the experience of Pentecost, having been baptized in holy spirit, proclaimed to the people: "And in no one else is there salvation, for there is no other name under heaven that has been given among people, by which we must be saved" [Acts 4:12 REV]. Either Peter told the people the truth—or he was greatly mistaken. People must decide for themselves. The Apostle John writes to the Church: "And this is the testimony: that God gave to us life *in the* Age *to come*, and this life is in his Son. Whoever has [believes in] the Son has life; whoever does not have the Son of God does not have life" [1 John 5:11,12 REV]. Either

John told the truth, or he was greatly mistaken. And Paul states: That "if you confess with your mouth 'Jesus is Lord,' and believe in your heart that God raised him out from *the* dead, you will be saved. For with the heart a person believes resulting in righteousness, and with the mouth confession is made, resulting in salvation" [Romans 10:9,10 REV]. Either Paul told the truth, or he was greatly mistaken. And Jesus Himself proclaimed: "I am the way, and the truth, and the life; No one comes to the Father except through me" [John 14:6 REV]. Either Jesus told the truth, or He was greatly mistaken. People must decide for themselves.

Some may argue: "What about the people who never get to hear the gospel of Jesus Christ—such as some lost tribe in the jungle. Or what about little children who die in time of war, or in fires, or drownings, or other accidents, who never had a chance to grow up and hear the gospel and make a decision for themselves?" One thing is clear from the scope of the Bible: God is a God of love, of compassion, of mercy, and of justice. 1 John 4:16 (REV) assures us: "And we have known and have believed the love God has for us. God is love...." And 2 Corinthians 1:3 (REV): "Blessed *be* the God and Father of our Lord Jesus Christ, the Father of mercies and God of all comfort." And Isaiah 30:18 (NKJV): "For the Lord *is* a God of justice; blessed are all those who wait for Him." God is the ultimate Judge of every person's destiny. 1 Corinthians 7:14 (REV) provides some remarkable insight into this dilemma: "For the unbelieving husband is made holy because of the wife, and the unbelieving wife is made holy because of the brother. Otherwise your children would be unclean, but now they are holy." This is the wonderful *extension* of the New Birth! Even if only one of the spouses in a marriage is a born-again believer, the other spouse is also saved. The reason for this grace is because God sees the married couple as "one flesh" [Ephesians 5:31]. And the children of such a couple are likewise "saved." But what about the children of unbelieving couples who died prematurely? In Revelation 20 (REV), John states that near the conclusion of the Millennial Kingdom: "And I saw a great white throne, and him who sat on it, from whose face the earth and the heavens fled away....And I saw the dead, the great and the small, standing before the throne, and books were opened, and another book was opened, which is *the book* of life, and the dead were judged out of the things which were written in the books, according to their works. And the sea gave up the dead who were in it, and death and the grave gave up the dead who were in them, and they were judged, each one, according to their works. And death and the grave were thrown into the lake of fire. This is the second death, *even* the lake of fire. And if anyone was not found written in the book of life, he was thrown into the lake of fire" [verses 11-15]. The "book of life" is also called "the book of life of the Lamb" in Revelation 13:8, and is mentioned in Philippians 4:13 and Revelation 3:5. In context it contains the names of all saved persons who will live forever. Consider this: Luke 18:15 and 16 (REV) informs us: "And they [the crowd] were also bringing to him their babies so that he would touch them; but when the disciples saw it, they rebuked them. But Jesus called them to him, saying, 'Permit the little children to come to me, and do not forbid them, *for to such belongs the Kingdom of God* [italics supplied].'" Indeed, in the Gospels we see the Lord's tender heart for all children. In Matthew 18:1-6 (REV), "In that hour the disciples came to Jesus, saying, 'Who is greatest in the Kingdom of Heaven?' And he (Jesus) called to him a little child and set him in the midst of them, and said, 'Truly I say to you, unless you change and become as little children, you absolutely will not enter the Kingdom of Heaven. Therefore, whoever humbles himself as this little child is the greatest in the Kingdom of Heaven. And whoever receives one such little child in my name receives me, but whoever causes one of these little ones who believes in me to fall away, it would be better for him to have a millstone turned by a donkey hung about his neck, and to be sunk in the depth of the sea.'" The Lord's willingness to devote time to children, in recognition of their social status, and His zeal for protecting their innocence, demonstrates His love and compassion for them. At the great white throne judgment at the conclusion of the Millennial Kingdom, John writes: "...the books were opened." In a spiritual sense, God has kept a "book" on every human being who has ever lived. "And another book was opened, which is *the book* of life." Could it be that God, in His love, His mercy and compassion, and in the name of justice, has included in this special "book of life" the names of anyone—including little children who died prematurely—who never had the chance to hear the good news of Jesus Christ—and that by His grace and love He will consider them worthy to enter the Everlasting Kingdom. I believe that's our God of love, mercy, and justice.

The Body of Christ

In a prophecy foreshadowing the Day of Pentecost and immediately prior to His ascension to the Father, Jesus tells His disciples: "John baptized with water, but you will be baptized in holy spirit not many days from now" [Acts 1:5 REV]. When a believer is baptized in holy spirit, not only is he "saved," "born again," and "made whole," instantaneously he becomes a member of the spiritual Body of Christ. Paul explains: "And he [God] put all things in subjection under his [Christ's] feet, and gave him *to be* head over all things for the congregation, which is his body, the fullness of the *one* filling all things in all" [Ephesians 1:22,23 REV]. Paul continues: "So then you are no longer strangers and foreigners, but you are fellow citizens with the holy *ones* and members of the household of God, having been built on the foundation of the apostles and prophets, Christ himself being the chief cornerstone, in whom the whole building, being fitted together, grows into a holy sanctuary in the Lord, in whom you also are being built together by means of the spirit into a dwelling place of God" [Ephesians 2:19-22 REV].

Paul continues: "*There is* one body and one spirit, even as you were called in one hope of your calling, one Lord, one trust, one baptism, one God and Father of all, who is over all, and through all, and in all. Now each one of us has been given grace according to the measured portion of Christ's gift. This is why it says, 'When he ascended on high, he led captivity captive, and gave gifts to people'....And he gave some apostles, and some, prophets, and some, evangelists, and some pastors and teachers, for the equipping of the holy *ones*, for the work of ministry, with a view to the building up of the body of Christ, until we all attain to the unity of the Faith, and of the knowledge of the Son of God, to a mature man, *and* to the measure of Christ's full stature, so that we are no longer children, tossed to and fro and carried about with every wind of doctrine, by human trickery, by *people's* craftiness in deceitful scheming. Instead, speaking the truth in love, let us grow up in every way into *union with* him who is the head, *into* Christ, from whom the whole body, being fitted together and united through that which every joint supplies, by the working of each individual part in its proper measure, produces the growth of the body for the building of itself in love" [Ephesians 4:4-8, 11-16 REV]. Moreover, Peter tells us in his first letter to the Church: "As you come to him [Christ], a living stone rejected by man but chosen *and* precious in the sight of God, you also, as living stones, are built up *into* a spiritual house, to be a holy priesthood, to offer up spiritual sacrifices that are acceptable to God through Jesus Christ" [1 Peter 2:4,5 REV]. This "spiritual house" is described in 1 Corinthians 3:16 and 17 (REV): "Do you not know that you are a sanctuary of God, and *that* the spirit of God lives in you? If anyone mars the sanctuary of God, God will mar him, for the sanctuary of God, which you are, is holy;" and in Ephesians 2:21 (REV): "…in whom the whole building, being fitted together, grows into a holy sanctuary in the Lord."

Paul further describes and explains the purpose of the one Body of Christ in 1 Corinthians 12 (REV): "For as the [human] body has many parts, but all the parts of the body, being many, are one body, so also is Christ. For we were all baptized in one spirit into one body, whether Jews or Greeks, whether bond or free, and were all made to drink of one spirit. For the body is not one part, but many. If the foot says, 'Because I am not the hand, I am not of the body,' it is not because of that not *part* of the body. And if the ear says, 'Because I am not the eye, I am not of the body,' it is not because of that not *part* of the body. If the whole body *were* an eye, where *would be* the hearing? If the whole *were* hearing, where *would be* the smelling? But now God has set the parts, each one of them, in the body, even as it pleased him. And if they were all the same part, where *would be* the body? But now there are many parts, but one body. And the eye is not able to say to the hand, 'I have no need of you,' or again the head to the feet, 'I have no need of you.' On the contrary, those parts of the body that seem to be weaker are much more necessary, and those *parts* of the body we think to be less honorable, on these we bestow more abundant honor; and our unrespectable *parts* have more abundant respect, whereas our respectable *parts* have no need. But God has combined *the parts of* the body, giving more abundant honor to that *part* that lacked, so that there is no schism in the body, but *that* the members have the same concern for one another. And if one part suffers, all the parts suffer with it, or *if one* part is honored, all the parts rejoice with it. Now you are *the* body of Christ, and individually parts of it. And God has set some in the congregation, first apostles, secondly prophets, thirdly teachers, then miracles, then gifts of healings, helps, governments, *various* kinds of tongues. Are all apostles? Are all prophets? Are all teachers? Are all *workers of* miracles? Do all have gifts of healings? Do all speak in tongues? Do all interpret? But earnestly desire the greater gifts" [*charisma*—"a favor which one receives without any merit of his own"] [1 Corinthians12:12-31 REV]. Our response to Paul's series of rhetorical questions is obvious—not all members of the Body of Christ are apostles, prophets, workers of miracles, etc. The "greater gifts" are those most needful in the local church--"for God has set the parts, each one of them, in the body just as it pleased him."

Diversities of gifts

In Romans 12 (REV) Paul encourages members of the Body of Christ to use their gifts: "For just as we have many parts in one body, and all the parts do not have the same function, in the same way, we who are many are one body in Christ, and individually parts of one another. But since we have gifts that differ according to the grace that was given to us, *let us use them accordingly.* If prophecy, *let us prophesy* according to the proportion of our trust; if serving [*diakonia*—"service"], *let us give ourselves* to our serving; or the one who teaches, to teaching; or the one who encourages, to encouragement; the one who gives, *do it* with liberality; the one who leads, with diligence; the one who shows mercy, with cheerfulness" [verses 4-8]. "But since we have gifts…." Here the word is *charisma* in the Greek text, meaning "a favor which one receives without any merit of his own," "a gift of grace," "a divine gratuity." The reality is, God has endowed each member of the Body of Christ with specific gifts of "divine grace" which one receives without any merit of his own. As each member of the Body of Christ matures spiritually in his or her Christian walk, he ought to become more and more self-aware of himself—that is, he begins to discover and recognize the special abilities, skills, and long suits with which God has blessed him. He discovers that which he does best and that which he loves to do in service to his Lord and to the local church of which he is a part. Experience is a great teacher. As each member of the Body discovers what he does best, he also learns what he is not very good at and what he needs to leave to others. Even in retrospect as he matures spiritually, he may look back on experiences he had serving the church and take into account how the experience affected him emotionally and psychologically. Was the experience energizing or was it discouraging? Christian ministry as the result of God's gifts functioning in a believer can accomplish the purposes of God in significant ways, "for it is God who is working in you both to want *to do,* and to do, His good pleasure" [Philippians 2:13 REV]. 1 Peter 4:10 (REV) says: "As each one has received a gift [*charisma*], use it to serve one another, as good house-managers of the many-sided grace of God." In Hebrews 6:10 (REV) Paul writes: "For God *is* not *so* unrighteous *as to* forget your work and the love that you showed toward his name, by having ministered to the holy *ones,* and in your continuing to minister." And Proverbs 18:16 (NKJV): "A man's gift makes room for him, and brings him before great men." This "self discovery" of how a believer best serves in the Body is all with a view toward edifying—building up—the Body in love as it grows into "a holy sanctuary" in the Lord.

A spiritually mature believer who has discovered his gifts and who is serving in the Body of Christ—the Church—effectively, understands that he must remain in spiritual alignment and harmony with the head of the Body—Christ. Serious problems can develop in the local church whenever members "lose connection" with the Lord's guidance. This may occur whenever a member becomes "puffed up" with pride and seeks to do things his or her own way rather than following the lead of the Lord via the holy spirit. "Let no one disqualify you for the prize by delighting in *false* humility and *the* worshipping of angels, taking his stand on what he has seen, puffed up without reason by his fleshly mind, and not holding fast to the Head, from whom the entire body, being supported and held together by the ligaments and those things that tie it together, grows with the growth that is from God" [Colossians 2:18,19 REV].

It is important to note that in 1 Corinthians 12:1(NKJV) where Paul writes: "Now concerning spiritual *gifts,* brethren, I do not want you to be ignorant," the word *gifts* is in italics in most English versions of the Bible. (The REV correctly states: "Now concerning spiritual *matters*....) Unfortunately, in the NKJV this is a misinterpretation of the Greek word *pneumatikos* which means "things of the spirit or "spiritual *matters.*" The word *gifts* was incorrectly added by the translators. Paul says in verse 4 that "there are diversities of gifts [*charisma,* correctly translated "gifts"] but the same Spirit. Then Paul states in verse 7: "But [in contrast to gifts] the manifestation of the Spirit is given to each one for the profit of all." The word "manifestation" [*phanerosis*] means "evidence," "exhibition," "expression." Then in verses 8-10 Paul lists seven manifestations or "expressions" of the holy spirit—and here he is talking about the potential manifestations of the one gift of holy spirit which every believer enjoys—word of wisdom, word of knowledge, faith, gifts [*charisma*] of healing, working of miracles, prophecy, discerning of spirits, different kinds of tongues, interpretation of tongues. These manifestations or evidences of the spirit are *enablements* via the gift of holy spirit born in every believer. They are not individual gifts which, it has been taught by some, God gives to different believers at different times. Every believer has been enabled by the Lord via the holy spirit to operate each of these manifestations of the spirit in a church setting or in his private life, depending on his understanding of their purpose and his believing trust to do so. Much confusion has resulted in the churches as the result of the misinterpretation of 1 Corinthians 12:1 and the misunderstanding of the manifestations of the spirit.

Years ago while I was a deacon in a church in Florida, we decided that each of us on the leadership council ought to take one of the popular spiritual gifts assessment tests to help us to more clearly identify our God-given gifts. Prior to my service in this church, I had enjoyed more than thirteen years as a teacher and leader in a major biblical research and teaching ministry with a Charismatic perspective so that I was knowledgeable and even adept at a number of the manifestations of the spirit. As the result, I scored very high in a number of the manifestations which the test incorrectly presented as individual gifts—making me the most impressively "gifted" member of the leadership council. I knew that this was not true because I understood that the manifestations of the spirit are not individual gifts at all. Fortunately I was able to use this error in the test's parameters as a teaching moment in the church. Alas, all of the spiritual gifts assessment tests that I've explored are flawed and only moderately helpful.

Following is a brief definition of each of the nine manifestations of the spirit that Paul discusses in 1 Corinthians 12-14 (NKJV): "Speaking in tongues" is the ability to speak a language you have never learned by your senses—"though I speak with the tongues of men and of angels" [1 Corinthians 13:1]—as the spirit born in the believer gives the utterance. All believers have this enablement but, alas, not all will speak in tongues, even though Paul says in 1 Corinthians 14:5: "I wish you all spoke with tongues." The "interpretation of tongues" is the ability of a believer to give the "gist" or interpretation of a message he has spoken out loud in tongues in a fellowship of believers. 1 Corinthians 14:13: "Therefore let him who speaks in a tongue pray [believe] that he may interpret;" and verse 27: "…let one [*heis*—"same one"] interpret." "Prophecy" is a spoken message of edification, exhortation, or comfort in a fellowship of believers. It is not the same as a message from a person with the gift ministry of a prophet in the local church. A "word of knowledge" is specific information received from the Lord via the gift of holy spirit born in a believer regarding a situation about which the believer could not have known on his own. A "word of wisdom" is information received from the Lord via the holy spirit instructing the believer *what to do* regarding the word of knowledge received. The "discerning of spirits" is the ability to recognize and understand via the holy spirit the presence and identity of a demon spirit or spirits in a given situation. "Faith" is the ability to believe with absolute conviction that what the Lord has revealed by a word of knowledge and a word of wisdom will come to pass. The "working of miracles" is the ability to bring to pass a miracle in one's life or in praying for and ministering to others after having received a word of knowledge and a word of wisdom from the Lord while having absolute believing trust that what the Lord has promised will come to pass. "Gifts of healings" is the ability to bring to pass a gift [*charisma*] of healing after having received from the Lord via the spirit a word of knowledge and a word of wisdom and having absolute believing trust that what the Lord has promised will come to pass as a miraculous gift of healing. Clearly, many of these manifestations of the spirit may *flow together dynamically* in the ministry of a faithful believer who is "walking by the spirit."

"...gifted artisans"
-Exodus 35:10 (NKJV)

Old Testament records reveal how God "gifted" certain faithful believers for His specific purposes. Exodus 35 (NKJV) tells of Moses' instruction to the Children of Israel for the construction of the tabernacle [*miskan*—"dwelling place"] where God would meet with His chosen people: "All who are gifted artisans among you shall come and make all that the Lord has commanded [verse 10]; "All the women who were gifted artisans spun yarn with their hands, and brought what they had spun, of blue, purple, and scarlet, and fine linen" [verse 25]. "And Moses said to the children of Israel, 'See, the Lord has called by name Bezalel the son of Uri, the son of Hur, of the tribe of Judah; and He has filled him with the Spirit of God, in wisdom and understanding, in knowledge and all manner of workmanship, to design artistic works, to work in gold and silver and bronze, in cutting jewels for setting, in carving wood, and to work all manner of artistic workmanship. And He has put in his heart the ability to teach, in him and Aholiab the son of Ahisamach, of the tribe of Dan. He has filled them with skill to do all manner of work of the engraver and the designer and the tapestry maker, in blue, purple, and scarlet thread, and fine linen, and of the weaver—those who do every work and those who design artistic works" [verses 30-35]. "And Bezalel and Aholiab, and every gifted artisan in whom the Lord has put wisdom and understanding, to know how to do all manner of work for the service of the sanctuary, shall do all that the Lord has commanded. Then Moses called Bezalel and Aholiab, and every gifted artisan in whose heart the Lord had put wisdom, everyone whose heart was stirred, to come to do the work" [Exodus 36:1,2 NKJV].

Clearly God blessed many Old Testament faithful believers with special gifts and skills in order to inspire them, guide and enable them in the design, construction, and decorating of the tabernacle. And God has done—and will do—nothing less for faithful members of the Body of Christ in the edifying and growth of "a holy sanctuary in the Lord," for "a dwelling place of God [Ephesians 2:21,22 REV].

A remarkable episode in 1 Samuel 16 (NKJV) tells how David the shepherd boy was able to minister to King Saul in a skillful way: "Then

Samuel took the horn of oil and anointed him [David] in the midst of his brothers; and the Spirit of the Lord came upon David from that day forward. So Samuel arose and went to Ramah. But the Spirit of the Lord departed from Saul, and a distressing spirit from the Lord [idiom of permission—God allowed it] troubled him. And Saul's servant said to him, 'Surely, a distressing spirit from God is troubling you. Let our master now command our servants, who are before you, to seek out a man who is a skillful player on the harp. And it shall be that he shall play it with his hand when the distressing spirit from God is upon you, and you shall be well.' So Saul said to his servants, 'Provide me now a man who can play well, and bring him to me.' Then one of the servants answered and said, 'Look, I have seen a son of Jesse the Bethlehamite, who is skilled in playing, a mighty man of valor, a man of war, prudent in speech, and a handsome person; and the Lord is with him.' Therefore Saul sent messengers to Jesse, and said, 'Send me your son David, who is with the sheep....' So David came to Saul and stood before him. And he [Saul] loved him greatly, and he became his armor bearer. Then Saul sent to Jesse, saying, 'Please let David stand before me, for he has found favor in my sight.' And so it was, that whenever the [distressing] spirit from God was on Saul, that David would take a harp and play it with his hand. Then Saul would become refreshed and well, and the distressing spirit would depart from him" [16:13-23].

God is informing us in this wonderful record in His word that music *inspired by God* and played skillfully not only can induce "refreshment of the soul," it can also bring healing to the heart. This should be of great encouragement to the gifted Christian musicians, composers, singers and songwriters who have a heart to inspire and bless God's people by their God-given talents.

The Gifts of Ministry

Throughout the gospel records and the New Testament, the word "gifts" has several subtle but different meanings. Romans 5:17 (REV), for example, talks about "the gift [*dorea*—"gratuity"] of righteousness...." Ephesians 2:8 (REV): it is "the gift [*doron*—"expression of honor"] of God...." Matthew 7:11 (REV) and Ephesians 4:8 (REV): "If you then, being evil, know how to give good gifts [*doma*—"a passive gift"] to your children;" and "he led captivity captive, and gave gifts [*doma*] to people." James 1:17 (REV): "All giving that is good [*dosis*—"act of giving"] and every gift that is perfect [*dosis*] is from above, coming down from the Father of lights...." Romans 12:6 (REV): "But since we have gifts [*charisma*—"gift of grace"] differing...."

It is possible to place the spiritual gifts of the Church Epistles that are specifically for the members of the Body of Christ in two general categories: gifts of ministry and motivational gifts. The gifts listed in 1 Corinthians 12, Romans 12, and Ephesians 4 are not exhaustive. Clearly the wonderful gifts of artistry, design, weaving, painting, carving, music, and others discussed in the Old Testament may be prominent in believers today.

Specific gifts of ministry are listed by Paul in Ephesians 4:8-13 (REV): "This is why it says: 'When he ascended on high, he led captivity captive, and gave gifts to people'....And he gave some apostles, and some, prophets, and some, evangelists, and some, pastors and teachers, for the equipping of the holy *ones*, for the work of ministry, with a view to the building up of the body of Christ, until we all attain to the unity of the Faith and of the knowledge of the Son of God, to a mature man, *and* to the measure of Christ's full stature." In the Greek text the word for "gifts" here is *doma*. It means "a present," "a good gift," in a passive rather than active sense because in this case the gift from Christ is the ministry or way of serving of the men and women to whom the gift ministry is imparted. Thus the purpose and the work of the gift ministries in the Church is leadership in a variety of ways. In the Greek the word "equipping" in verse 12 [some versions read "perfecting"] is *katartismos*, meaning "complete furnishing." These five gift ministries are not titles. They are functions in the Body of Christ. To be a true apostle or prophet, for example, is a Christ-given function and not an office or honor bestowed on oneself out of a sense of pride or subterfuge. The Lord imparts these gift ministries on certain men and women who have continued in the fellowship of faith and have shown themselves to be effective "stewards of the mysteries of God" [1 Corinthians 4:1], and whenever a particular ministry is needed in a local church or association of churches.

Apostle: An apostle is a spiritual builder, a dynamic leader sent by Christ to make disciples and to oversee the planting and building of churches. He is a visionary trailblazer adept at developing a community of believers. An apostle may be gifted with a number of the motivational gifts as well as enjoy additional gift ministries such as prophet or evangelist or teacher. First Century Church apostles were the original twelve chosen by Christ plus Mathias [after Judas committed suicide] who witnessed the birth of the Church on the Day of Pentecost, as well as Paul, Barnabas, Adronicus, and Junia who came later [Romans 16:7].

Prophet: A prophet is a spokesman for God and/or the Lord Jesus Christ, one who, in a sense, "sees" or "hears" the voice of the Lord and brings the Lord's instruction or admonition to the local church. Prophets are the "eyes and ears" of the Church of the Body and give spiritual direction. They may exhort, comfort, reprove and correct, foretell, direct, reveal character, interpret enigmas, or even have messages from the Lord for individuals. Prophets played a vital role in the establishment and growth of the First Century Church as recorded in the Book of Acts, and the prophet Agabus graphically portrayed what would happen to Paul [Acts 21] if he disobeyed God and traveled to Jerusalem for Pentecost.

Evangelist: An evangelist in the Church of the Body of Christ is one sent by the Lord, a messenger, to announce, proclaim, teach or preach specifically the good news of the gospel of Jesus Christ. An evangelist has a wonderful God-given ability to set forth the truths of redemption in Christ and to guide the hearers to a point of decision. Philip is the only person in the

New Testament specifically called an evangelist [Acts 21:8], but Jesus Christ demonstrated the fullness of the evangelistic ministry, especially in the first half of His ministry as He was announcing that "the kingdom of God is at hand" [Mark 1:15].

Teacher: The teacher in the Church is one who effectively sets forth sound biblical doctrine. He is fully prepared by means of study, research, and experience, well versed and energized by the truths of God's word to set forth what is true and right in order to instruct and encourage the hearers in wisdom. He has a relentless desire to hold forth truth-- understanding that, prior to His trial and crucifixion, as Jesus prayed to God for His friends in the Garden of Gethsemane, He said: "Make them holy by your truth. Your word is truth" [John 17:16b REV]. Nehemiah 8:8 (NKJV) provides a succinct definition of the ministry of the teacher (both Old and New Testament teachers) as the Levites "read distinctly from the book, in the Law of God; and they gave the sense, and helped them to understand the reading."

Pastor: The pastor is one who is energized by the Lord to tend to the flock. He or she excels in shepherding God's people and healing the broken hearted. The 23rd Psalm (NKJV) beautifully describes the heart of the true pastor: "The Lord is my shepherd; I shall not want... He restores my soul." The pastor cares deeply for the welfare of his people. He leads with gentleness and patience. Oftentimes "pastor" is the default title for the overseer of a congregation, but many times that overseer will not enjoy the true gift ministry of the pastor. Rather, he or she may have the true ministry of a teacher or evangelist, for example, but not be a true pastor. The pastor is a "protector of the sheep" and will be spiritually enabled and equipped to understand, deal with, and alert individual believers to satanic assaults as well as personal failings of sin nature—and to know the difference in counseling.

The Motivational Gifts

"But since we have gifts [*charisma*] that differ according to the grace that was given to us," Paul writes in Romans 12:6 (REV), "*let us use them accordingly.*" Prior to this exhortation, however, he writes in verses 1 and 2: "I urge you therefore, brothers, by the mercies of God, to present your bodies as a living sacrifice, holy, pleasing to God, which is your reasonable service. And do not be conformed to the pattern of this age, but be transformed by the renewing of your mind, so that you can test and approve what the will of God is—the thing that is good and pleasing and perfect." What does Paul mean by "do not be conformed to the pattern of this world"? In the Greek the word for "conformed" is *systhematizesthe,* meaning "a systemization of fashioning to worldly desires." In his first letter to the Church, John says: "For all that is in the world—the lust of the flesh, the lust of the eyes, and the pride of life—is not of the Father but is of the world (NKJV)." Most people, including most Christians, are affected by, and subject to, the very sins that John warns against. People "conformed" to such cravings of the world are, for the most part, defeated or frustrated in their life's desires and goals. This is the sad story of human nature. But Paul says there is a way to overcome: "...but [in contrast to being "conformed to the world"] be transformed by the renewing of your mind...." In the Greek the word "transformed" is *metamorphoo,* meaning "transfigured"—"to change into another form." This is the same word used in Matthew 17:2 and Mark 9:2 where Jesus took three of His disciples to a high mountain and was "transfigured" before them. And what is this transformation that we experience by the "renewing" of our minds?—it is a change into the very character of the living Christ. The word "renewing" is *anakainosis* in the Greek, meaning "a complete change for the better." By not being "conformed to this world," but by being "transformed" by the "renewing of your mind," Paul says "we may test and approve what the will of God is" for our lives. But what is it that we must "renew our minds" to? Clearly it's the word of God—"For the word of God is living, and active, and sharper than any two-edged sword, piercing as far as the dividing of soul and spirit, of both joints and marrow, and is able to judge the considerations and intentions of the heart" [Hebrews 4:12 REV]. Therefore, as a faithful believer and student of the Bible enjoys this ongoing process in his life of the renewing of his mind, he learns more and more effectively how to "walk by trust, not by sight" [2 Corinthians 5:7 REV], and he discerns with increased clarity his unique position as a member of the Body of Christ in functioning in his spiritual gifts.

> **Exhortation:** The word in the Greek is *paraklesis*, meaning "to come alongside of someone." A believer with the motivational gift of exhortation "sees the glass half full" in any situation and has the gift of speaking encouraging and uplifting words in a timely manner.

> **Giving:** A believer with the gift of giving shares his or her material resources with liberality and cheerfulness without any thought of return. Romans 12:8.

> **Leadership:** A gifted leader in the local church attends to the direction of the local Body of Christ with care and diligence so as to motivate others to involvement in accomplishing goals.

> **Mercy/Compassion:** The believer with the gift of mercy/compassion is especially sensitive to those who are suffering. He or she is guided by the heart rather than the head and reveals the love of God by showing kindness and concern for others.

> **Helps/Service:** The believer with this motivational gift is one who simply loves to be of help in any situation, especially if it involves hands-on activity. This person is able to identify undone tasks in God's work, freeing others up for ministry. Philippians 2:3 and 4 (REV) reveal

the servant's heart: "Do nothing out of selfish ambition or out of empty conceit, but in humility regard others better than yourselves. Let each of you not *just* look out for his own interests, but each of you also *looking out* for the interests of others."

Administration: This gifted believer is one who is able to guide the local body toward accomplishing goals and directives of the leaders by planning, organizing, and supervising. Greek: *kubernesis*—"steer," "guide," "helmsman."

Hospitality: A believer with the gift of hospitality warmly welcomes others, even strangers, into one's home or into the church as a means of serving those in need of food or lodging or simply as an encouragement and blessing to others. Greek: *philoxenos*—"love of strangers."

Martyrdom: One who gives over one's life in suffering or to die for the cause of the gospel of Jesus Christ. Revelation 20:4 (REV): "and I *saw* the souls of those who had been beheaded for the testimony of Jesus and for the word of God...."

Celibacy: The spiritual gift that allows a believer to voluntarily remain unmarried without regret and with the ability to maintain control of his or her sexual desires in order to serve the Lord with minimal distraction.

Missionary: This gifted believer is able to minister effectively in another culture. Ephesians 3:8 (REV): "To me, who am less than the least of all *the* holy *ones*, this grace was given, to tell to the Gentiles the good news of the unsearchable riches of Christ."

Intercession: The intercessor has a deep desire and the ability to pray for others for periods of time on a regular basis and believe to see specific answers to their prayers. Colossians 4:12 (REV): "Epaphras, who is one of you, a servant of Jesus Christ, greets you. He is always struggling on your behalf in his prayers...."

Music/Artisan: It is clear in both Old Testament records and the New Testament that certain believers were gifted by God in music or in some other artistry. Exodus 35 names Bezalel and Aholiab as "gifted artisans," and 1 Samuel 16 tells how David played the harp skillfully in order to drive a "distressing spirit" out of King Saul. In Acts 9:39 Dorcas, raised from the dead by Peter, is praised for the wonderful "tunics and garments" which she had made. In the Body of Christ today certain believers are similarly gifted. These are men and women who have a wonderful talent to sing, compose music, paint, sculpt, or design artistically so as to uplift, inspire, and encourage others in the Body to a more worthy endeavor. These talented believers are those whose work is perceived by others as "anointed."

"...since we have gifts that differ..."
-Romans 12:6 (REV)

Most Christians who are active participants in a local church or Christian assembly will discover over time that they have more than one gift—usually in the category of *charisma*, ["gift of divine grace"]. For each member of the Body, God helps us to focus our wonderful gifting so that we work together and remain dependent on one another in order to grasp and understand the larger truth of the one Body in Christ. To some degree, each one in the Body may minister in areas which may not be his or her primary area of gifting. Indeed, over time, we may find ourselves moved to minister in several areas of the *charisma* gifts even though the way we function best in the Body will normally be affected by our primary gift or gifts.

For example, we are all called to exhort one another. Hebrews 3:13

(REV): "But exhort one another day after day, so long as it is *still* called 'today,' lest any one of you is hardened by the deceitfulness of sin." But one who enjoys the gift of **Exhortation** will excel in this area. We all need to be generous in the church with our abundance. Luke 6:38 (REV): "Give, and it will be given to you, good measure, pressed down, shaken together, *and* running over will they give into your lap. For with whatever measure you measure, it will be measured to you again." But one who enjoys the gift of **Giving** will excel in this area. Many believers are called to be leaders in various ways and at different times. Mark 10:42,43 (REV): "You know that those who are recognized as rulers over the Gentiles lord it over them, and their great ones exercise authority over them. But it is not so among you, but whoever wants to be great among you will be your servant." And Matthew 25:21 (REV): "Well done, good and faithful slave. You have been faithful over a few things, I will set you over many things." But a believer who enjoys the gift of **Leadership** or **Administration** makes his gift known in due time and will excel in this area.

The spirit of Christ born in every Christian compels us to show mercy and have compassion for anyone in need. Matthew 5:7 (REV): "Blessed are the merciful, for they will obtain mercy." And 1 Peter 3:8 (REV): "Finally, all of you be likeminded, compassionate, having brotherly affection, tenderhearted, humble minded…." Yet the one who enjoys the gift of **Mercy** will excel in this area. All believers are called to be helpers and to serve in the local church in one way or another. John 12:26 (REV): "If anyone serves me, let him follow me, and where I am, there will my servant be also. If anyone serves me, the Father will honor him." And Galatians 5:13 (REV): "For you, brothers, have been called to freedom; only do not *use* the freedom for an opportunity to *indulge* the flesh, but through love serve [*douleuo*—"obey," "be devoted to"] one another." But the one who enjoys the gift of **Service** will find many opportunities to excel in this area. All Christians are called to use hospitality to bless others. 1 Peter 4:9 (REV): "Show hospitality [*philoxenos*—"generous to guests"] to one another without grumbling." Yet the believer who enjoys the gift of **Hospitality** will excel in this area. We are all encouraged to pray for one another. Luke 18:1 (NKJV): "…men ought always to pray and not lose heart…." And 1

Thessalonians 5:16,17 (REV): "Rejoice always, pray without ceasing; in everything give thanks; for this is the will of God for you in Christ Jesus." But the believer who enjoys the gift of **Intercession** will excel in this area. Every Christian is called to be a teacher of God's word and the love of Christ in our day-by-day relationships. Colossians 3:16 (REV): "Let the word of Christ dwell in you richly, teaching [*didasko*— "instruct"] and admonishing one another with all wisdom, with psalms, hymns *and* spiritual songs, singing with thankfulness in your hearts to God." But the believer to whom the Lord has imparted the gift [*doma*] ministry of a **Teacher** takes on a much greater responsibility and, in due time, will excel in this area. And finally, every Christian ought to be compelled by the love of Christ to share the gospel of Jesus Christ with others. In Mark 16:15 and 16 (REV) Jesus said: "Go into all the world and proclaim the Good News to every creature. Whoever believes and is baptized will be saved, but whoever does not believe will be condemned." And 1 Peter 3:15 (REV): "but in your hearts, set the Lord Christ apart as holy, *and* always *be* ready to give an answer to everyone who asks you for a reason for the hope that is in you, yet *do it* with meekness and respect...." But the believer to whom the Lord has imparted the gift [*doma*] ministry of an **Evangelist** will excel in this area. To such a one the words of Paul are like a clarion call: "I solemnly charge *you:* preach the word: be ready when it is convenient and when it is not convenient; reprove, rebuke, exhort with all longsuffering and teaching. For the time will come when they will not put up with sound teaching, but, having itching ears, will heap to themselves teachers to suit their own desires; and will turn their ears away from the truth, and turn aside to fables" [2 Timothy 4:2-4 REV]. All Christians are called to undershepherd one another: "Let the word of Christ dwell in you richly in all wisdom, teaching and admonishing one another in psalms and hymns and spiritual songs..." [Colossians 3:16 REV]. Yet the believer with the gift ministry [*doma*] of a **Pastor** will recognize his or her calling in due time and be recognized: "I exhort the elders among you...Shepherd the flock of God that is among you, exercising oversight, not out of compulsion but willingly..." [1 Peter 5:1,2 REV].

"...who saved us and called
us with a holy calling"
-2 Timothy 1:9 (REV)

Paul declares in Ephesians 4:4: "*There is* one body and one spirit, even as also you were called in one hope of your calling...." In the Greek text the word for "called" is *kaleo*. It means "to bid," "to call by name." This same word is used in many other verses including: Matthew 1:23 (REV): "Look!, the virgin will be with child, and will give birth to a son, and they will call his name Immanuel, (which translated, means, 'God with us')." Romans 8:30 (REV): "and those whom he [God] decided in advance, these he also called...." I Thessalonians 2:12 (REV): "encouraging you, and comforting *you*, and urging you to walk in a manner worthy of God, who calls you into his own kingdom and glory." 2 Timothy 1:9 (REV): "...who saved us and called us with a holy calling...." 1 Peter 2:9 (REV): "...that you can proclaim the glorious attributes of him who called you out of darkness into his marvelous light." Romans 9:7 (REV): "...neither, because they are Abraham's seed, are they all children, but, 'Through Isaac your seed will be called.'"

Another key word in the Greek translated "calling" or "call" is *klesis*, meaning "a divine invitation to embrace salvation." Among many verses where this word is used: 1 Corinthians 1:26 (REV): "For consider your calling, brothers, that not many wise according to the flesh, not many powerful, not many of noble birth, *are called*." Romans 11:29 (REV): "For the gifts and the calling of God are irrevocable." Philippians 3:14 (REV): "I press toward the goal to *win* the prize of the high calling of God *in connection with* Christ Jesus."

The "call" to Christ—a holy "bidding," "a divine invitation to embrace salvation"--is the foundational and ultimate calling in any person's life. Indeed, Jesus says in Matthew 22:14: "For many are called, but few are chosen." And Paul writes in 1 Timothy 2:4 (REV) that God "wants everyone to be saved and to come to a full knowledge of the truth." Why is it, then, that "few are chosen"? The truth is, not everyone who is called and invited to enter into God's kingdom will do so. This brings us to the hotly debated subject of "predestination" and the "foreknowledge" of God. The classical or Calvinist view is that God, in

His omniscience and foreknowledge, knows everything—past, present, and future, and that His plans are eternally fixed. This view--that God has exhaustive foreknowledge--has its thorny implications regarding evil and "hell" and requires extensive theological consideration, which will not happen here. The "open view," which many contemporary theists have embraced, is that God is omniscient and omnipotent and knows every detail of the past and the present, but that the future is not entirely set, not settled, and so allows for free choices. In this view God is the God of "probabilities." As the God of the "possible," He decides among possibilities as He moves along with us in time.

In Romans 8:29 and 30 (NKJV), Paul says: "For whom He foreknew, He also predestined to be conformed to the image of His Son...." And in Ephesians 1:4 and 5 (NKJV) he writes: "just as He chose us in Him before the foundation of the world, that we should be holy and without blame before Him in love, having predestined us to adoption by Jesus Christ to Himself, according to the good pleasure of His will." Here the word "foreknew" in the Greek is *proginosko,* meaning simply "foreordain" or "foresee." The word "predestined" in the Greek is *proorizo,* meaning "predetermined," "preordained." In the classical view, these definitions suggest that God has determined who will be saved and who will be lost and therefore has predestined certain people for salvation and others for "hell." This seems to preclude the possibility of "free will." In the "open view," some argue that God, in His omniscience and His omnipotence, is able to predict and prophesy the future with precision without overstepping the free will of individuals. In other words, God does not "micromanage" everything concerning our future but has limitless knowledge and understanding about what decisions and courses people will take as well as unlimited resources and ability to bring His predictions to pass. I tend toward this "open view." When Paul says in Ephesians 1:4 (REV) that God "chose us in him before *the* foundation of the world," the word "us" refers to the Church in general, not to individual believers. Thus it is an individual's free will to make a decision to become a member of the Church—the Body of Christ—by receiving God's Son as Lord and Savior. Certainly God is *omniscient*-- He knows every detail of the past and present from the beginning to the end and, as the God of probabilities, in His omnipotence He is able to predict and prophesy future potential. God knew, for example, that it would take a long time—hundreds of years of human history—before the Son of God could be born of a woman who would confess absolute faith in His plan and purpose when the angel Gabriel appeared to Mary in Nazareth: "And the angel answered and said to her, '*The* Holy Spirit will come upon you, and the power of the Most High will overshadow you, and for that reason the holy one to be born will be called the Son of God'….And Mary said, 'Lo! *I am* the servant of the Lord! May it be done to me according to your word'" [Luke 1:35,38 REV]. It took hundreds of years for God's plan to come to pass because His plan required a woman of absolute faith like Mary. And yet God knew in His foreknowledge that eventually His purpose would prevail. 1 John 3:20 (REV) says: "that if our heart condemns us, God is greater than our heart, and knows all things." This verse could support both the classical view and the "open view" of God's foreknowledge. Likewise, Psalm 139:15 & 16 (NKJV): "My frame was not hidden from You, when I was made in secret, and skillfully wrought in the lower parts of the earth. Your eyes saw my substance, being yet unformed. And in Your book they all were written, the days fashioned for me, when as yet there were none of them." This confession of David the psalmist seems to support the classical view--that God knew every detail of David's formation as an embryo, as well as all the days "fashioned" for him, even before he was born. However, eminent teacher John Gill [1697-1771] presents us with some interesting insight into the possible "open view" interpretation of this obscure verse. He writes: "…in the book of God's eternal mind, and designs, the plan of the human body was drawn, all the parts of it described, and their form, places, and uses fixed, even as yet not one of them was in actual being, but in due time they are all exactly formed and fashioned according to the model of them in the mind of God; who has as perfect knowledge of them beforehand as if they were written down in a book before him….not only each of the members of the body were put down in the book, but each of the days in which they should be formed and come into order: when as yet there was 'none of them;' none of those days, before they took place, even before all time."★

Therefore, in His omniscience and in His foreknowledge of "possibilities," God knows who will *likely* accept His "divine invitation to salvation" and who will reject it. And that's why Jesus said: "Many are called but few are chosen." God knows the precise probabilities of who will accept His invitation and be "chosen." Thus, "For whom He foreknew, He also predestined to be conformed to the image of His Son." In no way does this "open view" of predestination and God's foreknowledge preclude an individual's freedom of will to choose good or evil, to accept the gospel "call" or to reject it, to love God or to sin and rebel against Him. In fact most life choices people make day to day are according to each one's freedom of will to choose, not because God has already determined our choices.

As well, the Scriptures reveal the truth that there are certain things in God's will that He has decided will absolutely happen in His timing— and the "timing" of God often depends on human cooperation. In His foreknowledge, God knew that there would be enmity between the seed of the serpent and the seed of the woman [Genesis 3:15]. In His foreknowledge He knew that "There shall come forth a Root from the stem of Jesse, and a Branch [foretelling the coming of Christ] shall grow out of his roots" [Isaiah 11:1,2 NKJV]. In His foreknowledge God knows that "Look! he is coming with the clouds, and every eye will see him, even they who pierced him, and all the tribes of the earth will mourn because of him" [Revelation 1:7 REV]. Therefore, in a real sense, He has "predestined" certain events in the scope of history—and eternity. God pre-determined—predestined—the first coming of Christ, even though it took hundreds of years of human history for His plan and purpose to come to pass--and no amount of human unbelief or satanic interference kept the Son of God from fulfilling the will of God in God's timing. And no amount of human unbelief or scoffing or satanic interference will keep Christ from returning to the earth and establishing His Millennial Kingdom in God's timing.

In "the book of God's eternal mind," even before the "foundation of the world," God "saw" the probability that you, a faithful believer in Christ, would accept His call to salvation and become a member of the Body of Christ. Even "before all time," God knew the probabilities that His Son would bless you with wonderful spiritual gifts, and that in your desire to bless God and to love and serve your brothers and sisters in the Body, by your free will you would learn to recognize them and to function in them effectively. And so, "when as yet there was none of them...before they took place, even before all time," God *ordained* that "the gifts and the calling of God"—*your* gifts and *your* calling—"*are irrevocable.*" They will go with you and be an essential part of who you are *forever.*

---

*John Gill: *An Exposition of the Old Testament,* 1748, Bible Study Online, https:www. Christianity/john-gill. In the public domain.

FOUR

The judgment seat of Christ

"For we will all stand before the
judgment seat of God."
-Romans 14:10 (REV)

THE APOSTLE PAUL DISCUSSES SOME remarkable truths regarding the judgment seat of Christ in three of his letters to the Church: "Therefore also we make it our aim, whether at home or away from home, to be pleasing to him. For we must all be exposed before the judgment seat of Christ, so that each one may be repaid for the things *done* in the body, according to what he has made a practice of doing, whether good or worthless. Therefore knowing the fear of the Lord, we are persuading others. Now we have been made *completely* visible to God..." [2 Corinthians 5:8-11 REV].

In Romans 14:10-12 (REV) Paul says: "For we will all stand before the judgment seat of God. For it is written, **As I live, says the Lord, every knee will bow to me, and every tongue will confess to God.** So then each of us shall give account of himself to God."

And in 1 Corinthians 3:8-15 (REV) Paul writes: "Now the one who plants and the one who waters are one, but each will receive his own reward according to his own labor. For we are God's fellow workers; you are God's field, God's building. According to the grace of God that was given to me, as a wise master-builder I laid a foundation, and another is building on it. But let each one be careful how he builds on it. For no one is able to lay a foundation other than *the one* which has already been laid, which is Jesus Christ. But if anyone builds on *this* foundation using gold, silver, costly stones, wood, hay, straw--each one's work will become plainly seen, for the Day will make it clear, because it will be revealed by fire, and the fire itself will test each one's work, *and show* of what kind it is. If anyone's work that he has built on it remains, he will receive a reward. If anyone's work is burned, he will suffer loss, but he himself will be saved, but it will be like escaping through a fire."

Some Christians believe that God judges people today, either by rewarding good behavior or allowing bad things to happen because of bad behavior—or when they die allowing them into heaven or consigning them to "hell." But that's not what the Bible teaches. The Scriptures inform us that a foundational truth for every Christian believer is that we are "justified in the name of the Lord Jesus and by the Spirit of God" [1 Corinthians 6:11 NKJV], and "therefore, having been justified by faith, we have peace with God through our Lord Jesus Christ" [Romans 5:1 NKJV]. As well, we are "sanctified" [*hagiazo*][1 Corinthians 6:11 (NKJV)]—which means "consecrated," "cleansed," "purified," and "accepted"—"He made us accepted in the Beloved" [Ephesians 1:6 NKJV]. However, other verses clearly state that some Christians who die without confessing their sins and repenting—which is to express sincere regret for their wrongdoing—or who have simply wasted much of their lives caught up in the cares of this world, will appear before the judgment seat of Christ, be judged by the Lord Himself, and suffer loss and shame. "If anyone's work is burned, he will suffer loss, but he himself will be saved" [2 Corinthians 5:10]. "For we must all appear before the judgment seat of Christ, that each one may receive the things *done* in the body, whether good or worthless. Knowing, therefore, the fear of the Lord, we are persuading others..." [2 Corinthians 5:10,11 REV]. And Colossians 3:23-25 (NKJV): "And whatsoever you do, do it heartily, as to the Lord and not to men, knowing that from the Lord you will receive the reward of the inheritance; for you serve the Lord Christ. But he who does wrong will be repaid for what he has done, and there is no partiality." And 2 Timothy 2:12 (NKJV): "If we endure, we shall also reign with *Him* [in the Millennial and Everlasting Kingdoms]. If we deny *Him*, He also will deny us." And 1 John 2:28: "And now, little children, abide in him, that when he appears, we will have confidence and not be ashamed before him at his coming."

Thus it is clear that some Christians, although they are "saved, justified, sanctified, and accepted in the beloved" in terms of salvation, will nevertheless be "ashamed before him at his coming." Paul says: "Knowing, therefore, the fear of the Lord, we persuade men...." In the Greek text the word for "fear" is *phobos*, meaning "to fear exceedingly," "that which strikes terror." This "fear of the Lord" is what some Christians will experience as they stand on the *bema* face to face with Jesus Christ as all of heaven is made aware of the woeful failure of their Christian walk, allowing themselves to be conformed [*syschematizo*] to the satanic systemization of the "lust of the flesh, the lust of the eyes, and the pride in possessions" [1 John 2:16 REV]. Although professing themselves to be Christian, they actually continued to live as "children of wrath" [Ephesians 2:3]. At the judgment seat of Christ they will forfeit rewards they might have won and will suffer loss in terms of the full inheritance they might have received. It's not entirely clear what losses might be suffered by some, but it will become obvious as we continue this study that some Christians will not only have less honorable functions and responsibilities than others in the Millennial Kingdom, they will also enjoy less spiritual authority and missionary assignments in their everlasting lives. And—please take note—this is *forever.*

The Bible makes it clear that Christians will receive what we are due for the way we have lived in our short mortal lives—which is a proving ground for our future everlasting lives. Moreover, it becomes clear in the Scriptures that how well believers identify and discover their spiritual gifts and how well they effectively learn to function in these gifts in service in the Church and in their everyday lives will play a significant role in the quality of their rewards in their everlasting lives, beginning in the Millennial Kingdom and carrying into the Everlasting Kingdom.

Paul declares in 2 Timothy 4:1-8 (NKJV): "I charge *you* [Timothy] therefore before God and the Lord Jesus Christ, who will judge the living and the dead at His appearing and His kingdom: Preach the word! Be ready in season *and* out of season. Convince, rebuke, exhort, with all longsuffering and teaching. For the time will come when they will not endure sound doctrine, but according to their own desires, *because* they have itching ears, they will heap up for themselves teachers; and they will turn *their* ears away from the truth, and be turned aside to fables." Unquestionably this has happened time and again to different Christian sects down through the centuries since Paul's prophecy—and it is happening in our times. But to those who remain faithful to the Lord and obey His commandments, Paul says in 4:8: "Finally, there is laid up for me the crown of righteousness, which the Lord, the righteous Judge, will give to me on that Day [the Day of His appearing leading to the judgment seat of Christ], and not to me only but to all who have loved His appearing."

As well, Paul presents a foundational treatise on judgment in his letter to the Church at Rome: "And do you think this, O man, you who judge those who practice such things [previously delineated in Romans 1], and doing the same, that you will escape the judgment of God? Or do you despise the riches of His goodness, forbearance, and longsuffering, knowing that the goodness of God leads you to repentance? But in accordance with your hardness and impenitent heart you are treasuring up for yourself wrath in the day of wrath and revelation of the righteous judgment of God, who will render to each according to His deeds, eternal life to those who by patient continuance in doing good seek for glory, honor, and immortality; but to those who are self-seeking and do not obey the truth, but obey unrighteousness— indignation and wrath, tribulation and anguish, on every soul of man who does evil, of the Jew first and also of the Greek; but glory, honor, and peace to everyone who works what is good, to the Jew first and also to the Greek. For as many who have sinned without law will also perish without law, and as many who have sinned in the law will be judged by the law (for not the hearers of the law are justified in the sight of God, but the doers of the law will be justified;)…in the day when God will judge the secrets of man by Jesus Christ, according to my gospel" [Romans 2:3-16 NKJV]. Again, he says in 1 Corinthians 4:5 (REV): "So then, do not pass judgments before the proper time, until the

Lord comes, who will both bring to light the hidden things of darkness, and reveal the motives of *people's* hearts, and then each one will have his praise from God." Finally, Revelation 22:12 (REV) states unequivocally: "Look! I am coming quickly, and my reward is with me, to render to each one according to his work."

Peter sheds more light on judgment this way: Christ has given us "exceedingly great and precious promises, that through these you may be partakers of the divine nature, having escaped the corruption that is in the world through lust. But also for this very reason, giving all diligence, add to your faith virtue [*arête*—"moral goodness"], to virtue knowledge, to knowledge self-control, to self-control perseverance, to perseverance godliness [*eusebeia*—"reverence"], to godliness brotherly kindness, and to brotherly kindness love [*agape*—"benevolence"]. For if these things are yours and abound, you will be neither barren nor unfruitful in the knowledge of our Lord Jesus Christ. For he who lacks these things is shortsighted, even to blindness, and has forgotten that he was cleansed from his old sins. Therefore, brethren, be even more diligent to make your call and election secure, for if you do these things you will never stumble; for so an entrance will be supplied to you abundantly into the everlasting kingdom of our Lord and Savior Jesus Christ" [2 Peter 1:4-11 NKJV]. What Christian in his right mind does not hope for an entrance supplied "abundantly into the everlasting kingdom of our Lord and Savior Jesus Christ"?

Students of the Bible must not confuse the judgment seat of Christ with the "great white throne" judgment of Revelation 20. The judgment seat of Christ is exclusively for Christians—those who have confessed Jesus Christ as their Lord and Savior and believe in their hearts that God has raised Him from the dead" [Romans 10:9 NKJV], who have been baptized in holy spirit which Titus 3:5 calls a spiritual "washing of regeneration," and who are members of the spiritual Body of Christ. This spiritual Body is composed of both Jews and Gentiles since the Day of Pentecost, which was the onset of "the dispensation of God's grace" [Ephesians 3:2]. Old Testament faithful believers will not participate in the Rapture of the Church or the judgment seat of Christ. Those early believers in God and the Messiah are destined for "the resurrection of life," also referred to as the resurrection of the just, prophesied by

Jesus [John 5:29], Daniel [12:2], and Ezekiel [37:1-4]. This resurrection will occur shortly after Jesus returns to the earth and establishes His Millennial Kingdom. The second resurrection that Jesus prophesies in John 5:29 is the "resurrection of condemnation." All God-rejecters since the beginning of time not found written in the Lamb's Book of Life [Revelation 20:11-15 NKJV] are destined for this final ominous resurrection: "Then I [John] saw a great white throne and Him who sat on it, from whose face the earth and the heavens fled away. And there was found no place for them. And I saw the dead, small and great, standing before God, and books were opened. And another book was opened, which is the Book of Life, and the dead were judged according to their works, by the things which were written in the books. The sea gave up the dead who were in it, and death and Hades [the grave] delivered up the dead who were in them. And they were judged, each one according to his works. Then death and Hades were cast into the lake of fire. This is the second death. And anyone not found written in the Book of Life was cast into the lake of fire."

"...we will be like him..."
-1John 3:2 (REV)

Questions arise: When will the judgment seat of Christ occur? How long will it last? What will it be like? According to 1 Thessalonians 4, the event or events of the judgment seat of Christ will occur sometime after the Rapture of the Body of Christ—the true Church—after the dead in Christ are raised from the dead first, and after "we who are alive and remain [are] caught up together with them in the clouds to meet the Lord in the air" [verses 16a,17]. It seems possible from the Scriptures that all raptured believers will instantly at that time be "transformed" by the Lord and "conformed to His glorious body," as Paul prophesies in Philippians 3:20 and 21. Paul writes in 1 Corinthians 15:51 and 52 (REV): "Look!, I tell you a sacred secret: We will not all sleep, but we will all be changed. In a moment, in the blink of an eye, at the last trumpet. For the trumpet will sound, and the dead will be raised incorruptible, and we will be changed." 1 John 3:2 (REV) gives us a further clue: "Beloved, we are children of God now; and what we will be has not yet been revealed. We know that when it is revealed, we will be like him, because we will see him just as he is." And 1 Corinthians 13:12 (REV) informs us: "For now we see in a mirror, darkly, but then face to face." So it is possible that at the very moment the raptured saint sees the Lord *face to face,* his "lowly body" will be "changed"--transformed instantly into a likeness of Christ's glorious body, "according to the working by which He is able even to subdue all things to Himself" [Philippians 3:21b]. However, it's not entirely clear from these scriptures that every Christian will be transformed into the likeness of the glorified Christ at the Rapture. Indeed, it's possible that this change will occur later at the judgment seat of Christ. And it's even possible that the quality of an individual's "transformation" may be in relation and proportion to the quality of his or her rewards.

And so a feature of the Rapture of the Church--wherein all Christians, both the living and those raised from the dead—is that we will be "caught up together" for a meeting with the Lord in the air, and in this manner we will always be with the Lord" [1 Thessalonians 4:17b REV]. In the Greek the word for "meeting" is *apantesis.* In three occurrences of this word in the Greek text, it means "a friendly encounter" with a further sense of "extended activities." This "meeting" with the Lord and the inference of extended activities includes the events of the judgment seat of Christ. These extended activities may last the full seven years of the catastrophic tribulation on the earth which will be occurring at the same time. Thus at the Rapture of the Church, all Christians will have a "meeting with the Lord in the air," spend time with Him in heaven at the judgment seat of Christ, and then return with Him to the earth to fight the battle of Armageddon and reign with Him in the Millennial Kingdom.

Since the Lord will "transform our lowly body that it may be conformed to His glorious body," what will our new body be like? Revelation 1:12-16 (REV) gives us a brilliant picture of the glorified Christ: "And I [John] turned to see the voice that spoke with me. And when I turned I saw seven golden lampstands, and in the midst of the lampstands *was* like a Son of Man, clothed with a garment reaching down to the feet, and girded across at the chest with a golden sash. And his head and his hair were white as white wool, *white* as snow, and his eyes were like a flame of fire, and his feet like burnished brass, as if it had been refined in a furnace, and his voice as the sound of many waters. And he had in the right hand seven stars, and out of his mouth came a sharp two-edged broadsword, and his face was like the sun shining in its *full* strength."

However, the Lord's appearance to His disciples after His resurrection and before He ascended to heaven gives us a different picture: On the morning following His resurrection, Jesus appeared to Mary outside the garden tomb where he had been buried: "When she had said this [to the two angels], she turned around and sees Jesus standing, but did not know that it was Jesus. Jesus says to her, 'Woman, why are you crying? Who are you looking for?' She, supposing him to be the gardener, says to him, 'Lord, if you have carried him from here, tell me where you have laid him, and I will take him away.' Jesus says to her, 'Mary.' She turns herself, and says to him in Hebrew, 'Rabboni!' (meaning "Teacher"). Jesus says to her, 'Do not touch me, for I have not yet gone up to the Father. But go to my brothers and say to them, 'I am going up to my Father and your Father, and my God and your God'" [John 20:14-17 REV]. Upon first seeing Jesus in the garden, Mary "supposed Him to be the gardener." Thus He appeared to her as an ordinary man since He had not yet been glorified.

Luke 24 gives us more insight into the Lord's appearance on earth prior to His ascension to the Father. On the dusty road to a village called Emmaus, after His resurrection, Jesus appeared to two of His disciples: "So it was, while they conversed and reasoned, Jesus Himself drew near and went with them. But their eyes were restrained, so that they did not know Him." Thus Jesus appeared to the two disciples as an ordinary traveler like themselves until, at the end of their journey together, "they constrained Him, saying, 'Abide with us, for it is toward evening, and the day is far spent.' And He went in to stay with them. Now it came to pass, as He sat at the table with them, that He took bread, blessed it and broke it, and gave it to them. Then their eyes were opened and they knew Him, and He vanished from their sight" [verses 15,16,29-31 NKJV]. Evidently Jesus was seen by His disciples at first as an ordinary traveler. However, when "their eyes were opened and they knew Him"—"He vanished from their sight." Therefore it's clear that even prior to His ascension to the Father, in His resurrection body He possessed what may have been new and miraculous powers.

Luke 24:36-43 (NKJV) tell us of the Lord's appearance in a gathering of His disciples in Jerusalem: "Now as they said these things, Jesus Himself stood in the midst of them, and said to them, 'Peace to you.' But they were terrified and frightened, and supposed they had seen a spirit. And He said to them, 'Why are you troubled? And why do doubts arise in your hearts? Behold My hands and My feet, that it is I Myself. Handle Me and see, for a spirit does not have flesh and bones as you see I have.' When He had said this, He showed them His hands and His feet. But while they still did not believe for joy, He said to them, 'Have you any food here?' So they gave Him a piece of a broiled fish and some honeycomb. And He took it and ate in their presence."

It's clear in these records in Luke, that the Lord, after His resurrection and prior to His ascension, had the ability to appear and disappear miraculously. In the gathering of His disciples in Jerusalem, He "stood in their midst" so that they thought they were seeing a spirit. And yet He showed them His hands and His feet and ate fish and honeycomb in their sight so that they realized that He was a man "of flesh and bone" like themselves. As well, Acts 1:3 (REV) informs us that the Lord "After his suffering showed himself alive by many convincing proofs, appearing to them over *a period* of forty days and speaking of the things concerning the Kingdom of God." Thus the Scriptures provide us with two remarkable pictures of the Lord after His resurrection—that of an ordinary traveler or gardener or journeyman (albeit with miraculous abilities), and that of John's brilliant vision of Christ in His glory in heaven.

One might ask, "How long will the events of the judgment seat of Christ last?" At the Rapture of the Church, literally millions of people who have confessed Jesus Christ as their Lord and Savior since the Day of Pentecost some 2000 years ago will be raised from the dead, plus those who are alive and will be "caught up together with them in the clouds for a meeting with the Lord in the air." It's logical to assume, therefore, that if "we must all appear before the judgment seat of Christ, that each one may receive the things done in the body, according to what one has done, whether good or worthless" [2 Corinthians 5:10 REV], that this may take considerable time. No one will get shortchanged. "Each one" will receive a full and complete assessment and reckoning in the sight of God, the Lord Jesus Christ, the angels ["host of heaven"], and all brothers and sisters in Christ. Prophetically, Solomon concludes his discourse in Ecclesiastes this way: "Let us hear the conclusion of the whole matter: Fear God and keep His commandments, for this is man's all. For God will bring every work into judgment, including every secret thing, whether good or bad" [12:13,14 NKJV]. And Paul states in 1 Corinthians 4:5 (REV): "So then, do not pass judgments before the proper time, before the Lord comes, who will both bring to light the hidden things of darkness and reveal the motives of people's hearts. And then each one will have his praise from God."

We can deduce from the prophet Daniel's visionary "seventy weeks of years" [Daniel 7:25 and 9:24] corresponding to the 3 ½ years of tribulation plus another 3 ½ years of "great tribulation" on the earth in John's revelation [Revelation 7:14 and 13:5], that the Christian saints will spend either three and one-half years or possibly seven full years in heaven with the Lord. It is possible, then, that the events of the judgment seat of Christ will take seven years until all is complete and the Lord is ready to return to the earth on the Mount of Olives [Zachariah 14:4], and fight the battle of Armageddon "with all His saints" [1 Thessalonians 3:13 NKJV].

"...the mystery...hidden from ages and from generations"
-Colossians 1:26 (NKJV)

In Daniel 9:25 and 26, Daniel is told by Gabriel, God's messenger angel, that the Messiah will be "cut off after seven weeks and sixty-two weeks," beginning with God's command to "rebuild and restore Jerusalem." It has been determined by scholars that "69 sevens" of years equals 483 years after God's decree to rebuild Jerusalem when the Messiah would be "cut off." Biblical historians generally agree that 483 years passed from the time of the decree to rebuild Jerusalem to the crucifixion [the "cutting off"] of Jesus Christ. That left one seven-year period yet to be fulfilled according to Daniel 9:24 (NKJV): "To finish the transgression, to make an end of sins, to make reconciliation for iniquity, to bring in everlasting righteousness, to seal up vision and prophecy, and to anoint the Most Holy." This single seven-year period of prophecy *is* the tribulation of God's judgment on Israel and on unrepentant humanity.

But that leaves us with a mysterious "gap"—a period of time between the "69 sevens of years" and the actual onset of the 70th "weeks of years" of Daniel's prophecy. Amazingly, God determined to interrupt and suspend the fulfillment of the prophecy [of the tribulation] by what Paul describes as the "mystery"--"the dispensation of the grace of God." "For this reason I, Paul, the prisoner of Christ Jesus for you Gentiles—if indeed you have heard of the dispensation of the grace of God which was given to me for you, how that by revelation He made known to me the mystery (as I have briefly written already, by which, when you read, you may understand my knowledge in the mystery of Christ), which in other ages was not made known to the sons of men, as it has now been revealed by the Spirit to His holy apostles and prophets: that the Gentiles should be fellow heirs, of the same body, and partakers of His promise in Christ through the gospel..." [Ephesians 3:1-6 NKJV]. Paul declares in Colossians 1:26 and 27 (REV): "...I became a servant, in accord with the administration of God that was given to me for you to complete the word of God, the Sacred Secret, which has been hidden for ages and generations, but now has been revealed to his holy ones. God wanted to make known to them what is the riches of the glory of this Sacred Secret among the Gentiles, which is Christ in you, the hope of glory." So it is a remarkable truth that God determined that a *pause* should occur between the conclusion of the 69th week of Daniel's prophecy— the "cutting off," i.e., the crucifixion of Christ—and the beginning of the 70th week—the tribulation of God's wrath--a "parenthesis" in prophetic history allowing for the inception of the Church of the Body of Christ which has now lasted about 2000 years! And when this present "dispensation of the grace of God" comes to an end with the Rapture of the Church, then will begin the final seven year period of Daniel's prophecy—the tribulation.

The wrath of God is coming on Israel and the nations "to make reconciliation for iniquity" and to "bring in everlasting righteousness."

But one thing is certain for the Christian: "Jesus, our Deliverer from the wrath to come" [1 Thessalonians 1:10 REV], and Romans 5:9 (REV): "Since we have now been declared righteous by his blood, much more *surely* then we will be saved from the wrath through him." However, it is uncertain if being delivered from "the wrath to come" refers to being saved from the full seven years of the tribulation or only from the three and one-half years of "great tribulation." Many Bible scholars believe in a "pre-tribulation" Rapture while others suggest a "mid-tribulation" Rapture. "Nevertheless the solid foundation of God stands, having this seal: 'The Lord knows who are his...'" [2 Timothy 2:19 REV].

"...each one's work will become plainly seen..."
-1 Corinthians 3:13 (REV)

What will the events of the judgment seat of Christ be like? For many Christians it will be a time of rejoicing, unparalleled celebration, and divine fellowship—a magnificent family reunion and homecoming. The words "judgement seat" are one word in the Greek text—*bema*—which means "a raised place or platform." In ancient Greek culture, the *bema* referred to a seat of judgment and a platform where athletes were awarded for their performance in the Olympic Games. It also referred to a platform where Greek or Roman magistrates could address a public assembly or administer justice. In heaven the judgment seat of Christ will be a place of an ongoing incomparable awards ceremony. Each Christian will be called forth in the halls of heaven to stand on the *bema*. Nothing in this mortal life can compare to the magnificent honor and privilege to be bestowed on each faithful believer in the giving of praise and eternal rewards—presented personally by Jesus Christ Himself. Joy and delight will be overwhelming for each faithful believer when Christ Himself smiles on each one, embraces each one, and announces to the holy gathering of the host of heaven the fabulous eternal rewards each one has earned, not only for his or her accumulated years of service to Christ, but because he or she endeavored to use their God-given spiritual gifts to the edification of the Body of Christ in the love of God and His Son. Every Christian will experience a thorough and complete evaluation process at the *bema:* "each one's work will become plainly seen, for the Day will make it clear, because it will be revealed by [holy] fire; and the fire itself will test [*dokimazo*—"prove," "discern," "examine"] each one's work, *and show* of what kind it is. If anyone's work which he has built on it remains, he will receive a reward. If anyone's work is burned, he will suffer loss, but he himself will be saved, But it will be like escaping through fire" [1 Corinthians 3:13-15 REV]. Paul says in Galatians 6:7 (REV): "Do not be deceived: God is not mocked, for whatever a person sows, that will he also reap."

Surely every Christian will experience the gamut of intense emotions as he or she stands *face to face* with the Lord Jesus Christ at the *bema*. For some, confidence because of their lifelong devotion to Christ. For others, unspeakable joy for their having long anticipated and prayed for His "appearing" as they receive the "crown of righteousness" reserved for those who have longed for Christ's return and love His appearing, as described by Paul in 2 Timothy 4:8. Others will experience shock and shame [1 John 2:28] as the quality of their Christian life and works will not measure up to the test of holy fire. And others will experience a sense of fear when it is revealed how they devoted their words and deeds to the service of their selfish sin nature—or even denied the Lord and "turned from the holy commandment" [2 Peter 2:21] to serve idols. For such there will be deep sorrow when they learn how little eternal reward they earned because their words and works did little to reflect God's goodness and love. For such, a deep sense of guilt as their eyes are opened in the presence of heaven to see that their character shockingly missed the mark of the minimal quality God expects for His children.

At the *bema* every Christian son or daughter will give a full accounting of their character, conduct, words ["for by your words you will be declared righteous and by your words you will be condemned"— Matthew 12:37 (REV)], how well they learned to function in their spiritual gifts in the Body, and even their motives of the heart. Indeed, in Luke 12:1b-3 (REV) Jesus warns His followers: "Beware of the leaven of the Pharisees, which is hypocrisy. Indeed, there is nothing covered up that will not be revealed, and hidden that will not be known. Therefore, whatever you have said in the darkness will be heard in the light, and what you have spoken in the ear in inner rooms will be proclaimed from the housetops." In practice modern religious Pharisees rule many churches and denominations today and pride themselves on their many followers. In Matthew 15:7-9 (REV) the Lord says: "You hypocrites, rightly did Isaiah prophesy about you, saying: 'This people honors me with their lips, but their heart is far from me. Moreover in vain do they show devotion to me, teaching *as their* doctrines the commandments of men.'" At the judgment seat of Christ, our entire lives will be an "open book" to all of heaven itself. Thus not only will the Lord uncover and reveal "every secret thing" in our lives, He will fully examine the motivations of our hearts as to why we did it. He will examine and reveal the total pattern of our conduct in our mortal lives and reward us for those works, words, and motivations of goodness that pass the test. The judgment seat of Christ will issue forth the final verdict as to our eternal rewards and destiny in both the Millennial and Everlasting Kingdoms. Thus, for every Christian, it will be a time of joy and thanksgiving, humility and praise, shame and guilt, amazement and love, as every knee shall bow in the presence of the Lord—and then unspeakable *glory* as all believers rise and stand in heaven in their *transformed bodies* conformed to Christ's glorious body fitted and prepared for *eternity*.

The Five Crowns

In the Church Epistles God promises ways in which He will reward faithful Christians who go "above and beyond" in their service in the Body of Christ. In a sense, God has laid out an "extra credit" plan for believers. These incentives are referred to in the Scriptures as "crowns." Five "crowns" are available: the "incorruptible crown," the "crown of rejoicing," the "crown of righteousness," the "crown of life," and the "crown of glory."

> **Incorruptible Crown.** The "incorruptible crown" is mentioned in 1 Corinthians 9:25-27 (REV): "And everyone who is competing *in the games* exercises self-control *in* all things. Now they *do it* to obtain a corruptible crown, but we an incorruptible.

Therefore I do not run like one *who runs* aimlessly. I do not box as one beating the air, but I treat my body harshly and make it my slave, lest by any means, after that I have preached to others, I myself should be disqualified *for the prize.*" In essence, this "crown" will be given for exercising self-control and striving to be the best you can be in your life for the Lord. Paul discusses it in an athletic connotation. Athletes train hard to be the best they can be and endeavor constantly to improve. God implores His sons and daughters to have that kind of attitude and behavior. The Lord Jesus Christ will personally award worthy believers with this special "incorruptible crown" at the judgment seat of Christ.

Crown of Rejoicing. The "crown of rejoicing" is mentioned in 1 Thessalonians 2:19 (REV): "For who is our hope, or joy, or crown of boasting before our Lord Jesus at his coming? Is it not even you? For you are our glory and joy." This "crown" will be awarded to those who reach others with the word of God—the gospel of salvation—and help to bring them to a decision for Christ. Paul says in Romans 10:13 and 14 (NKJV): "For whoever calls on the name of the Lord shall be saved. How then shall they call on Him in whom they have not believed? And how shall they believe in Him of whom they have not heard? And how shall they hear without a preacher? And how shall they preach unless they are sent? As it is written: 'How beautiful are the feet of those who preach the gospel of peace, who bring glad tidings of good things.'" Not every believer is called by God to be an evangelist, but everyone is called to tell others the good news of the gospel of salvation. Witnessing to others the "good news" can sometimes be intimidating, and the hearer is not always appreciative. But the Lord Jesus Christ will personally award believers who do so with the "crown of rejoicing" at the judgment seat of Christ.

Crown of Righteousness. The "crown of righteousness" is mentioned in 2 Timothy 4:8 (REV): "In the future there is laid up for me the crown of righteousness, which the Lord, the righteous judge, will give to me at that day, and not to me only, but also to all those who have longed for his appearing." Certain Christians have such a love for and dedication to God's word, and for the intimacy of their fellowship with Christ, that they long for His return. Others who choose not to live a godly lifestyle because of the deceitfulness of sin do not look forward to the Lord's return. Christians who long for and love His appearing will be rewarded personally by Jesus Christ with the "crown of righteousness" at the judgment seat of Christ.

Crown of Life. The "crown of life" is described in James 1:2 and 3 and verse 12 (REV): "Count it all joy, when you fall into various temptations, knowing that the testing of your trust produces patience. Now let patience have *its* complete effect, so that you become mature and whole, lacking in nothing....Blessed is the man who endures temptation; for when he has been approved he will receive the crown of life which the Lord promised to those who love him." Thus the "crown of life" will be given to Christians who remain faithful through various trials and temptations. Certainly it is a challenge for Christians to remain faithful their entire lives "in the midst of a crooked and twisted generation" [Philippians 2:15 REV]. Too often some believers "cool off" in their zeal for the Lord at some point in their lives, just as Jesus describes in the Parable of the Sower: "A sower went out to sow his seed. And as he sowed, some fell by the wayside; and it was trampled down, and the birds of the air devoured it. Some fell on rock; and as soon as it sprang up, it withered away because it lacked moisture. And some fell among thorns, and the thorns sprang up with it and choked it. But others fell on good ground, sprang up, and yielded a crop a hundredfold....Now the parable is this: The seed is the word of God. Those by the wayside are the ones who hear, then the devil comes and takes away the word out of their hearts, lest they should believe and be saved. But the ones on the rock are those who, when they hear, receive the word with joy; and [but] these have no root, who believe for a while and in time of temptation fall away. Now the ones that fell among thorns are those who, when they have heard, go out and are choked with cares, riches, and pleasures of life, and bring no fruit to maturity. But the ones that fell on the good ground are those who, having heard the word with a noble and good heart, keep it and bear fruit with patience" [Luke 8:5-8;11-15 NKJV]. The "crown of life" will be personally awarded by the Lord at the judgment seat of Christ to those who persevere in their faithfulness to the Lord despite trials and temptations.

Crown of Glory. The "crown of glory" is mentioned in 1 Peter 5:2-4 (REV): "Shepherd the flock of God which is among you, exercising oversight, not out of compulsion, but willingly, as God would have you do it, and not for dishonorable gain, but eagerly, not lording it over those allotted to you, but being examples to the flock; and when the Chief Shepherd appears, you will receive the crown of glory that does not fade away." The "crown of glory" is for those who willingly and faithfully shepherd God's people. Too often in the local church pastors, elders, or overseers become discouraged because overseeing God's people, some of whom can be ungrateful or even disruptive, can be disappointing and difficult. Certain Old Testament records tell us that even God Himself occasionally became disgusted with the Children of Israel's attitudes and behavior. God understands that it is sometimes difficult and frustrating work to shepherd the people of God. Thus the Lord Jesus Christ, at the judgment seat of Christ, will personally present this special "crown of glory" to those who faithfully persevere in the shepherding of God's people.

The Parable of the Talents

The purpose of the Lord's parables—of which there are 40 recorded in the Synoptic Gospels—is to introduce in layman's terms the mysteries of the kingdom of God. In Luke 8:10 and in Mark 4:11 (REV), Jesus explains the purpose of His parables: "The Sacred Secret of the Kingdom of God has been given to you [disciples]. But to those who are outside, everything is done in parables, so that 'seeing they see but do not perceive, and hearing they hear but do not understand....'"

The word "parable" [*parabole*] means "figure," "comparison." It is a side-by-side placing, a comparing of earthly matters with heavenly truths to be understood. A parable of the Lord is often an expanded proverb. His parables are not merely illustrations, but internal analogies—the natural world becoming a witness for the spiritual realities. Jesus points out to His disciples that His parables can only be understood by those willing to learn with spiritual intuition: "He who has ears to hear, let him hear!" Jesus did not seek to conceal truth from those not understanding; rather He was differentiating those with "ears to hear" from those who cannot bring themselves to come to the light, thus exposing their unbelief and their sins.

The Parable of the Talents found in Matthew 25:15-30 (REV) is an analogy of what the kingdom of heaven will be like. Jesus relates the story of a master leaving his home for a while in order to travel. Before leaving he entrusts his possessions—his "goods" worth eight talents [*talanton*—"a certain weight," "sum of money"] to his servants. "And to one he gave five talents, and to another two, and to another one; to each according to his own ability; and *then* he went on his journey." While the master was away, the servant who had received five talents "went and traded with them, and gained another five talents. Likewise the one *who received* the two gained two more also. But the one who received the one *talent,* having gone out, dug in the earth and hid his lord's money.

"Now after a long time the lord of those slaves comes and settles accounts with them. And the one who received five talents came and brought five more talents, saying, 'Lord, you entrusted five talents to me. See, I have gained five more talents.' His lord said to him, 'Well done, good and faithful slave. You were faithful over a few things, I will set you over many things. Enter into the joy of your lord.' And the one who *received* the two talents also came and said, 'Lord, you entrusted two talents to me. See, I have gained two more talents. His lord said to him, 'Well done, good and faithful slave. You have been faithful over a few things, I will set you over many things. Enter into the joy of your lord.'

"And the one who had received the one talent also came and said, 'Lord, I knew that you are a hard man, reaping where you did not sow, and gathering where you did not scatter, and I was afraid, and went away and hid your talent in the earth. See, you have that which *is* yours.' But his lord answered and said to him, 'You wicked and lazy slave. You knew that I reap where I have not sowed, and I gather where I did not scatter, then you needed to deposit my money with the bankers, and at my coming I would have received back my own with interest. Therefore take away the talent from him and give it to the one who has the ten talents. For to everyone who has, *more* will be given, and he will have abundance. But from the one that does not have, even what he has will be taken away. And throw out the worthless slave into the extreme darkness; there will be the sobbing and the gnashing of teeth.'"

The Parable of the Talents is an encouragement, as well as a prophetic warning, specifically to Israel prior to the Lord's departure. Christ, their Lord, is leaving for a long time and delegates to them responsibility as stewards to care for the kingdom to come. He impresses on them the weight of that responsibility and the serious consequences of neglecting His instructions. It is a message specific to Israel, but its application is to all who have "ears to hear." In its application to the members of the Body of Christ, each one has been entrusted by the Lord with specific spiritual gifts [*charisma* or *doma*]—abilities, skills, perhaps even a gift ministry—to serve in the Church "causing growth in the body unto the building up of itself in love" [Ephesians 4:16]. How well each member discovers his gifts and learns to function in them in service to the Lord will determine who he or she will be in terms of the quality of their rewards—or lack of rewards—at the judgment seat of Christ and in the Millennial and Everlasting Kingdoms to come. As Christians we have been endowed with valuable resources—"talents"—to serve and to bless others. The value of what we do in this life will be multiplied abundantly both naturally and spiritually in our everlasting lives. Each one of us will be held accountable to the Lord for the "talents" we have been given.

FIVE

The Millennial Kingdom
Forever Young

"Repent, for the Kingdom of Heaven is at hand."
-Matthew 4:17 (REV)

THE SUBJECT AND SUBSTANCE OF the Lord's Beatitudes in the gospels is prescriptive and is *not* this mortal life, notwithstanding that there may indeed be application of the Lord's teaching for this present age. Essentially His teaching is of the future life—the Millennial Kingdom. The Beatitudes are recorded in both Matthew and Luke. When the reader of the Bible understands that Christ is teaching about Old Testament prophesies to be applied to His future kingdom, what He teaches is clear and simple. In Matthew chapter 5 Christ teaches to a crowd situated on a hillside, and so His teaching has been called the Sermon on the Mount. In Luke 6 He is teaching on a plain, and so His teaching has been called the Sermon on the Plain.

In Matthew 5:3 (REV) the Lord says to the gathered multitude: "Blessed are the poor in spirit [those who mourn], for theirs is the Kingdom of Heaven" [when the kingdom of heaven comes to pass]. Isaiah 61:2 and 3 (NKJV) prophesies of "the day of vengeance of our God," referring to the tribulation, and afterward "to comfort all who mourn, to console all those who mourn in Zion. To give them beauty for ashes, the oil of gladness for mourning." In Matthew 5:5 (REV) Jesus says: "Blessed are the meek, for they will inherit the earth." Isaiah 57:13b (NKJV) says to Israel: "But he who puts his trust in Me shall possess the land and shall inherit My holy mountain" [in the future kingdom]. And Psalm 37:11 (NKJV) says: "But the meek shall inherit the earth, and shall delight themselves in the abundance of peace." In Ezekiel 37:12 (NKJV) God tells the prophet: "Therefore prophesy and say to them [Israel], 'Thus says the Lord God, Behold, O My people. I will open your graves and cause you to come up [at the resurrection of life in the Millennial Kingdom] from your graves, and bring you into the land of Israel.'"

In Matthew 5:6 (REV) Jesus says: "Blessed are those who hunger and thirst after righteousness, for they will be filled." Unrighteousness exists on earth and will continue until Christ returns. 2 Corinthians 5:21 (REV) informs us that the individual Christian is righteous in God's reckoning: "He made him who did not know sin *to be* a sin offering on our behalf, so that through *union with* him, we would become the righteousness of God." Yet in a practical sense righteousness is not attainable in this mortal life because of our sin nature. Righteousness will become fully attainable and practical in the future kingdoms. 2 Peter 3:13 (REV) assures us: "But according to his promise, we look for new heavens and a new earth in which dwells righteousness." And for Israel: "The righteous shall inherit the land [in the Millennial Kingdom] and dwell in it forever." And Isaiah 11:4 (NKJV): "But with righteousness He shall judge the poor, and decide with equity for the meek of the earth."

Continuing in the Sermon on the Mount, Matthew 5:7 (REV): "Blessed are the merciful, for they will obtain mercy." Although mercy may be in short order for many in this mortal life, God will display great mercy for all who are destined for the Lord's Millennial Kingdom. Matthew 25:34-36 (REV): "Then the King will say to the ones on his right, 'Come, you who have been blessed by my Father, inherit the kingdom that has been prepared for you from the foundation of the world: for I was hungry and you gave me *something* to eat; I was thirsty and you gave me a drink; I was a stranger and you invited me in; naked, and you clothed me; I was sick, and you visited me; I was in prison and you came to me…." Then verses 45 and 46 conclude the parable: "Truly I say to you, in so far as you did not do *it* to one of these least, you did not do it to me.' And these will go away into punishment *in the* Age *to come;* but the righteous into life *in the* Age *to come*."

Matthew 5:8 (REV): "Blessed are the pure in heart, for they will see God." When will the pure in heart see God? "Look! the tabernacle of God is with man, and he will dwell with them, and they will be his people; and God himself will be with them *and be* their God" [Revelation 21:3 REV]. In Matthew 5:9 (REV) Jesus says: "Blessed are the peacemakers, for they will be called sons of God." Today God refers to His born-again believers as "sons of God" [Romans 8:14]. This prophecy in Matthew, however, refers to a psalm of David for Israel: """Mark the blameless man, and observe the upright; For the future of that man is peace. But the transgressors shall be destroyed together; The future of the wicked shall be cut off. But the salvation of the righteous is from the Lord" [Psalm 37:37,38 NKJV].

Matthew 5:10-12 (REV): "Blessed are those who have been persecuted for the sake of righteousness, for theirs is the Kingdom of Heaven [when the Kingdom of Heaven comes to pass]….Rejoice, and be exceedingly glad, for great is your reward [reserved] in heaven. For in the same way they persecuted the prophets who were before you." Hebrews 11 (REV) provides us with a summary of the persecution of righteous people in Old Testament times. Verse 35 says some of them "were tortured, not accepting their release, in order that they would obtain a better resurrection"—meaning the resurrection of life in the Millennial Kingdom specifically for the Old Testament faithful. Verses 13-16: "All these people were still living by trust when they died, not having received the promises [of inheriting the land], but they saw them from a distance, and saluted them, and professed that they were foreigners and temporary residents on the earth. For those who say such things make it clear that they are seeking a homeland. And indeed, if they had kept thinking of that *land* from which they came out, they would have had an opportunity to return. But as it is, they desire a better *land,* that is, a heavenly *one,* Therefore God is not ashamed to be called their God, for he has prepared a city for them"—meaning the New Jerusalem [Revelation 21:2].

In His Sermon on the Plain, Jesus is not preaching to the multitude but specifically to His disciples. In Luke 6:20 (REV) He says: "Blessed are *you* poor, for yours is the Kingdom of God." The Lord was talking to His disciples who were poor and not to poor people in general. Poverty does not gain anyone the kingdom of God, but faith and discipleship do. In verse 21 He says: "Blessed *are* you who hunger now, for you shall be filled." In His Sermon on the Mount, He told the multitude: "Blessed are those who hunger and thirst for righteousness, for they shall be filled." Thus there is a distinct difference to whom Christ is teaching and a distinct difference in the message. In His Sermon on the Mount, His tone is evangelistic. Not so in His Sermon on the Plain where He is teaching His disciples. In Luke 6:22 and 23 (REV) He says to His disciples: "Blessed are you when people hate you, and when they exclude you, and reproach you, and reject your name as evil, on account of the Son of Man. Rejoice in that day and leap *for joy*, for Look!, your reward is great [reserved by God] in heaven, for their fathers did the same things to the prophets." The Lord's promise here is similar to His promise to the multitude in Matthew 5:10-12. Records of the persecution of God's faithful people in Old Testament times are abundant. Indeed, the Lord prophesies that this will continue in the lives of His disciples. But His promise is for great reward in the Millennial Kingdom for those who remain faithful.

To say that the subject of the Lord's Beatitudes is prescriptive and is not this mortal life is not to say that they have no application for Christians today. Certainly they do! Peter says: "But, according to his promise, we look for new heavens and a new earth in which dwells righteousness" [2 Peter 3:13 REV]. Christians will be there! In this mortal life we need to prepare for that day. Thus the Lord's teaching in both the Sermon on the Mount and His Sermon on the Plain provides Christians with enlightening examples of God's promise of the return of Jesus Christ to the earth and our hope for both the Millennial and Everlasting Kingdoms to come. Such hope for the Christian is what Paul calls "an anchor of the soul" [Hebrews 6:19].

"Repent, for the Kingdom of Heaven is at hand."

–Matthew 4:17 (REV)

Jesus Christ's short earthly ministry can be viewed in two basic phases: the first—His proclamation that "the kingdom of heaven is at hand;" the second—His declaration and assessment of Israel's rejection of the kingdom. John chapter 2 (REV) tells of the miracle of His turning water into wine at a wedding: "This beginning of *his* signs Jesus did in Cana of Galilee, and revealed his glory; and his disciples believed in him" [verse 11]. However, Matthew 4:17 (REV) represents the actual beginning of the initial phase of His ministry: "From that time on [following His temptation by the devil in the wilderness] Jesus began to preach, and to say, 'Repent, for the Kingdom of Heaven is at hand.'" Verse 23: "And Jesus went throughout all Galilee, teaching in their synagogues and preaching the Good News of the kingdom." Matthew 5 records His Sermon on the Mount, which is the heart of His teaching regarding the advent of the kingdom of heaven. Matthew 9:35 shows Him continuing to preach the gospel of the kingdom as well as demonstrating His authority as the king: "And Jesus went about all the cities and villages, teaching in their synagogues, and preaching the gospel of the kingdom, and healing every sickness and every disease among the people." In Matthew 10:1 (REV) Jesus, in His authority as the king, gave them [His twelve disciples] "authority over unclean spirits, to cast them out, and to heal every kind of sickness and every kind of disease." And He commands them: "And as you go, preach, saying, 'The kingdom of heaven is at hand.'"

In Matthew 11:3 (REV) John the Baptist sends two of his disciples to Jesus, asking Him: "Are you the Coming One, or should we be looking for a different one?" In His authority as the king of the promised kingdom, Jesus replies: "Go and tell John the things that you hear and see: 'The blind receive their sight, and the lame walk; the people with skin diseases are cleansed, and the deaf hear, and the dead are raised, and the poor have Good News told to them., and blessed is the one who will not fall away because of me'" [verses 4-6]. In Matthew 11:15 Jesus continues to proclaim that the kingdom of heaven is "at hand" and Himself as the king in His authority displayed. However, Matthew 16:20 and 21 (REV) inform us that He now begins to understand that Israel would reject the kingdom as well as Himself as their Messiah and king: "Then he ordered his disciples that they should not tell anyone that he was the Christ. From that time Jesus began to show to his disciples that he must go to Jerusalem and suffer many things from the elders and chief priests and experts in the law, and be killed, and the third day be raised." Matthew 21:18 and 19 (REV): "Now in the morning, when he returned to the city, he was hungry. And having seen a lone fig tree by the road, he went up to it and found nothing on it but only leaves. And he says to it, 'Let there be no fruit from you any longer forever.' And immediately the fig tree withered." Few readers of the Bible understand this strange action of the Lord in cursing the fig tree. The fig tree was a symbol of national Israel. The Lord's cursing of the fig tree represented God's curse on Israel for their failure to recognize their "time of visitation," that is, their rejection of Christ as their Messiah, and thus their ultimate rejection of the kingdom of heaven which He had been announcing. In Luke 19:41-44 (REV) Jesus prophesies regarding Jerusalem: "And when he drew near and saw the city, he burst into sobs over it, saying 'If you had known on this your day, even you, the things that would bring peace...but now they have been hidden from your eyes. For the days will come upon you when your enemies will build an embankment around you, and surround you, and keep you in on every side, and will dash you to the ground, and your children with you, and they will not leave in you one stone *standing* on another because you did not know the time of your visitation." In Matthew 21:33-43 (REV) He relates a parable to His disciples about a landowner who planted a vineyard, "rented it out to some farmers. And *then* he went into another country. And when the season of fruit drew near, he sent his slaves to the farmers to receive his fruit." As it turns out, the farmers beat, stoned or killed all his servants. Then the landowner "sent to them his son, saying, 'They will respect my son.'" But the farmers "caught him, threw him out of the vineyard, and killed him." Jesus asks His disciples: "Therefore, when the lord of the vineyard comes, what will he do to those farmers? They say to Him, 'He will destroy them in a wretched way, and will rent out his vineyard to other farmers who will give him the fruit in its season.' Jesus said to them, 'Have you never read in the Scriptures: 'The stone that the builders rejected has become the chief cornerstone'....Therefore I say to you, the Kingdom of God will be taken away from you [Israel] and will be given to a nation [some versions read: "given to a people"] producing its fruits'" [verse 43].

As well, in Matthew 22 (REV), Jesus relates the parable of the king who arranged a marriage for his son and sent forth his servants to invite people to the wedding. "But they did not want to come…and went their ways, one to his own farm, another to his business, and the rest seized his slaves, mistreated and killed them.…Then he says to his slaves, 'The wedding feast is ready, but the ones who had not been invited were not worthy'" [verses 5,6,8]. In the end, the Lord concludes: "For many are called, but few are chosen" [verse 14]. This, too, is a verdict on Israel for their rejection of the king and the kingdom. And Matthew 23 (REV) records the Lord's ringing condemnation of Israel's religious leaders: "Woe to you, experts in the law and Pharisees, hypocrites! For you shut the Kingdom of Heaven *right* in front of people, for you do not enter, neither do you allow the ones entering to enter" [verse 15]. And in verses 37 and 38: "Jerusalem, Jerusalem, she who keeps on killing the prophets and stoning the ones who have been sent to her! How often I wanted to gather your children together, in the same way a hen gathers her chicks under her wings, and you were not willing! Look! Your house is left to you desolate."

Many students of the Bible have not understood these two basic phases of the Lord's earthly ministry. His own disciples, however, understood. Prior to His ascension, His disciples asked Him: "Lord, is it at this time you are going to restore the kingdom to Israel?" Remembering the Lord's frequent proclamation in the early phase of His ministry that the kingdom was "at hand," they were expecting Him in His resurrection authority to take charge over the nation and bring the kingdom to pass. Jesus answered: "It is not for you to know times or seasons that the Father has set within His own authority" [Acts 1:6,7 REV].

A few days later, at the hour of prayer in the temple in Jerusalem, His disciples were all baptized in holy spirit—ushering in the "administration [dispensation] of God's grace" which has continued for these 2000 years. And when this age of God's grace concludes with the Rapture of the Church, it will be followed by seven years of catastrophic tribulation on Israel for their rejection and crucifixion of their Messiah, and also on the rebellious nations—"Alas! For that day is great, so that none is like it: And it is the time of Jacob's trouble.... And there shall be a time of trouble, such as never was since there was a nation, even to that time. And at that time your people [Israel] shall be delivered, everyone who is found written in the book" [Jeremiah 30:7; Daniel 12:1; Matthew 24:15-22]. The Millennial Kingdom will then come to pass.

Waiting for their messiah

It must be understood that national Israel today is not the same as God's "chosen people" of Old Testament times. In 2021 the population of the nation of Israel was about 9,300,000, according to Wikipedia, the online encyclopedia. Of this total, about 75% were Jewish, 18.6% were Muslim, 2% were Christian, 3% other. Of the Jewish people, only about 20-25% identified with orthodox or ultra-orthodox Judaism which, for a variety of reasons, rejects Jesus Christ as the Messiah, believing that their "mashiach" (the "anointed one") is yet to come. Thus the majority of the Jewish population of Israel today is secular.

In Deuteronomy 7:6 (NKJV) God, with Moses as their mediator, said to the people of Israel: "For you are a holy people to the Lord your God; the Lord your God has chosen you to be a people for Himself, a special treasure above all the people on the face of the earth." This is not the case with national Israel today. First of all, times have changed. In this present age of the "dispensation of the grace of God" [Ephesians 3:2] in which we are living, God is not dealing directly with Israel as a nation, or with any nation, as He did in Old Testament times. In Matthew 28:18, following His resurrection, Jesus said to His eleven apostles: "All authority has been given to Me in heaven and on earth." Today, in this present age of God's grace, and in the age to come—the Millennial Kingdom—Jesus Christ has been given *"all authority in heaven and on earth."* Alas, for Israel as a national entity with Judaism as their religion, ever since Christ's earthly ministry unto this present time, they have rejected Jesus Christ as their Messiah and are waiting for another to come. Luke 19 informs us that as Jesus drew near to Jerusalem, "He saw the city and wept over it, saying 'If you had known, even you, especially in your day, the things that make for your peace! But now they are hidden from your eyes....because you did not know the time of your visitation'" [verses 41,42,44b]. The religious rulers of Israel, over the centuries, have never understood nor acknowledged "the time of [their] visitation."

In Romans 10:1-4 (REV), Paul laments over his people Israel: "Brothers, my heart's desire and my supplication to God for them is that they be saved. For I can testify about them that they have a zeal for God [in Paul's time], but not according to knowledge. For in their disregarding the righteousness [in Jesus Christ] that comes from God, and seeking to establish their own [via the law of Moses], they did not submit themselves to the righteousness of God. For Christ is the fulfillment [end] of the law, with the result that *now* there is righteousness for everyone who believes." And in Romans 9:27-29 (REV), Paul says "Isaiah cries out on behalf of Israel: **Though the number of the sons of Israel is as the sand of the sea** [*hypoleimma* – "smallest remnant"], *only* **the remnant will be saved, for the Lord will fulfill** *his* **Word upon the earth completely and quickly.** And just as Isaiah has foretold: **If the Lord of the Armies had not left us a seed, we would have been like Sodom, and would have been like Gomorrah.**"

Toward the conclusion of his revelation of the Great Tribulation across the face of the earth, John declares in Revelation 9:13-16 (REV): "And the sixth angel blew his trumpet, and I heard a voice from the horns of the golden altar that is before God, saying to the sixth angel that had one trumpet, 'Loose the four angels that are bound at the great river Euphrates [at the heart of the Middle East bordering Israel, Syria and Iraq]. And the four angels that had been prepared for the hour and day and month and year, were released to kill a third of mankind. And the number of the armies of the horsemen *was* twice 10,000 times 10,000 (I heard the number of them)." This incredible army described in Revelation 9 will be a military force—*200 million strong*—advancing from the North and East (perhaps a confederacy of Islamic nations--see Ezekiel 38:1-6 for a prophetic description) across the dried up bed of the Euphrates River in preparation for the *invasion of Israel.* John says: "And the sixth [angel] poured out his bowl on the great river, the *river* Euphrates, and its water was dried up to prepare the way for the kings that *come* from the east" [Revelation 16:12 REV]—for the invasion of Israel and in anticipation of the battle of Armageddon [verse 16].

The Prophet Zechariah tells of these awesome events before John was even born: "Behold, the day of the Lord is coming. And your spoil will be divided in your midst. For I will gather all the nations to battle against Jerusalem, the city shall be taken, the houses rifled, and the women ravished. Half of the city shall go into captivity, but the remnant of the people shall not be cut off from the city. Then the Lord will go forth and fight against these nations, as He fights in the day of battle. And on that day His feet will stand on the Mount of Olives, which faces Jerusalem on the east. And the Mount of Olives shall be split in two [as the result of a massive earthquake-- Revelation 16:18], from east to west, making a very large valley; Half of the mountain shall move toward the north, and half of it toward the south. Then you [the remnant of Israel] shall flee *through* My mountain valley, for the mountain valley shall reach toward Azal [the Mount of Olives and area]. Yes, you shall flee, as you fled from the earthquake in the days of Uzziah king of Judah. Thus the Lord my God will come, and all the saints with You" [Zechariah 14:1-5 NKJV]. With this majestic appearing of the Lord Jesus Christ on the Mount of Olives, it is likely that this event will cause many unbelieving Jews [the prophesied "remnant"] finally to recognize and acknowledge Jesus Christ as the true Messiah and Redeemer of Israel and, as the Apostle Paul prayed on behalf of Israel in Romans 10, to be "saved."

"Look!, he is coming with the clouds..."
-Revelation 1:7 (REV)

The Bible informs us that Jesus Christ will return to earth in God's timing and "will come in the same way as you saw him going into heaven" [Acts 1:11 REV]. Then, after winning the battle of Armageddon, He will at that time establish His prophesied kingdom of heaven which will last 1000 years. This kingdom will then be followed instantly by the Everlasting Kingdom described in Revelation 21 (REV): "And I saw a new heaven and a new earth, for the first heaven and first earth passed away, and the sea is no more. And I saw the holy city, New Jerusalem, coming down out of heaven from God...."

Paul writes in 1 Thessalonians 5:1-4 (REV): "But concerning the times and dates, brothers, you have no need that anything be written to you. For you yourselves know very well that the Day of the Lord will come like a thief in the night. When they [those who remain on the earth after the Rapture of the Church] are saying, 'Peace and safety,' then ruin will suddenly come upon them, like labor pains upon a pregnant woman, and they will surely not escape. But you, brothers, are not in darkness that the Day would overtake you like a thief." The Rapture of the Church, which Paul describes in the previous chapter, actually initiates "the Day of the Lord," which is a process in time including the Rapture, the judgment seat of Christ, the seven years of tribulation on the earth, and the second coming of Christ. It appears from Paul's statement that following the Rapture of the Church, with conspiracy theories abounding concerning what became of all the Christian believers, there may be a period of time when societies exclaim "peace and safety." This will be a time of increasing spiritual deception. Paul says in 2 Thessalonians 2:7 (REV): "For the sacred secret [mystery] of lawlessness is already at work...." Paul was fully aware in his time that "the whole world lies *under the sway* of the wicked one" [1 John 5:19], but he predicts that at this future time satanic deception will greatly increase throughout societies. In verses 9-12 he states: "The coming *of the lawless one* is in accord with the working of the Adversary with all kinds of power and signs and lying wonders, and with every kind of unrighteous deception for those who are destroying themselves because they refused to love the truth and so be saved. And because of this God sends them a deluding influence [idiom of permission for the surfeit of deceiving spirits] so they believe a lie. The result of this is that all the ones who did not believe the truth, but had pleasure in unrighteousness, will be judged." During this lull when the world proclaims "peace and safety," then sudden destruction comes upon them. This may actually represent the beginning of the seven years of tribulation. Jeremiah prophesies of that terrible time all across the face of the earth. "'For behold, I begin to bring calamity on the city which is called by My name, and should you be utterly unpunished? You shall not be unpunished, for I will call for a sword on all the inhabitants of the earth,' says the Lord of hosts. Therefore prophesy against them all these words, and say to them: 'The Lord will roar from on high, And utter His voice from His holy habitation; He will roar mightily against His fold. He will give a shout, as those who tread *the grapes,* against all the inhabitants of the earth. A noise will come to the ends of the earth—For the Lord has a controversy with the nations, He will plead His case with all flesh. He will give those *who are* wicked to the sword,' says the Lord. Thus says the Lord of hosts: 'Behold, disaster shall go forth from nation to nation, And a great whirlwind shall be raised up from the farthest parts of the earth. And at that day the slain of the Lord shall be from one end of the earth even to the *other* end of the earth. They shall not be lamented, or gathered, or buried; they shall become refuse on the ground" [Jeremiah 25:29-33 NKJV].

Toward the conclusion of the catastrophic seven years of tribulation on the earth, Christ returns in glory [an expansion of the prophecy in Acts 1:11]: "Look! he is coming with the clouds, and every eye will see him, even those who pierced him, and all the tribes of the earth will mourn because of him. So will it be, Amen" [Revelation 1:7 REV]. Christ wins the battle of Armageddon and conquers the earth: "But immediately after the [concluding hours of the] tribulation of those days, the sun will be darkened, and the moon will not give its light, and the stars will fall from heaven [asteroids? Or possibly the effects of volcanoes spewing fireballs], and the powers of the heavens will be shaken, and then the sign of the Son of Man will appear in heaven, and then all the tribes of the earth will mourn, and they will see the Son of Man coming on the clouds with power and great glory" [Matthew 24:29,30 REV]. I Thessalonians 3:13 (REV) adds to the drama of Christ's return: "...to the end he may establish your hearts blameless in holiness before our God and Father in the presence of our Lord Jesus with all his holy *ones.*" And Jude 14b (NKJB): "Behold, the Lord comes with ten thousands of His saints"—meaning the angels of His power and all raptured Christians.

Revelation 19:11-16 (REV) continues the prophecy of Christ's return: "And I saw the heavens opened, and Look!, a white horse, and he who sat on it called Faithful and True, and in righteousness he judges and makes war. And his eyes *are* a flame of fire, and on his head *are* many diadem, and he has a name written which no one knows except himself. And he is clothed in a robe sprinkled with blood, and his name is called The Word of God. And the armies that are in heaven [angels and raptured saints], followed him on white horses, clothed in fine linen, white *and* pure. And out of his mouth comes a sharp broadsword, so that with it he can strike down the nations (and he will rule them with a rod of iron), and he treads the winepress of the fury of the wrath of God, the Almighty. And he has on his garment and on his thigh a name written: KING OF KINGS, AND LORD OF LORDS." The fact that Christ will rule the nations "with a rod of iron" will be the fulfillment of the prophecy in Psalm 2:8 and 9 (NKJB) a thousand years before Jesus' birth in Bethlehem: "Ask of Me, and I will give You the nations for Your inheritance, and the ends of the earth for your possession. You shall break them with a rod of iron; You shall dash them to pieces like a potter's vessel."

It must be understood that the vast majority of the people remaining on the earth after all genuine Christian believers are raptured will be unbelievers--God-rejecters, those deceived by counterfeit religions, and those simply blinded by deceiving spirits. 2 Corinthians 4:3 and 4 (REV): ("But even if our Good News is veiled, it is veiled to those who are perishing, in whom the god of this world has blinded the minds of those who do not believe, to keep them from seeing *and shining forth* the light of the Good News of the glory of Christ, who is the image of God). This is why "all the tribes of the earth will mourn" at Christ's return and why the Lord will "rule them with a rod of iron" and "dash them to pieces like a potter's vessel" as He subdues the nations. Once He has subdued the nations, the devil is "chained" and the first resurrection—the resurrection of life—occurs in which the Old Testament faithful are raised from the dead [Ezekiel's prophecy of the "dry bones"], along with those who became believers in Christ during the seven years of tribulation and who were martyred [Revelation 13:15]. These people will be granted everlasting life and will reign with Christ throughout the 1000-year kingdom, along with all raptured saints.

"Mine eyes have seen the glory...."

Permit me a digression. One of my favorite Christian hymns is the stirring "Battle Hymn of the Republic." The lyrics are from a poem written by Julia Ward Howe in 1861 during the Civil War. She writes in her memoirs that following a public review of the Union troops the day before, she awoke in the twilight of the dawn with the words and stanzas of the poem beginning to swim in her mind. Quickly getting up out of bed, she found the stump of an old pencil which she had used the day before, and wrote down the words as they sprang into her mind. Perhaps she had no idea at the time how wonderfully the gift of holy spirit was moving in her soul and working in her mind. Julia Ward Howe's words to "The Battle Hymn of the Republic" are prophetic:

"Mine eyes have seen the glory of the coming of the Lord."

Yes! Our eyes have seen the glory! We have seen
the glory of His coming in the Word of God! We
have seen the glory of His coming in our mind's
eye, we have seen it in our spirit, we have seen it
in our soul! "Look!, he is coming with the clouds,
and every eye will see him...." [Revelation 1:7
REV]. "This Jesus, who was taken up from you into
heaven, will so come in the same way as you saw
him going into heaven." [Acts 1:11 REV]. "And then
they will see the Son of Man coming in clouds
with great power and glory" [Mark 13:26 REV].

"He is trampling out the vintage where the grapes of wrath are stored."

"And another angel came out from the altar, he
who has power over fire, and he called with a great
voice to him who had the sharp sickle, saying,
'Put in your sharp sickle, and gather the clusters
of the vine of the earth, for her grapes are fully
ripe.' And the angel swung his sickle onto the
earth, and gathered the vintage of the earth, and
threw it into the winepress, the great *winepress* of

the anger of God. And the winepress is trodden outside the city, and blood came out from the winepress, even to the bridles of the horses, as far as 1,600 stadia" [Revelation 14:18-20 REV].

"He has loosed the faithful lightning of His terrible swift sword."

"And I saw, and Look!, a white cloud, and sitting on the cloud *I saw* one like *the* Son of Man, having on his head a golden crown, and in his hand a sharp sickle. And another angel came out of the sanctuary, crying with a great voice to him who sat on the cloud, 'Put in your sickle and reap, for the hour to reap is come, because the harvest of the earth is ripe.' And he who sat on the cloud swung his sickle on the earth, and the earth was reaped" [Revelation 14:14-16 REV]. "For behold, the Lord will come with fire and with His chariots, like a whirlwind, to render His anger with fury, and His rebuke with flames of fire. For by fire and by His sword the Lord will judge all flesh; and the slain of the Lord shall be many" [Isaiah 66:15,16 NKJV].

"His truth is marching on."

"Blow the trumpet in Zion, and sound an alarm in My holy mountain! Let all the inhabitants of the land tremble; For the day of the Lord is coming" [Joel 2:1 NKJV]. "Oh, send out Your light and Your truth! Let them lead me; Let them bring me to Your holy hill and Your tabernacle" [Psalm 43:3 NKJV].

"He has sounded forth the trumpet that shall never call retreat."

"In a moment, in the blink of an eye, at the last trumpet, For the trumpet will sound, and the dead will be raised incorruptible, and we will be changed" [1Corinthians 15:52 REV].

**"He is sifting out the hearts of men
before His judgment seat."**
"For we must all be exposed before the judgment
seat of Christ, so that each one may be repaid
for the things *done* in the body, according to
what he has made a practice of doing, whether
good or worthless" [2 Corinthians 5:10 REV].
"God overlooked these times of ignorance, but now
he commands all people everywhere to repent,
because he has set a day in which he is about
to justly judge the inhabited world by the man
whom he has appointed" [Acts 17:30,31 REV].

"O be swift, my soul, to answer Him, be jubilant my feet."
"And if it seems evil to you to serve the Lord,
choose for yourselves this day whom you
will serve....But as for me and my house, we
will serve the Lord" [Joshua 24:15 NKJV].

"Our God is marching on."
"And Look!, I come quickly.
Blessed is the one who keeps the words of the
prophecy of this book" [Revelation 22:7 REV]

★

"Son of man, can these bones live?"
-Ezekiel 37:3 (NKJV)

Ezekiel's astonishing prophecy of Israel's future resurrection of life [Ezekiel 37:1-14 NKJV] is a clear revelation that God absolutely intends to honor His covenant with Abram--that Israel should "inherit the land:" "And the Lord said to Abram... 'Lift your eyes now and look from the place where you are—northward, southward, eastward, and westward; for the land which you see I give to you and your descendants forever'" [Genesis 13:14,15 NKJV]; "On the same day the Lord made a covenant with Abram, saying: 'To your descendants I have given this land, from the river of Egypt to the great river, the River Euphrates..."' [Genesis 15:18 NKJV]. Ezekiel's vision of the valley of dry bones is the prophetic announcement of the restoration of the nation of Israel during the Millennial Kingdom: "The hand of the Lord came upon me and brought me out in the Spirit of the Lord, and set me down in the midst of the valley, and it was full of bones. Then He caused me to pass by them all around, and behold, there were very many in the open valley; and indeed they were very dry. And He said to me, 'Son of man, can these bones live?' So I answered, 'O Lord God, You know.' Again He said to me, 'Prophesy to these bones, and say to them, 'O dry bones, hear the word of the Lord! Thus says the Lord God to these bones: 'Surely I will cause breath to enter into you, and you shall live. I will put sinews on you and bring flesh upon you, cover you with skin, and put breath in you; and you shall live. Then you shall know that I am the Lord.' So I prophesied as I was commanded, and as I prophesied there was a noise, and suddenly a rattling; and the bones came together, bone to bone. Indeed, as I looked, the sinews and the flesh came upon them, and the skin covered them over, but there was no breath in them. Also He said to me, 'Prophesy to the breath, prophesy, son of man, and say to the breath, 'Thus says the Lord God: Come from the four winds, O breath, and breathe on these slain, that they may live.' I prophesied as He commanded me, and breath came into them, and they lived, and stood upon their feet, an exceedingly great army. Then He said to me, 'Son of man, these bones are the whole house of Israel. They indeed say, 'Our bones are dry, our hope is lost, and we ourselves are cut off!' Therefore prophesy and say to them, 'Thus says the Lord God: 'Behold, O My people, I will open your graves and cause you to come up from your graves, and bring you into the land of Israel. Then you shall know that I am the Lord. When I have opened your graves, and brought you up from your graves. I will put My Spirit in you, and you shall live, and I will place you in your land. Then you shall know that I, the Lord, have spoken it and performed it,' says the Lord."

The Sheep and Goats Judgment

Billions of people will die as the result of the terrible events of the tribulation. Revelation 6:8 (REV) says: "And I saw, and Look!, a pale horse, and the one who sat on him, his name was Death, and the Grave was with him, following. And there was given to them authority over a fourth of the earth, to kill with broadsword, and with famine, and with death, and by the wild beasts of the earth." If in fact one fourth of humanity living at that time is killed, that could be as many as one to two billion people. The Pew Research Center estimates that presently there are about 2 1/2 billion Christians in the world—nearly 1/3 of the world's population. Of course, not all those who call themselves Christian are genuine Christians simply because they attend or are a member of a church or other assembly. To be a genuine Christian, one must be "born again" [1 Peter 1:23]; "sealed with the Holy Spirit of promise" [Ephesians 1:13]; and thus "*He saved us* through the washing of a new origin and a renewal by holy spirit" [Titus 3:5 REV]. But if as many as two billion Christians are taken out of this world by the Rapture, that might leave as many as six or seven billion unbelievers remaining on earth at the time of the catastrophic tribulation. Then Revelation 9:18 (REV) says: "By these three plagues [later in the three and one-half years of the Great Tribulation] a third of mankind was killed; by the fire and the smoke and the sulfur which came out of their mouths." One third of the earth's population still living at this time could represent another one to two billion people killed. One might wonder: After billions of Christians have been raptured and suddenly disappeared from human society, why would billions of people across the face of the earth continue to reject God? Paul explains in 2 Thessalonians 2:8-12 (NKJV) that following the Rapture of the Church, "The coming of the lawless one is according to the working of Satan, with all power, signs, and lying wonders, and with all unrighteous deception among those who perish, because they did not receive the love of the truth, that they might be saved. And for this reason God will send them strong delusion, that they should believe the lie, that they all may be condemned who did not believe the truth but had pleasure in unrighteousness." Billions will die during the tribulation--but billions will survive. Along with the Old Testament faithful and those martyred during the tribulation, billions of natural men and women, both Jews and Gentiles, will be alive at the onset of the Millennial Kingdom. Some of these the Lord will judge to be "worthy" and will be allowed to continue living in the kingdom. This judgment has come to be known as the "Sheep and Goats Judgment." It is not the same as the first resurrection—the resurrection of life--because it's not a resurrection, it's a judgment. Matthew 25:32-46 (REV) explains: At that time (in the Millennial Kingdom), "All the nations will be gathered before him, and he will separate them one from another, as the shepherd separates the sheep from the goats. And he will put the sheep on his right, but the goats on the left. Then the king will say to the ones on his right, 'Come, you who have been blessed by my Father, inherit the kingdom that has been prepared for you from the foundation of the world: for I was hungry and you gave me something to eat; I was thirsty and you gave me a drink; I was a stranger and you invited me in; naked, and you clothed me; I was sick, and you visited me; I was in prison, and you came to me.' Then the righteous will answer him, saying, 'Lord, when did we see you hungry and fed you? Or thirsty and gave you a drink? And when did we see you a stranger and took you in, or naked, and clothed you? And when did we see you sick, or in prison, and came to you?' And the King, answering, will say to them, 'Truly I say to you, in as much as you did it to one of these my brothers, *even* the least, you did it to me.' Then he will also say to those on the left hand, 'Depart from me, you cursed, into the fire of the *coming* Age, which has been prepared for the Slanderer and his angels. For I was hungry and you did not give me *anything* to eat; I was thirsty, and you gave me no drink; I was a stranger, and you did not invite me in, naked, and you did not clothe me, sick, and in prison, and you did not visit me.' Then they will also answer, saying, 'Lord, when did we see you hungry, or thirsty, or a stranger, or naked, or sick, or in prison, and did not serve you?' Then he will answer them, saying, 'Truly I say to you, in so far as you did not do *it* to one of these least, you did not do *it* to me.' And these will go away into punishment *in the* Age *to come*; but the righteous into life *in the* Age *to come*." Thus the Sheep and Goats Judgment may be God's answer to those who criticize a basic tenant of Christianity that only people "born again" in this present age of God's grace will enjoy everlasting life. As well, it's a remarkable prophecy in that it displays the Son of Man's great mercy and love, even regarding people who have been deceived by counterfeit religion or who otherwise have had their minds blinded from the truth by satanic spirits.

"Do you not know that the saints will judge the world?"
1 Corinthians 6:2 (NKJV)

Isaiah 65:20-25 (NKJV) describe conditions for both God's elect and the natural men and women living in the Millennial Kingdom: "No more shall an infant from there *live but a few* days, nor an old man who has not fulfilled his days; for the child shall die one hundred years old, but the sinner *being* one hundred years old shall be accursed. They shall build houses and inhabit them; they shall plant vineyards and eat their fruit. They shall not build and another inhabit; they shall not plant and another eat; for as the days of a tree, so shall be the days of My people, and My elect shall long enjoy the work of their hands. They shall not labor in vain, nor bring forth children for trouble; for they shall be the descendants of the blessed of the Lord, and their offspring with them. It shall come to pass that before they call, I will answer; and while they are still speaking, I will hear. The wolf and the lamb shall feed together, the lion shall eat straw like the ox. And dust shall be the serpent's food. They shall not hurt nor destroy in all My holy mountain, says the Lord."

The "natural" people spoken of in Isaiah 65 will grow naturally, marry, procreate, age, and die. Generation after generation over the 1000 years of the kingdom will mean that these natural people will increase "as the sand of the sea" [Revelation 20:8]. And because they will have the same sinful, rebellious nature as natural people have today—despite living in peace and enjoying the abundance of Paradise restored—Christ will need to rule them "with a rod of iron" [Psalm 1:9; Revelation 2:27]. In fact, Paul informs us in I Corinthians 6:2 and 3 (REV): "Or do you not know that the holy *ones* [saints] will judge *and administer* the world?...Do you not know that we will judge *and administer* angels?" Christians will reign alongside Christ in the Millennial Kingdom and, depending on their earned rewards [consider the Parable of the Talents], will exercise various degrees of spiritual authority and power in judging the nations by enforcing righteousness and even judging fallen angels [demons] at the conclusion of the kingdom when Satan and his minions are released for a time to deceive the world.

Revelation 20:4-6 (REV) sheds more light on the first resurrection—the resurrection of life: "And I saw thrones, and they sat on them, and judgment was given to them, and I saw the souls of those who had been beheaded for the testimony of Jesus and for the word of God [during the tribulation], and such as had not worshipped the beast, neither his image, and had not received the mark on their forehead and on their hand; and they came to life, and reigned with Christ 1,000 years. The rest of the dead did not come to life until the 1,000 years were finished [referring to the second resurrection—the resurrection to condemnation]. This is the first resurrection. Blessed and holy is whoever has part in the first resurrection [Old Testament believers and those martyred during the tribulation], over these *people* the second death has no power, but they will be priests of God and of Christ, and will reign with him 1,000 years."

"I will pour out My Spirit on all flesh..."
-Joel 2:28 (NKJV)

Remarkably, everyone living in the Millennial Kingdom who believes in Christ as Lord will receive the gift of holy spirit, including Old Testament believers and those martyred during the tribulation. Of course, all raptured Christians will have already received the gift of holy spirit in their mortal lifetimes. Over the generations of the Millennial Kingdom, natural people who will be born and grow up may ultimately rebel against Christ's rule and therefore will not be born of the spirit and thus will not be allowed to enter the Everlasting Kingdom. Others who accept Christ during their lifetimes and who remain faithful will be granted eternal life and will be allowed to enter the Everlasting Kingdom at the conclusion of the Millennial Kingdom. Joel 2:28,29 (NKJV) inform us: "And it shall come to pass afterward [after the tribulation and after the Lord establishes His kingdom on earth] that I will pour out My Spirit on all flesh; your sons and your daughters shall prophesy, your old men shall dream dreams, your young men shall see visions. And also on My menservants and on My maidservants I will pour out My Spirit in those days." This is a prophecy for Israel for the future time in the Millennial Kingdom, but Joel's phrase "all flesh" will apply to all who will believe in the Lord at that time.

A major purpose of the Millennial Kingdom is to fulfill God's promise to His chosen people, Israel. Indeed, every covenant God made with Abraham and with Israel will be fulfilled in the Millennial Kingdom. Without the Millennial Kingdom, many of God's promises to His chosen people would be like empty wind. But another vital purpose of the kingdom is to fulfill God's promises of the "inheritance" and rewards for the millions of Christians who remain faithful throughout the centuries of this "age of the grace of God." Paul says: "Brothers, I do not consider myself as having grasped *it* yet, but one thing *I do*, letting go of the things that are behind, and straining forward to the things that are before, I press toward the goal to win the prize of the high calling of God in *connection with* Christ Jesus" [Philippians 3:13,14 REV].

And another principal purpose of the Millennial Kingdom is for God to demonstrate conclusively to humanity that even with the devil bound for 1,000 years and with Jesus Christ governing over all the earth, along with millions of faithful believers in their new and glorious bodies, that the natural people living at that time, in their sin nature, will still be susceptible to deception and rebellion. Revelation 20 (REV) tells us that toward the end of the Millennial Kingdom, Satan, who had been bound for 1,000 years and cast into "the abyss" [verse 3], must be released for a while. Verses 7-10: "And when the 1,000 years are finished, the Adversary will be loosed out of his prison and will come out to deceive the nations [natural men and women] that are in the four corners of the earth, Gog and Magog [perhaps symbolic for the same general confederacy of nations which will have invaded Israel toward the conclusion of the Great Tribulation], to gather them together to the war, the number of whom is as the sand of the sea. And they went up over the breadth of the earth and surrounded the camp of the holy *ones* and the beloved city, and fire came down out of heaven and devoured them. And the Slanderer, who deceived them, was thrown into the lake of fire and sulfur where both the beast and the false prophet *had been thrown*, and they will be tormented day and night to the ages of ages."

Thus the millennial reign of Christ will be the ultimate test of humanity's recognition of and faithfulness to the goodness, love, benevolence and authority of God. After the "great white throne" judgment, which immediately follows the destruction of Satan and his minions, mankind will have been thoroughly purged of his rebellious nature and will enter into the Everlasting Kingdom: "Look!, the tabernacle of God is with man, and he will dwell with them, and they will be his people. God himself will be with them *and be* their God. And he will wipe away every tear from their eyes, and death will be no more, neither will there be mourning, nor crying, nor pain, anymore; the former things have passed away. Then he who sits on the throne said, 'Look!, I make all things new.' And he says, 'Write, for these words are faithful and true'" [Revelation 21:3-5 REV].

Paradise restored

"He has made everything beautiful in its time. Also He has put eternity in their hearts, except that no one can find out the work that God does from beginning to end" [Ecclesiastes 3:11 NKJV]. Mankind's nostalgia for Paradise is among the strongest nostalgias that haunt human beings. Such nostalgia is understood because Genesis tells us that man [primordial humanoids notwithstanding] began life in Paradise—the magnificent garden of Eden—free of sorrow, disease, and death. The singer Joni Mitchell phrased it well in her song from "Woodstock," suggesting that we are "stardust" and that we are "golden," and that somehow we need to "get back to the garden."

Throughout the Bible we read of the hope of the future Paradise. "For the Lord will comfort Zion ["Promised Land"], He will comfort all her waste places; He will make her wilderness like Eden, and her desert like the garden of the Lord; Joy and gladness will be found in it, thanksgiving and the voice of melody" [Isaiah 51:3 NKJV]. And Isaiah 35:1-10 (NKJV) tell us: "The wilderness and the wasteland shall be glad for them, and the desert shall rejoice and blossom as the rose; It shall blossom abundantly and rejoice, even with joy and singing. The glory of Lebanon shall be given to it, the excellence of Carmel and Sharon. They shall see the glory of the Lord, the excellency of our God. Strengthen the weak hands, and make firm the feeble knees. Say to those who are fearful-hearted, 'Be strong, do not fear! Behold, your God will come *with* vengeance, *with* the recompense of God; He will come to save you.' Then the eyes of the blind shall be opened, and the ears of the deaf shall be unstopped. Then the lame shall leap like a deer, and the tongue of the dumb sing. For waters shall burst forth in the wilderness, and streams in the desert. The parched ground shall become a pool, and the thirsty land springs of water; In the habitation of jackals where they lay, *there shall be* grass with reeds and rushes. A highway shall be there, and a road. And it shall be called the Highway of Holiness. The unclean shall not pass over it, but it shall be for others. Whoever walks the road, although a fool, shall not go astray. No lion shall be there, nor shall *any* ravenous beast go up on it; it shall not be found there. But the redeemed shall walk *there*, and the ransomed of the Lord shall return, and come to Zion with singing, with everlasting joy on their heads. They shall obtain joy and gladness. And sorrow and sighing shall flee away."

The immediate consequences of Adam's and Eve's treasonous disobedience in original Eden were disastrous: "Cursed *is* the ground for your sake; In toil you shall eat *of* it all the days of your life. Both thorns and thistles it shall bring forth for you, and you shall eat the herb of the field. In the sweat of your face you shall eat bread till you return to the ground, for out of it you were taken; for dust you *are*, and to dust you shall return" [Genesis 3:17-19 NKJV]. Indeed, Psalm 90:10 (NKJV) informs us: "The days of our lives *are* seventy years; and if by reason of strength *they are* eighty years, yet their boast *is* only labor and sorrow; For it is soon cut off, and we fly away."

Man's fall from God's grace brought him toil, sorrow, and death. Man's redemption in Christ will ultimately reward him with Paradise *restored*—"For waters shall burst forth in the wilderness, and streams in the desert." For redeemed mankind living in Paradise restored, "they shall obtain joy and gladness, and sorrow and sighing shall flee away." In Paradise restored, Christ will reign as King of Kings and Lord of Lords [Revelation 19:16]: "The Lord of hosts shall reign on Mount Zion, and in Jerusalem, and before His elders gloriously' [Isaiah 24:23 NKJV]. "Yes, all kings shall fall down before Him; All nations shall serve Him; for He will deliver the needy [natural man] when he cries, the poor also, and him who has no helper. He will spare the poor and needy, and will save the souls of the needy [as the Lord prophesied in the Beatitudes]. He will redeem their life from oppression and violence; and precious shall be their blood in His sight. And He shall live; and the gold of Sheba will be given to Him; Prayers [of thanksgiving] also shall be made for Him continually, and daily He shall be praised. There will be an abundance of grain in the earth, on the top of the mountains; its fruit shall wave like Lebanon; and those of the city shall flourish like grass of the earth. His name shall endure forever; His name shall continue as long as the sun. All men shall be blessed in Him; All nations shall call Him blessed" [Psalm 72:11-17 NKJV]. "Yes, many peoples and strong nations shall come to seek the Lord of hosts in Jerusalem, and to pray before the Lord" [Zechariah 8:22 NKJV].

Not only will humanity be delivered from Adam's curse, the animal kingdom also will experience remarkable changes. "The wolf also shall dwell with the lamb, the leopard shall lie down with the young goat, the calf and the young lion and the fatling together; and a little child shall lead them. The cow and the bear shall graze; their young ones shall lie down together; and the lion shall eat straw like the ox. The nursing child shall play by the cobra's hole. And the weaned child shall put his hand in the viper's den. They shall not hurt nor destroy in all My holy mountain, for the earth shall be full of the knowledge of the Lord as the waters cover the sea" [Isaiah 11:6-9 NKJV].

The wolf, the lion, the leopard, the bear—all animals carnivorous and dangerous to humans in this present age—will be plant eaters, docile and harmless in Paradise restored. Even the cobra and viper will be harmless. A little child shall be able to lead a gentle lion or leopard around like a household pet or play safely by the viper's den. "For the earth shall be full of the knowledge of the Lord!"

"THE LORD OUR RIGHTEOUSNESS"
-Jeremiah 23:6 (NKJV)

In Paradise restored, Christ will reign with justice prevailing. The corruption of this present age—the hatred, bribery, bigotry, intolerance and injustice of this present age--will be a thing of the past. Other consequences of man's fall from grace will also be reversed. Government will be purified: "Behold, *the* days are coming, says the Lord, that I will raise to David a Branch of righteousness [Christ]; a King shall reign and prosper, and execute judgment and righteousness in the earth. In His days Judah will be saved, and Israel will dwell safely; now this is His name by which He will be called: THE LORD OUR RIGHTEOUSNESS" [Jeremiah 23:5,6 NKJV].

In Paradise restored, war and bloodshed will be abolished. "Now it shall come to pass in the latter days *that* the mountain of the Lord's house shall be established on the top of the mountains, and shall be exalted above the hills; and all nations shall flow to it. Many people [of the nations] shall come and say, 'Come, let us go up to the mountain of the Lord, to the house of the God of Jacob; He will teach us His ways, and we shall walk in His paths.' For out of Zion shall go forth the law, and the word of the Lord from Jerusalem. He shall judge between the nations, and rebuke many people; they shall beat their swords into plowshares and their spears into pruning hooks; nation shall not lift up sword against nation, neither shall they learn war anymore" [Isaiah 2:2-4 NKJV].

Isaiah 25:6-8 (NKJV) gives us a prophetic description of the abundance that will be available to everyone in Paradise restored: "And in this mountain the Lord of hosts will make for all people a feast of choice pieces, a feast of wines on the lees, of fat things full of marrow, of well-refined wines on the lees [fermenting and aging]. And He will destroy on this mountain the surface of the covering cast over all people, and the veil that is spread over all nations. He will swallow up death forever, and the Lord God will wipe away tears from all faces; the rebuke of His people [anti-Semitism?] He will take away from all the earth; for the Lord has spoken."

In this present age the fear of death is like a veil "spread over all nations." Hebrews 2:14 and 15 (REV) state this reality: "Now since the children participate fully in blood and flesh, in a similar way he also himself shared the same so that through death he could make ineffective the one who holds the power of death, that is, the Slanderer, and free all those who were held in slavery all their lives by their fear of death." Although natural men and women will marry and procreate, grow old and die during the Millennial Kingdom, toward the conclusion of this kingdom approaching the advent of the Everlasting Kingdom, God will abolish death and the grave altogether [Revelation 20:14].

In many ways medical science has been a blessing and a benefit to humanity in this present age, but it has failed to cure many human sicknesses and diseases. In Paradise restored, Christ will change that: "And the inhabitants will not say, 'I am sick;' the people who dwell in it *will* be forgiven *their* iniquity'" [Isaiah 33:24 NKJV]. "In that day the deaf shall hear the words of the book, and the eyes of the blind shall see out of obscurity and out of darkness. The humble shall increase their joy in the Lord, and the poor among men shall rejoice in the Holy One of Israel" [Isaiah 29:18,19 NKJV]. "Then the eyes of the blind shall be opened, and the ears of the deaf shall be unstopped. Then the lame shall leap like a deer, and the tongue of the dumb sing" [Isaiah 35:5,6 NKJV]. "For behold, the day is coming, burning like an oven, and all the proud, yes, all who do wickedly will be stubble. And the day which is coming shall burn them up, says the Lord of hosts, that will leave them neither roof nor branch. But to you who fear My name the Sun of Righteousness shall arise with healing in His wings; and you shall go out and grow fat like stall-fed calves" [Malachi 4:1,2 NKJV].

In Paradise restored all immortals [the resurrected Old Testament faithful, all raptured saints, and those who turn to the Lord in the Millennial Kingdom] will enjoy perfect health. Natural men and women living at that time may get sick, grow old and die. However, Revelation 22:1 and 2 (REV) give us an astonishing picture: "And he showed me a river of water of life, bright as crystal, proceeding out of the throne of God and of the Lamb, in the middle of the street. And on this side of the river and on that *side was* the tree of life, bearing twelve *manner of* fruit, yielding its fruit every month. And the leaves of the tree were for the healing of the nations." In context, it seems that the "tree of life" will be a feature of the Everlasting Kingdom and may or may not be present in the Millennial Kingdom. However, this begs the question: If only those populating the Everlasting Kingdom will be immortals who will never get sick and never die, what's the need for "the healing of the nations" from the leaves of the tree of life? It seems that some mysteries of the coming ages are still to be revealed.

Genesis chapter 11(NKJV) relates the story of how rebellious humanity determined to build a tower "whose top is in the heavens" on a plain in the land of Shinar, and how the Lord God confused their language and "scattered them over the face of all the earth" [verses 2,7,8]. In Paradise restored all language barriers will be eliminated. "For then I will restore to the peoples a pure language, that they all may call on the name of the Lord, to serve Him with one accord" [Zephaniah 3:9 NKJV]. Compare Paul's prophecy in 1 Corinthians 13:8 (REV): "Love never fails, but where *there are* prophecies, they will be done away; whether *there are* tongues, they will cease; where *there is a message of* knowledge, it will be done away."

In this present age all nations face such serious threats as hurricanes, tornadoes, tsunamis, oppressive heat, catastrophic wildfires, etc. Not so in Paradise restored. The whole earth (or much of it) will be turned into an exquisite Eden similar to the original Paradise. This global garden will enjoy complete weather control. Mark 4:39 (REV) tells how Jesus "rebuked the wind, and said to the sea, 'Hush!, Be bound!' And the wind ceased, and there was a great calm." And his disciples exclaimed to one another, "Who then is this, that even the wind and the sea obey him?" [verse 41].

Throughout the Millennial Kingdom people of every nation will be allowed to visit Jerusalem and even to sacrifice in the new temple, not just Jews. "Now it shall come to pass in the latter days that the mountain of the Lord's house shall be established on the top of the mountains [very likely Mount Moriah], and shall be exalted above the hills; and all nations shall flow to it. Many people shall come and say, 'Come, and let us go up to the mountain of the Lord, to the house of the God of Jacob; He will teach us His ways, and we shall walk in His paths'" [Isaiah 2:2,3 NKJV]. "Also the sons of the foreigner who join themselves to the Lord, to serve Him, and to love the name of the Lord, to be His servants—everyone who keeps from defiling the Sabbath, and holds fast My covenant—even them I will bring to My holy mountain, and make them joyful in My house of prayer. Their burnt offerings and their sacrifices will be accepted on My altar, for My house shall be called a house of prayer for all nations" [Isaiah 56:6,7 NKJV]. "'Then they shall bring all your brethren for an offering to the Lord out of all nations, on horses and on chariots and on litters, on mules and on camels, to My holy mountain in Jerusalem,' says the Lord, 'as the children of Israel bring an offering in a clean vessel into the house of the Lord. And I will also take some of them for priests and Levites'" [Isaiah 66:20,21 NKJV]. Commentators have noted that the "burnt offerings and...sacrifices accepted on My altar" during the Millennial Kingdom will not be for the covering and forgiveness of sins, as they were during Old Testament times. Rather, the burnt offerings and sacrifices to be brought by the children of Israel, and others, during this time will point Israel to the sacrifice of the Lamb of God, a continuous reminder of all that Christ their Messiah, their Redeemer, accomplished for them. Similarly, today in this age of God's grace, many Christians regularly participate in the Eucharist—the rite of Holy Communion--as a reminder of Christ's sacrifice, just as the Lord commanded: "This is my body which is given for you; do this in remembrance of me....This cup is the new covenant in my blood, which is being poured out for you" [Luke 22:19b;20b REV].

"...an anchor for the soul"
-Hebrews 6:19 (REV)

Paul says to the Church in Colossians 1:24-27 (REV): "Now I rejoice in my sufferings for you, and I fill up in my flesh that which is lacking in the afflictions of Christ. *I do this* for the sake of his body, which is the Church, of which I was made a servant, in accord with the administration of God that was given to me for you to complete the word of God, the Sacred Secret, which has been hidden for ages and generations, but now has been revealed to his holy ones. God wanted to make known to them what is the riches of the glory of this Sacred Secret among the Gentiles: which is Christ in you, the hope of glory."

And in Hebrews 6:17-19 (REV) Paul writes: "God, intending to show more convincingly to the heirs of the promise the unchangeableness of his purpose, guaranteed it with an oath, so that by two unchangeable things, in *each of* which it is impossible for God to lie, we have strong encouragement, we who have found refuge in laying hold of the hope set before us. We have this *hope* as an anchor for the soul, both sure and steadfast, and extending into the inner part of the veil, where as a forerunner, Jesus entered for us...."

"Christ in you, the hope of glory" is the promise of God echoing down through the ages for all who are faithful to Him and to His Son Jesus Christ. This hope we hold as an anchor for our souls—the hope of the glorious transformation of our lowly bodies that they may be conformed to Christ's glorious body—and the hope of everlasting life in the ages to come.

Certainly our mortal lives in this present age would be more joyous if only our bodies remained youthful and healthy. Christ's promise of a new and glorious body that will last forever is something to rejoice about—and a promise worth sharing with others who do not yet understand this truth and who do not appreciate this hope. God states that our new bodies will be spiritual and not natural: "So also it is written, The first man Adam became a living soul [*psyche*—"soul," "breath life"—Genesis 2:7 NKJV]. The last Adam *became* a life-giving spirit. But the spiritual is not first, on the contrary, the soul *body* is; after that is the spiritual. The first man is of the earth, made of dust; the second man is of heaven. Like the *one* made of dust, so too are those who are of the dust; and like the heavenly *man*, so too *will be* the heavenly *ones*. And just as we have born the image of the *man* made of dust, we will also bear the image of the heavenly *man*" [1 Corinthians 15:45-49 REV]. Our new heavenly bodies will be energized—made alive—by spirit life rather than soul life—that is, "breath life." Genesis 2:7 tells us that "God breathed into his [Adam's] nostrils the breath of life, and man became a living soul." In contrast to Adam, Jesus became a "life-giving spirit" at His resurrection. This does not mean that He shed His physical body, as has been pointed out in an earlier chapter. He told His disciples in person that He was not a "spirit." "Look at my hands and my feet, that it is I myself. Handle me and see, for a spirit does not have flesh and bones, as you see that I have" [Luke 24:39 REV]. In His physical body after His resurrection, Jesus appeared suddenly inside locked rooms or to friends on the dusty road to Emmaus. So He moved instantaneously from one place to another, and He traveled through the sky to heaven at His ascension. It is quite likely that immortal Christians in our new and glorious bodies like Christ's will be able to do similar feats. We will have physical bodies of "flesh and bones" and still be capable of unimagined supernatural activities.

It's interesting to realize that in manifesting Himself to His disciples after His resurrection that the Lord used the phrase "flesh and bone" and not flesh and blood. I Corinthians 15 informs us that the life force of the Christian's new body will be "spirit" and not "breath life." "So it is with the resurrection of the dead. It is sown in corruption, it is raised in incorruption. It is sown in dishonor, it is raised in glory. It is sown in weakness, it is raised in power. It is sown a soul body, it is raised a spiritual body. Since there is a soul body, there is also a spiritual one. So also it is written, the first man, Adam, became a living soul. The last Adam *became* a life-giving spirit" [1 Corinthians 15:42-45 REV]. Since Leviticus 17:11 (NKJV) informs us that in our present physical bodies "the life of the flesh is in the blood," it's unclear whether or not our new and glorious bodies will have blood in our veins. Nevertheless Philippians 3:21 assures us that our new and transformed bodies will be conformed to Christ's glorious body—and Christ is in heaven at the right hand of the throne of God. We have seen John's vision of the glorified Christ in heaven [Revelation 1:13-16]. Thus it is likely that some worthy saints in the Millennial Kingdom will have glorious bodies similar to Christ's body as He appears in heaven, depending on the quality of their rewards. Indeed, three of the Four Gospels include the record of Jesus' transfiguration, which was a vision of His glorious appearance when He comes "in His kingdom:" "For the Son of Man is about to come with his angels in the glory of His Father, and then he will repay each *person* according to what he has done. Truly I say to you, there are some of those who stand here who will absolutely not taste of death until they see [in a vision] the Son of Man coming in his kingdom. And after six days Jesus takes with him Peter, and James and his brother John, and brings them by themselves up onto a high mountain. And he was transfigured before them, and his face shone like the sun, and His garments became white as the light" [Matthew 16:27,28;17:1,2 REV]. Mark 9:3 (REV) says: "and his garments became radiant, exceedingly white such as no launderer on earth is able to whiten them." As we have seen, Revelation 1:13-16 gives us a picture of Christ glorified in heaven, and the gospels provide a vision of the Lord "coming in His kingdom." And so it is likely that some saints in Paradise will take on aspects of Christ's glorious appearance in their new bodies as a reward, just as Jesus promised—"according to [their] works" in this mortal life.

The Everlasting Kingdom

Revelation 21 and 22, the final two chapters of the Bible, provide us with remarkable insights into the features of the Everlasting Kingdom immediately following the conclusion of the Millennial Kingdom. John writes in Revelation 21:1-3 (REV): "And I saw a new heaven and a new earth, for the first heaven and the first earth passed away, and the sea is no more. And I saw the holy city, New Jerusalem, coming down out of heaven from God, made ready as a bride adorned for her husband. And I heard a great voice out of the throne saying, 'Look!, the tabernacle of God is with man, and he will dwell with them, and they will be his people, and God himself will be with them, *and be* their God.'" This glorious event occurs following the Great White Throne Judgment and ushers in the Everlasting Kingdom.

These chapters, and others, reveal many similarities between the Millennial Kingdom and the Eternal Kingdom, and yet some significant differences. At the close of the Millennial Kingdom, the devil and all demon spirits [fallen angels] will be cast into the "lake of fire and sulfur where both the beast and the false prophet had been thrown" [Revelation 20:10 REV]. Nothing evil will be present in the Eternal Kingdom. As well, only immortal individuals will populate this kingdom. All God-rejectors will have been judged and cast into the lake of fire [Revelation 20:11-15].

In the Everlasting Kingdom death will be abolished. In the New Jerusalem where God and Christ will reign, there will be no temple and no sacrifices like in the Millennial Kingdom because "the Lord God the Almighty and the Lamb, are its sanctuary. And the city [New Jerusalem] has no need of the sun, nor of the moon, to shine on it, for the glory of God has illuminated it, and its lamp *is* the Lamb" [Revelation 21:22,23

REV]. And in the Everlasting Kingdom, God will be personally present to commune with His people, just as He was in original Eden.

We have seen in the abundance of revelation in Isaiah, the gospels, and elsewhere that the vision provided by the prophets of old is, in a real sense, a vision of a "full circle" return to God's original plan for mankind—paradise on earth with wonderful, healthy, physical bodies. Indeed our new bodies will be similar to the old, but immortal and with some measure of supernatural ability. After God made Adam and Eve of the dust of the ground and breathed into their nostrils "the breath of life" in original Eden, He "saw everything that He had made, and indeed it was very good" [Genesis 1:31 NKJV]. God was pleased with His design for mankind in the beginning. Nothing in the Bible suggests that God was dissatisfied with His original design of man [humanity's descent into immorality and rejection of God notwithstanding] or that He wants to eliminate the "flesh and bone" design and turn people into spirit beings like the angels.

In our new and everlasting lives in Paradise restored, people will still remember friends, family, and experiences from their mortal lives. Some features of the Millennial Kingdom indicate this. For example, Ezekiel chapter 48 is an extensive prophecy of the division of the land among the tribes of Israel in the Millennial Kingdom, and Revelation 21:10 and 11 (REV) inform us that "the holy Jerusalem"…will have "a wall great and high, having 12 gates, and at the gates 12 angels, and names written on it, which are *the names* of the 12 tribes of the sons of Israel." Also, verse 14 says: "And the wall of the city had 12 foundations, and on them 12 names of the 12 apostles of the Lamb." This would all be meaningless if people did not remember the tribes of Israel or the Lord's apostles.

As well, we have seen that at the Judgment Seat of Christ in heaven, "each one's work will become clear" [1 Corinthians 3:13 REV], "that each one may receive the things done in the body, according to what he has done, whether good or worthless" [2 Corinthians 5:10 REV]. If raptured saints will have no remembrance of their previous lives, this would all be pointless. And as we have seen, 1 John 2:28 warns us that some Christians will be "ashamed before Him at His coming"—shame because of failures remembered from their former lives. 2 Timothy 2:11

(NKJV) and 12 is another ominous warning: "This is a faithful saying: For if we died with Him, we shall also live with Him. If we deny Him [by our wayward lifestyle], He also will deny us" [in the loss of eternal rewards]. Although Isaiah 65:17 (NKJV) says: "For behold, I create new heavens and a new earth [at the onset of the Everlasting Kingdom]; and the former shall not be remembered or come to mind," it will not be as if people will not be able to remember anything from their mortal lives. But in the joy of their everlasting lives in Paradise restored, tears and painful memories from the past will have faded away: And God "will wipe away every tear from their eyes, and death will be no more, neither will there be mourning, nor crying, nor pain, any more; the former things have passed away. And he who sits on the throne said, 'Look!, I make all things new.' And he says, 'Write, for these words are faithful and true'" [Revelation 21:4-6 REV].

"Therefore, brothers, be all the more diligent to be sure of your calling and choice, for if you do these things, you will absolutely not stumble, for in this way the entrance into the kingdom of our Lord and Savior Jesus Christ will be richly provided to you in the Age *to come*" [2 Peter 1:10,11 REV].

---

*Howe, Julia Ward, *Reminiscenses,* 1819-1899, Houghton, Mifflin, New York, 1899, p. 275.

SIX

Recognizing Your Spiritual Gifts

"For the gifts and the calling of God are irrevocable."
-Romans 11:29 (REV)

OVER THE MORE THAN SEVENTY-EIGHT years of my life, I have dreamed from time to time that, by the power of my imagination, and by using my hands and arms as thrusters, I am able to push myself upward from the land and, depending on the severity of the challenge or stress I seem to be facing, I can fly! At times in the dream it seems I have difficulty "lifting off" and can't manage to fly very high. Other times I seem to be able to soar upward and, gazing down over the land, I marvel that the people on the ground don't even notice that I'm flying! A "dream dictionary" I consulted on the web suggested that dreams of flying are a common universal dream image and that they generally represent some form of ascension—rising above our mundane lives—and that it is always a feeling of joy or freedom.

I believe that in my everlasting life in Paradise restored that I will actually be able to fly. And possibly so will you! In fact I believe that my ability to fly will be a feature of my eternal inheritance. After His resurrection, Jesus appeared to His friends and disappeared at will. As well, angels "fly." In a number of records in the Bible, angels "fly" in the sense that they move quickly or even instantaneously from place to place [Daniel 4:13 and 9:21; Revelation 14:6]. And seraphim fly [Isaiah 6:2,6]. Certainly some Christians in their everlasting lives in Paradise restored will enjoy such miraculous abilities no less than the angels! In John 14:12 (REV) Jesus prophesies: "Most assuredly, I say to you, he who believes in Me, the works that I do he will do also, and greater *works* than these he will do, because I go to the Father." What works did Jesus do? And what are the "greater works" that we will do? He told His disciples: "Go and tell John the things you have seen and heard: that *the* blind see, *the* lame walk, *the* lepers are cleansed, *the* deaf hear, *the* dead are raised, *the* poor have the gospel preached to them" [Luke 7:22 REV].

In my Christian ministry over the years, I've often longed to do more of the works that Jesus did. I have longed to be able to heal the sick, to unstop the ears of the deaf, to open the eyes of the [spiritually] blind. By the grace of God, I've enjoyed limited success, but over time I've come to understand that, in this sophisticated Western world especially, suffocating unbelief often defeats the promises of God. Certain anointed ministers in other parts of the world—India, Africa, South America, for example—have enjoyed more success because people there have been hungry for God and for God's healing touch. In the Millennial Kingdom to come, many believers who have longed to take the Lord at His word and do the works that He did in His earthly ministry will have sensational success. We will absolutely heal the sick, open the eyes of the blind, unstop the ears of the deaf, cause the lame to walk, and even raise the dead. There will be great need among the natural peoples who repopulate the earth, and many Christians who have longed to walk "in His steps" in this mortal life will be supernaturally enabled in their everlasting lives.

God promises rewards to believers for their faithfulness and obedience. Along with the many verses we have already seen, consider: "I, the Lord, search the heart, *I* test the mind, even to give every man according to his ways, according to the fruit of his doings" [Jeremiah 17:10 NKJV]. The psalmist says: "Also to You, Lord, *belongs* mercy; For You render to each one according to his work" [Psalm 62:12 NKJV]. Paul writes in Romans 2:6 (REV): "...who [God] will repay each *person* according to his works;" and in 1 Corinthians 3:8 (REV): "Now the one who plants and the one who waters are one, but` each one will receive his own reward according to his own labor." In Matthew 16:27 (REV) Jesus says: "For the Son of Man is about to come with his angels in the glory of his Father, and then he will repay each *person* according to what he has done." Other significant verses speak of future rewards: To Israel under the law—"Therefore whoever breaks one of the least of these commandments and teaches others *to do* the same, will be called least in the Kingdom of Heaven, but whoever does *them* and teaches *them* will be called great in the Kingdom of Heaven. For I say to you, that unless your righteousness exceeds *the righteousness* of the experts in the law and Pharisees, you will absolutely not enter into the Kingdom of Heaven" [Matthew 5:19,20 REV]. Also: "And whoever gives one of these little ones even a cup of cold water to drink in the name of a disciple, truly I say to you, he will not ever lose his reward" [Matthew 10:42 REV]. And in Matthew 18:1-4 (REV): "In that hour the disciples came to Jesus, saying, 'Who is greatest in the Kingdom of Heaven?' And he called to him a little child and set him in the midst of them, and said, 'Truly, I say to you, unless you change and become as little children, you will absolutely not enter into the Kingdom of Heaven. Therefore, whoever will humble himself as this little child, that one is the greatest in the Kingdom of Heaven."

And to Christians not under the law ["For Christ is the fulfillment of the law, with the result that *now* there is righteousness for everyone who believes"--Romans 10:4 REV]: "...each one's work will become plainly seen; for the Day [His appearing] will make it clear, because it will be revealed by fire; and the fire itself will test each one's work, *and show* of what kind it is. If anyone's work which he has built on it remains, he will receive a reward" [1 Corinthians 3:13,14 REV]. And 2 John 1:8 (REV): "Watch yourselves, so that you do not lose those things what we have worked for, but that you receive a full reward."

Moreover, it is clear from other sections of the Scriptures that some people who have thought of themselves as Israel or as Christians will be shocked and ashamed at Christ's appearing: "For whoever is ashamed of me and of my words, of that person will the Son of Man be ashamed when he comes in his glory, and *the glory* of the Father, and of the holy angels" [Luke 9:26 REV]. And 1 Thessalonians 4:3-6 (REV): "For this is the will of God, your holiness [*hagiasmos*—"consecration"]: that you abstain from sexual immorality; that each of you know how to take control of his own vessel in holiness and honor, not in lustful passion, like the Gentiles who do not know God, *and* that no one overstep proper boundaries and take advantage of his brother in this matter, because the Lord is an avenger in all these things, even as we told you before and solemnly warned you." Also, 1 John 2:28 (REV): "And now, little children, abide in him, so that when he appears, we will have confidence and not shrink back from him in shame at his coming." And 2 Timothy 2:11-13 (REV): "This statement is trustworthy: For if we died with him, we shall also live with him. If we endure, we will also reign with him. If we deny him, he also will deny us. If we are unfaithful, he remains faithful, for he is not able to deny himself." And 1 Corinthians 10:7-12 (REV): "Do not be idolaters as were some of them [Children of Israel in the wilderness]....We must not commit sexual immorality, as some of them committed, and 23,000 fell in one day. We must not tempt the Lord, as some of them tempted, and perished by the serpents. We must not grumble, as some of them grumbled, and were destroyed by the destroyer. Now these things happened to them as an example, and they were written for our admonition, upon whom the ends of the ages have come. So then, let the one who thinks he stands watch out, lest he fall."

Thus it becomes obvious that salvation and everlasting life for the believer in God and in Christ in the ages to come does not automatically mean everlasting rewards. Everlasting life is by the grace of God ["For by grace you have been saved through trust, and this is not of yourselves; *it is* the gift of God, not as a result of works, so that no one can boast"— Ephesians 2:8,9 REV], whereas rewards in the ages to come are earned in this mortal life here and now. And it is likely that the degree of spiritual authority one will enjoy in his everlasting life will be in relation to the functions and the missions of power that the believer will be assigned by the Lord Himself. We realize from certain sections of the Scriptures that some angels are more powerful and have a higher status in heaven than others [Daniel 10:12-14; Ezekiel 28:12-14; Revelation 10:1;18:21]. And consider Colossians 1:16 (REV): "For by him all things were created in heaven and on earth, the visible and the invisible, whether thrones or lordships or rulerships or authorities, through him and for him all things have been created." Thus it is possible that the status or station one might enjoy and the miraculous abilities that a believer might possess in the Millennial Kingdom will be in relation to the rewards he has earned in his mortal life.

"Then the Lord God took the man and put him in the garden of Eden to tend and keep it."
–Genesis 2:15 (NKJV)

In original Eden God gave Adam and Eve work to do. "Then the Lord God took the man and put him in the garden to tend and keep it." Other versions of the Bible read "to cultivate it and keep it" and "to work it and take care of it." Adam and Eve were given the task and the responsibility of cultivating and tending to the garden, just as any farmer today must work the soil and take care of his plants and trees. Thus various types of work and responsibilities in Paradise restored will be needed and required of the inhabitants. For example, Isaiah 60:10, 61:4, Ezekiel 36:10, Amos 9:13, and others [all verses here (NKJV)] inform us that there will be "builders." Isaiah 30:23 and 24, Jeremiah 31:5, Ezekiel 36:9, Amos 9:13, and others, speak of "farmers," and "sowers." Isaiah 60:6,7; 61:5, Jeremiah 31:12, and others, mention or imply "herdsmen." Isaiah 60:13—"landscapers." Isaiah 2:4, 60:17, Micah 4:3—"metalworkers." Ezekiel 47:10—"fishermen." Ezekiel 44:10-16—"temple duties." Isaiah 25:6, 62:9; Jeremiah 31:12—"vinedressers." Ezekiel 39:14,15—"gravediggers." Isaiah 14:2—"servants and maids." And many other verses inform us that there will be cooks, bakers, weavers, musicians, seamstresses, administrators, and many other duties required in the Millennial Kingdom. Even though there will be differences in the assignments people will receive in the kingdom, no one will be stressed out or be in want. In general, immortal believers as well as the natural men and women living in the Millennial Kingdom, will work and play, eat and drink, sing and dance, and enjoy fellowship with the Lord and with one another in Paradise restored. Indeed, the Bible describes a future age that will be in many ways similar to life today except without disease and sickness, without war, injustice, hunger or want.

Many of the tasks and responsibilities listed above will be carried out by the natural men and women living at that time. However, certain immortal believers who in their mortal lives passed much of their time as "still of the flesh" Christians [1 Corinthians 3:3 REV] and who may even have denied the Lord by rejecting or ignoring Christian principles [2 Timothy 2:12 REV], and who failed to recognize their God-given spiritual gifts and failed to function in them in love in service to the Lord and to the Body of Christ, and who will have appeared at the judgment seat of Christ with unconfessed sin, will be shocked and ashamed at the Lord's appearing and will forfeit most of the rewards they might have enjoyed had they remained faithful to the Lord's commandments. Therefore, it's likely that their tasks and assignments in the Millennial Kingdom will be similar to those of the natural men and women who will be their neighbors—farmers, shepherds, builders, etc. However, as immortals, it's unlikely that their days will be days of stress and disappointment in Paradise. And again I say—this is *everlasting life*.

Along with John 3:16, another verse that is set like a many-faceted diamond in the living word of God—as we discussed earlier but which is so vitally important--is Romans 12:2 (REV): "And do not be conformed to the pattern of this age, but be transformed by the renewing of your mind, so that you can test and approve what the will of God is—the thing that is good and pleasing and perfect." The important guidelines presented in this remarkable verse and how well the believer acts on these commandments will absolutely affect how well he or she is able to function in their spiritual gifts and skills in the Body of Christ—thereby affecting the quality of their rewards in Paradise restored.

In the Greek text the word for "conformed" is *syschematizesthe*. It means "to conform or fashion one's mind and character to another's pattern." Many Christians allow themselves to be "conformed" in their attitudes and actions to the superficial patterns of this world which are heavily influenced by "the god of this age" [2 Corinthians 4:4 REV]. Galatians 5:17 (REV) testifies to this reality: "For the flesh sets its desire against the spirit, and the spirit against the flesh; indeed, these oppose each other, with the result that you are not doing what you want." In other words, the Christian who allows himself or herself to be conformed continually to the deceitful patterns of this world will absolutely be thwarted in his or her desire to fulfill their ministry of *charisma* in the Church.

In Romans 12:2 the word for "transformed" in the Greek text is *metamorphoo* which means "transfigure," "change into another form." By way of a picture of what is available in our mortal lives and ultimately in our everlasting lives, God presents us with the remarkable scene of Christ's transfiguration on the mountain [Matthew 17:2 and Mark 9:2,3] when He was transformed and "began to shine brightly with divine and regal glory" [Matthew 17:2, AMP]. God encourages us that as we persistently "renew our minds" to God's living word instead of to the deceitful patterns of this world, we will experience progressively a transformation of our character in this mortal life and, in the ages to come, our living presence may indeed "shine brightly with divine and regal glory." Moreover, in the Greek text the word for "renewing" in Romans 12:2 is *anakainosis* which means "renovation"—"a complete change for the better."

The fact is, God exhorts His people to meditate on His word. To the Children of Israel, in preparation for entering "the land which I swore to their fathers to give them" [Joshua 1:6 NKJV], God said: "This Book of the Law shall not depart from your mouth, but you shall meditate in it day and night, that you may observe to do according to all that is written in it. For then you will make your way prosperous, and then you will have good success" [verse 8]. As well, the psalmist assures us: "Blessed *is* the man who walks not in the counsel of the ungodly, nor stands in the path of sinners, nor sits in the seat of the scornful; But his delight is in the law of the Lord, and in His law he meditates day and night. He shall be like a tree planted by the rivers of water, that brings forth its fruit in its season, whose leaf also shall not wither; and whatever he does shall prosper" [Psalm 1:1-3 NKJV]. Moreover, Jesus says in His Parable of the Sower: "And these are the ones [the seed of the word] who were sown on the good ground: those who go on hearing the word, and go on accepting it, and go on bearing fruit, thirtyfold, and sixtyfold, and a hundredfold" [Mark 4:20 REV]. In the Hebrew text [Joshua and the Psalms] the word for "meditate" is *hagah,* meaning "utter," "muse," "study," "moan," "growl." Psalm 1:1-3 (NKJV) encourages the reader: "Blessed *is* the man who walks not in the counsel of the ungodly, Nor stands in the path of sinners, Nor sits in the seat of the scornful; But his delight is in the law of the Lord, and in His law he meditates ["muse," "study," "utter,"] day and night." Paul says in 2 Timothy 2:15 (REV): "Make a diligent [*spoudason*—"study," "labor"] effort to present yourself approved before God, a workman who does not need to be ashamed, rightly handling the word of truth." When we meditate on God's word—study it faithfully, muse on it—it becomes a part of our being, it increases our faith, it becomes "a lamp to [our] feet and a light to [our] path" [Psalm 119:105 NKJV]. Indeed, Psalm 119:162 (NKJV) says: "I rejoice at Your word as one who finds great treasure." *Great treasure!* As we faithfully sow the seed of God's word on the good ground of our minds and hearts: "For then you will make your way prosperous, and then you will have good success."

The Parable of the Sower

As we learn more about recognizing and learning to function in our spiritual gifts in the Church, we are reminded not only of the Lord's Parable of the Talents, but also of His Parable of the Sower. Matthew 13:3-9 (REV): "The sower went out to sow, and as he sowed, some *seeds* fell along the path; and the birds came and devoured them. And others fell on the rocky places, where they did not have much earth, and immediately they sprang up, because they had no depth of earth. And when the sun rose they were scorched, and because they had no root, they withered away. And others fell among the thorns, and the thorns grew up and choked them. And others fell on the good ground, and yielded fruit: some a hundredfold, some sixty, some thirty. Anyone who has ears had better listen!" Then in verses 18-23 Jesus explains this parable to His disciples: "Hear, then, the parable of the sower: When anyone hears the message about the kingdom and does not understand *it*, the Wicked *one* comes and snatches away that which has been sown in his heart. This is the one who was sown along the path. And the seed that was sown on the rocky places, this is the one who hears the word, and immediately with joy receives it, yet he does not have *any* root in himself, but is short-lived. When tribulation or persecution arises because of the word, immediately he falls away. Now the one that was sown among the thorns, this is the one who hears the word, but the worry of this age and the deceitfulness of wealth chokes the word, and it becomes unfruitful. And the one who was sown on the good ground, this is the one who hears the word, and understands *it*, who indeed bears fruit, and yields, some a hundredfold, some sixty, some thirty."

People have always responded in different ways to the preaching of the word of God. The "good ground" represents the minds and hearts of those who hear and receive God's word and allow it to take root and grow in their lives. Jesus teaches the importance of the states of our attitude and heart in terms of producing "fruit" in our lives now, because not only will it affect the quality of our rewards in Paradise restored, it will enhance the quality of our lives in these mortal years. Some Christians by endeavoring to "renew their minds" to the living word of God throughout their lives will produce fruit—"some a hundredfold, some sixty, some thirty," depending on their faithfulness and their effectiveness in functioning in their spiritual gifts in the Body of Christ.

"For he whom God sent continues to speak the words of God...
-John 3:34 (REV)

In His brief earthly ministry, Jesus Christ displayed many of the spiritual gifts He has bestowed on the members of His spiritual Body, the Church. John 3:34 (REV) informs us that even in His earthly ministry, the Lord enjoyed the spirit "without measure:" "For he whom God sent continues to speak the words of God, for He continues to give to *him* the spirit without measure." As the **Teacher**, Christ taught the people and preached in a way no one had ever preached before, manifesting His spiritual authority by healing the sick, opening the eyes of the blind, casting out demons, raising the dead. Mark 1:22 (REV) tells us that the people "were astonished at his teaching, for he taught them as *one* having authority and not as the experts in the law [scribes]." This is the gift ministry of an anointed Teacher.

As well, the Lord's teaching in the Sermon on the Mount, the

Sermon on the Plain, in His parables, and on many other occasions, were words of pure prophecy—not simply forth-telling truths to His disciples for the here and now, but also foretelling truths for future appreciation in the age to come. Matthew 25:31-33 (REV): "But when the Son of Man comes in his glory, and all the angels with him, then he will sit on his glorious throne [in Jerusalem in the Millennial Kingdom]. And all the nations will be gathered before him, and he will separate them one from another, as the shepherd separates the sheep from the goats. And he will put the sheep on his right, but the goats on the left." This is a prophecy of the Sheep and Goats Judgment to occur at the onset of the Millennial Kingdom.

Prophetically, Jesus saw into individual's hearts and lives and spoke accordingly: To the woman at the well He said: "You have rightly said, 'I have no husband,' for you have had five husbands, and he whom you now have is not your husband. This you have said truly" [John 4:17,18 REV]. And to the Pharisees he said: "You offspring of vipers! How are you, being evil, able to speak good things? For out of the abundance of the heart the mouth speaks" [Matthew 12:34 REV]. Jesus was and is God's **Prophet** for all time.

Moreover, He was the pre-eminent **Evangelist**: "Come to me, all you who are laboring and have been loaded down with burdens, and I will give you rest. Take my yoke upon you and learn from me, because I am meek and humble in heart, and you will find rest for your souls. For my yoke is kind and my burden is light" [Matthew 11:28-30 REV]. Even the Pharisees confirmed his excellence as a gifted Evangelist, saying among themselves: "Look, the world has gone after him" [John 12:19 REV].

And Jesus was and is God's **Apostle**: "I am the light of the world. The one who continues to follow me will not ever walk in darkness, but will have the light of life" [John 8:12 REV]; and Luke 9:1 and 2 (REV): "And he called the twelve together, and gave them power and authority over all demons, and to cure diseases. And he sent them out to preach the Kingdom of God and to heal the sick."

And Jesus was and continues to be the most loving **Pastor**: "I am the good shepherd. The good shepherd gives his life for the sheep....I am the good shepherd. And I know my own, and my own know me"

[John 10:11,14 REV]. "But when he saw the multitudes, he was moved with compassion for them, because they were distressed and scattered, like sheep without a shepherd" [Matthew 9:36 REV].

Thus Christ was and is the embodiment of the five gift ministries which He has given to certain faithful believers in the Church "for the equipping of the holy *ones* for the work of ministry, with a view to the building up of the body of Christ..." [Ephesians 4:12 REV].

"The harvest indeed is abundant, but the laborers are few..."
-Luke 10:2 (REV)

We can discern in the Lord's earthly ministry how He functioned in a variety of other gifts [*charisma*]. As a **Server/Helper**: "*Jesus*, knowing that the Father had given all things into his hands, and that he had come from God and was going to God, gets up from supper and lays aside his outer garments, and he took a towel and tied it around himself. Then he pours water into the basin and began to wash the disciples' feet and to wipe them with the towel that was tied around him" [John 13:3-5 REV]. And Mark 10:43-45 (REV): "...whoever wants to become great among you will be your servant, and whoever wants to be first among you will be slave of all. For even the Son of Man did not come to be served, but to serve, and to give his life a ransom for many."

As a persistent **Exhorter**, Jesus said: "Blessed are those who hunger and thirst after righteousness, for they will be filled." And: "...let your light shine before people so that they can see your good works and glorify your Father who is in heaven" [Matthew 5:6,16 REV]. As one who shows **Mercy/Compassion**: To the woman caught in the act of adultery: "'Woman, where are those accusers of yours? Has no one condemned you?' She said, 'No one, Lord.' And Jesus said to her, 'Neither do I condemn you; go and sin no more'" [John 8:10b,11 REV]. And Matthew 5:7 (REV): "Blessed are the merciful, for they will obtain mercy." At the tomb of Lazarus, Jesus said, "'Where have you laid him?' They say to him, 'Lord, come and see.' Jesus burst into tears" [John 11:34,35 REV]. And Matthew 9:36 (REV): "But when he saw the multitudes, he was moved with compassion for them because they were distressed and scattered, like sheep without shepherd."

As one who exhibits **Leadership**: "To him the doorkeeper opens and the sheep hear his voice, and he calls his own sheep by name and leads them out. When he has brought out all his own, he goes before them, and the sheep follow him because they know his voice" [John 10:3,4 REV]. Also: "I am the way, and the truth, and the life. No one comes to the Father except through me" [John 14:6 REV]. As an **Administrator**: "Now after these things the Lord appointed 72 others and sent them two and two before his face into every city and place where he himself was about to go. And he said to them, 'The harvest indeed is abundant, but the laborers are few. Therefore, implore the Lord of the harvest to send out laborers into his harvest'" [Luke 10:1,2 REV].

As one who is a **Giver**: "And he commanded the multitude to sit down on the ground, and he took the seven loaves and the fish and he gave thanks and broke *them*, and gave to the disciples, and the disciples *gave* to the multitudes. And they all ate and were filled, and they took up what remained of the broken pieces, seven baskets full. And those who ate were 4,000 men, besides women and children" [Matthew 15:35-38 REV]. Also: "This is my commandment, that you love one another just as I have loved you. No one has greater love than this—that one would lay down his life for his friends" [John 15:12,13 REV].

Recognizing Your Spiritual Gifts

Here we consider a listing of all the spiritual gifts [*doma* and *charisma*] mentioned or suggested in the Bible, as we have previously noted. Along with each gift listed is a series of affirmations specifically describing the nature or function of that gift in a believer's life. The purpose of this listing and the affirmations is to help guide the believer into recognizing a particular gift at work in his or her life and ministry in the Church. If one agrees wholeheartedly with a majority of the affirmations describing a particular gift, it is likely that he recognizes that gift at work in his life. Some may recognize more than one gift as their primary gift while at the same time discover that another gift or two may also be at work secondarily or occasionally. This is quite common in the Body of Christ.

Regarding the five gift ministries Paul lists in Ephesians 4, we present four of them here. The gift ministry of an Apostle is rare and entirely God's doing. If a believer is endowed by God to serve the Body of Christ as an Apostle, no series of tests or affirmations will cause him to discover it. As for the other gift ministries, oftentimes when a faithful believer in a local church or assembly is ordained to the Christian ministry by the laying on of hands and prophetic prayer of the leaders of the group, if he or she has in fact been given a gift ministry by the Lord, that ministry is revealed in this process. But not always.

Note: A variety of spiritual gifts assessment tests are readily available on the internet or even from your church or denomination. Unfortunately, most of these tests include the nine manifestations of the spirit (which Paul presents in 1 Corinthians 12) as individual gifts in their testing. As we have pointed out earlier, these manifestations of the spirit are *not* individual gifts—they are enablements—expressions— of the gift of holy spirit with which every born-again believer has been baptized. Thus a person using one or more of these tests can unintentionally be misguided.

Teacher

*   I feel that consistent Bible study is foundational to understanding the purpose of life.
*   I enjoy presenting the truth of God's word in a logical, systematic way.
*   I prefer teaching the word of God to individuals or to groups rather than participating in evangelism.
*   Sometimes I get a bit upset when I see other teachers or individuals use the Scriptures out of context.
*   I believe that biblical truth has the power to produce change in a person's life.
*   I enjoy doing Bible word studies and other research projects.
*   Other believers have encouraged and even applauded me for my ability to make a biblical point clearly and persuasively in a group setting.

If you agree with a majority of these affirmations and even recognize them in your convictions, then you may function in the gift ministry of a Teacher in the Body of Christ.

Prophet

* I tend to have strong convictions and opinions.
* I view the Bible as the word of God and the basis for truth, faith, and spiritual authority.
* I can easily perceive the character of individuals from their words or statement of beliefs.
* I tend to see people's actions or even most situations as black or white with little compromise.
* In my church or assembly I love to faithfully promote the spiritual growth of individuals and groups.
* In my life I tend to be introspective.
* Most of the time I can quickly identify good and evil in a situation, and I hate evil.

If you agree with or recognize a majority of these affirmations in your life and in your participation in your church or assembly, you may sometimes function in the gift ministry of a Prophet.

Evangelist

* I love to present the good news of the gospel of Jesus Christ to individuals or to groups whenever available.
* Other believers in my church or group have recognized and applauded my passion for effectively preaching the good news of the gospel.
* I have a deep desire to present Jesus Christ, when the opportunity arises, to anyone who will listen, and I actively seek those opportunities.
* I have a heartfelt desire to lead others to a point of decision for Jesus Christ.

If you agree with or even recognize these affirmations in your life, you may sometimes function in the gift ministry of an Evangelist. Note: In 2 Timothy 4:5 (REV), Paul tells Timothy: "But you, always be clear-minded, endure suffering, do the work of an evangelist, fulfill your ministry." Church history suggests that Timothy was a skilled evangelist. Sometimes, however, in the local church or assembly, it's important for believers who are not specifically called by the Lord in the gift ministry of an evangelist, nevertheless to "do the work of an evangelist" in order to grow the church.

Pastor

* ★ I have a passion to tend to "the flock of God" and feel energized and called by God to do so.
* ★ I long to "heal the brokenhearted" and "bring deliverance to the captives," just as Jesus desired.
* ★ I have a deep desire to minister to a group of believers, practicing patience and forbearance, gentleness and concern for the quality of their individual walks with Christ, as well as their relationships with one another.
* ★ Others in my church have let it be known to me that my counseling is a gift of God.
* ★ I wholeheartedly believe in the Lord's Great Commission, especially in "teaching them to observe all that I commanded you" [Matthew 28:20 REV].

If you agree with the guidelines of these affirmations, you may function in the gift ministry of a Pastor.

★

And now we turn to the more common gifts of God's divine favor—*charisma*.

Exhortation

* ★ I am often inspired to encourage and edify others with words from the Bible or even general encouragement toward a more worthy endeavor in their lives.

151

★ I am not one to research and teach the Bible, but I love to encourage others with the words of wisdom I have learned.

★ Others in my church have told me that I have a way with words and a facility for communicating inspiring points of view.

★ When I am inspired to speak words of encouragement to an individual or to a group, I try to speak words of specific practical application.

★ I expect a lot of myself in my walk with Christ, and I love to encourage others to expect a lot of themselves.

If you recognize and agree with these affirmations for yourself, you may often function in the gift of Exhortation.

Server/Helps

★ I tend to recognize undone tasks in our church and take pleasure in assisting or being of use in a variety of ways.

★ I know I work well with my hands and seem to be able to do almost anything that requires manual skill.

★ I enjoy working on short-term projects—something I can help finish in a foreseeable amount of time—and prefer to leave the long-term goals to others.

★ I don't consider myself a leader in a given project, but as a faithful follower. My motto is: "What can I do to help?" I get frustrated if I am asked to lead.

★ Jesus said, "If anyone serves me, let him follow me" [John 12:26 REV]. I think of my service in my church as the practical application of Christianity.

If you agree with the majority of these affirmations for yourself, you may be enjoying the gift of Service/Helps.

Giver

★ I enjoy sharing my resources—whether money or other abundance—with our church or with anyone in need.

*   I never want credit for my giving. I just want to please my Heavenly Father.
*   I long to help in any way I can in ministries that I give to financially—to pray for them or assist in practical ways, or to advance them in other ways.
*   I've always been good at stewarding money—careful, cautious, even frugal.
*   I believe that everything I have—money and all my possessions—ultimately belongs to the Lord. I'm just the steward.

If you recognize the majority of these affirmations in your life, you may have the gift of the Giver.

Hospitality

*   I love to welcome and entertain others—even strangers—into my home or during church get-togethers, as a means of blessing them abundantly.
*   I believe in the motto: "Do not forget to show love to strangers, for by *doing* this some have entertained angels without knowing it" [Hebrews 13:1 REV].
*   People love to just "hang out" at my place.
*   I love to meet new people at church or at other group gatherings and to help them feel warmly welcomed.

If you recognize these affirmations in your life, you may have the gift of Hospitality.

Mercy/Compassion

*   I have always felt especially sensitive to those who are suffering.
*   I can often sense how others are feeling, and I do my best to respond to it with love and understanding.
*   I believe my sensitivity to those who are suffering is a gift of God.
*   I am often motivated to pray for or to help the handicapped, the elderly, the sick, or the wounded in spirit.

- ★ I think of myself as a humble person aware of my own weaknesses and failures.

If you recognize these traits in your life and agree with these affirmations, you may have the gift of Mercy/Compassion. The person with this gift may also have the gift of Intercession.

Intercession

- ★ I am often moved by the spirit of God to pray on behalf of others for an extended period of time and to believe for and see specific answers to prayer.
- ★ I often sense a sweet intimacy with God in the spirit and seem to be able to discern an understanding of the Lord's heart and mind for someone who may be hurting.

If you recognize these traits in your life on a regular basis, you may have the gift of Intercession as well as the gift of Mercy/Compassion.

Administration

- ★ I am one to "dig in" and help to organize or develop a project in our church.
- ★ I have been known to "step in" and take charge of a project when it requires a focused leader.
- ★ Others have recognized that I am able to communicate my ideas clearly and effectively.
- ★ I seem to be good at making long-range plans, supervising others, and coordinating projects in the church that take a lot of planning and time.
- ★ I am a "people person." I enjoy getting to know and interacting with others and learning how to work with others effectively.

If you recognize these traits and agree with these affirmations, you may have the gift of Administration.

Leadership

- ★ I feel that I am called by the Lord to lead, assist, protect, and care for others in our church.
- ★ Others in our church have told me that I seem inspired to guide fellow believers into a deeper relationship with the Lord.
- ★ I love to help the church set goals in accordance with Christ's guidance for the Church's growth.
- ★ I am highly motivated to inspire, guide, and work with others harmoniously to effectively do the work of our church.
- ★ In a variety of different groups of which I have been a member, oftentimes others have expected me to assume a leadership role sooner or later.

If you recognize these traits in your life and agree with these affirmations, you may have the gift of Leadership.

★

Other gifts [*charisma*] of the spirit mentioned in the New Testament are more or less self-explanatory: Celibacy, Martyrdom, Missionary. These have been discussed briefly earlier in this study—except for this one note: As pointed out in chapter three, Celibacy is the spiritual gift that allows a believer to voluntarily remain unmarried without regret and with the ability to maintain control of his or her sexual desires in order to serve the Lord without distraction. In 1 Corinthians 7:7 (REV) Paul says: "…for I would like everyone to be just like I myself [unmarried]. But each has his own gift from God, one of one kind and one of another." Let it be said that Celibacy as a gift [*charisma*] of God is not the same as celibacy as a manner of life required of certain individuals in some churches, denominations, or religious groups for full participation in their religious order.

★

Certain other gifts noted throughout the Bible—Singers, Musicians, Artists, Poets, Composers, and others—will be discussed in more detail in the next chapter.

"...having been born again, not of corruptible seed but incorruptible..."
1 Peter 1:23 (REV)

Recognizing and learning to function in your spiritual gifts in the Body of Christ will increase the joy of the Lord in your life. You may be surprised or amazed at this discovery, or you may realize that you have been functioning naturally in your gifts all along. As well, you may begin to understand that you function in and enjoy certain gifts other than your primary gift and that some gifts seem to overlap in certain circumstances. Understanding your spiritual gifts and their purposes in the Body of Christ will help you to make wise choices and decisions and provide for you a more fulfilling sense of value and purpose in the Church and in your walk with the Lord.

God says: "... so that we are no longer children, tossed to and fro, and carried about with every wind of doctrine, by human trickery, by *people's* craftiness in deceitful scheming. Instead, speaking the truth in love, let us grow up in every way into *union with* him who is the head, *into* Christ, from whom the whole body, being fitted together and united through that which every joint supplies, by the working *of each individual part in its proper measure* [italics supplied], produces the growth of the body for the building up of itself in love" [Ephesians 4:14-16 REV].

Who you will be in Paradise restored in the Millennial Kingdom will be dependent on several primary factors—

* You must be "born again" [1 Peter 1:23 REV], "sealed with the promised holy spirit" [Ephesians 1:13 REV], and washed with "the water of regeneration" [Titus 3:5 NKJV]. In other words, "saved" [Romans 10:9]. "For God did not send the Son into the world to judge the world, but that the world should be saved through him. Whoever believes in him is not condemned, but whoever does not believe is condemned already, because he has not believed in the name of the only begotten Son of God" [John 3:17,18 REV].

* To the best of your ability you have embraced the word of God in your life, and have done your best to work patiently at

renewing your mind to the wisdom of the Bible so as not to be conformed to the deceitful patterns of this world, but instead endeavoring to be transformed—changed—in your character, slowly but surely, to the character of Jesus Christ.

★ You have recognized your God-given spiritual gifts and have patiently and diligently learned to function in them in your church or assembly and in your life in order to bless and edify your fellow believers in the Body of Christ.

★ With a willing heart and mind you have endeavored to live the love of God in your renewed mind in evidence in your mortal life since you became a Christian, whether early or later in life—despite the many turns and disruptions and challenges along the way.

"I came so that they can have life, and have it abundantly."
-John 10:10 (REV)

In this biblical research study, I have endeavored to present the high standard of God's Word regarding the Christian's challenge to live up to the Lord's promise in John 10:10b (REV): "I came so that they can have life, and have it abundantly," both now and in the age to come. At times in our lives we fall short of God's high standard of Christian living, sometimes miserably so, myself included. But we thank God for His healing grace and abundant mercy. Proverbs 24:16 (NKJV) encourages us: "For a righteous *man* may fall seven times and rise again, but the wicked shall fall by calamity." In other words, every Christian believer will face challenges to his faith in his or her life—perhaps many times. And although he or she may "fall" from God's grace for a time, we rise again and persevere, unlike the unbeliever. The psalmist says: "Bless the Lord, O my soul; And all that is within me, *bless* His holy name! Bless the Lord, O my soul, And forget not all His benefits: Who forgives all your iniquities…" [Psalm 103:1-3 NKJV]. In Matthew 6:14 and 15 (REV), Jesus says: "For if you forgive people their transgressions, your

157

heavenly Father will also forgive you. But if you do not forgive people their transgressions, your Father will not forgive your transgressions." And 1 John 1:9 and 10 (REV) instruct believers: "If we confess our sins, he (God) is faithful and righteous to forgive us our sins and to cleanse us from all unrighteousness. If we say that we have not sinned, we make him a liar, and his word is not in us." Again, we thank God for His grace and abundant mercy.

★

We live in a world where many seek after fame and fortune and in a society which tends to see people as "somebodies" and "nobodies." But that's not how God sees people. I Samuel 16 (NKJV) records how God worked in the Prophet Samuel's ministry to anoint David the shepherd boy king over Israel. Samuel went to visit Jesse, the father of David, on a mission. One by one the sons of Jesse appeared before Samuel to see if he would choose them to be king. As each one stood before the prophet: "...the Lord said to Samuel, do not look at his appearance or at his physical stature, because I have refused him. For the Lord does not see as man sees; for man looks at the outward appearance, but the Lord looks at the heart" [verse 7]. And so it is not so much what one accomplishes in his or her life according to this world's ideals that is ultimately important, but *one's life's motive is everything.* How well we have exhibited these truths listed above will absolutely determine the quality of our rewards when we stand with the Lord Jesus Christ *face to face* at the judgment seat of Christ. It will absolutely determine the quality of our spiritual authority and our eternal commissioning on behalf of the Lord in our *everlasting life.*

As one who is an exhorter, I say to each reader: May it echo throughout eternity when you stand on the *bema* with all the host of heaven looking on, perhaps with members of your own family standing along side you, and with all your brothers and sisters in Christ gathered around, as the Lord Jesus Christ Himself smiles at you and says for everyone to hear: "Well done, My good and faithful servant! Enter into the joy of your Lord!" [paraphrased from Matthew 25:21 and 23].

SEVEN

Who will you be in Paradise?

"Truly I say to you today, you will
be with me in Paradise."
-Luke 23:43 (REV)

THREE CATEGORIES OF PEOPLE WILL inhabit the Millennial
Kingdom—which will be Paradise restored. First--saved
Christians living at the Rapture of the Church at the close of the
Age of God's Grace when they will have met Christ "in the air," along
with all fellow Christians raised from the dead [1 Thessalonians 4:17].
Following the events of the judgment seat of Christ, they will return
with the Lord to the earth [2 Thessalonians 3:13]. Second--faithful Old
Testament and Gospel Age believers in God and in the promise of the
Messiah [the Children of Israel and others] who lived and died prior to
the Day of Pentecost, along with those who become believers in Christ
during the seven-year tribulation on the earth and who will have been
martyred for their faith. These people will be resurrected as immortals
at the resurrection of life—the first resurrection promised by Jesus in
John 5:29. This will occur early at the onset of the Millennial Kingdom.
Third--"natural" men and women who will survive the tribulation. Of
these people, possibly as many as several billion, some will be judged
"worthy" by the Lord at the Sheep and Goats Judgment [Matthew 25

(REV)] early in the Millennial Kingdom and will "inherit the kingdom." Matthew 25:46 says that they will gain eternal life. Those not judged worthy will "go away into everlasting punishment." It is likely that they will simply die during the Millennial Kingdom and be raised from the dead and judged at the Great White Throne Judgment.

"But many who are first will be last..."

In Matthew 19:16–30 (REV), a rich young ruler asks Jesus: "Teacher, what good thing must I do in order to have life *in the* Age?" Jesus answers: "...keep the commandments." The young man says: "All these things I have kept, what do I still lack?" Jesus replies: "If you *really* want to reach the goal, go, sell your possessions and give to the poor, and you will have treasure in heaven, and come, follow me." The young man "went away grieved, for he had many possessions."

Jesus tells His disciples: "Truly I say to you, it is hard for a rich man to enter the Kingdom of Heaven. And again I say to you, it is easier for a camel to go through a needle's eye than for a rich person to enter the kingdom of God." Astonished, His disciples reply: "Who then can be saved?" Jesus says: "With people this is impossible, but with God all things are possible." Peter said: "See, we have left everything and followed you, so what will we have?" Jesus replies: "Truly I say to you, that you who have followed me, in the New Beginning, when the Son of Man sits on the throne of his glory, you also will sit on 12 thrones, judging the 12 tribes of Israel. And everyone who has left houses, or brothers, or sisters, or father, or mother, or children, or lands, for my name's sake, will receive a hundredfold, and will inherit life *in the* Age *to come*. But many *who are* first will be last, and *the* last first."

The primary point that the Lord was making in this discourse with His disciples was that those who are rich and have great privilege in their lives are often the last to realize their need for a savior, whereas those who may have little in the way of resources and privilege in society in this life are often among the first. Consider Paul's teaching in 1 Corinthians 1:26 and 27 (REV): "For consider your calling, brothers, that not many wise according to the flesh, not many powerful, not many of noble birth, *are called*. But God chose the no good things of the world to put to shame those who are wise, and God chose the weak things of the world to put to shame the things which are strong...." In a deeper sense, Jesus is indicating that those who have sacrificed much in this life for the sake of the gospel will receive "a hundredfold," along with eternal life, in the age to come in terms of spiritual authority and blessings. But the many who are "first" in riches, privilege, and power in this life will be "last" in terms of inheritance in the age to come— assuming they are even saved and counted worthy of everlasting life.

In the Millennial Kingdom--

Apostle

★   If a person with the gift ministry of an Apostle has been faithful and effective in his mortal-life ministry, it is likely that he or she will work directly with the Lord Jesus Christ in the Millennial Kingdom. His ministry will be to both Christians and to the natural men and women who will inhabit the Millennial Kingdom. Billions of people will survive the catastrophic seven-year tribulation on earth. They will marry, procreate, and repopulate the earth. Apostles will be supernaturally empowered and will work in coordination with other Christian leaders as spiritual builders—developing communities of new believers among the natural men and women. According to the guidelines of the Lord's Parable of the Talents, apostles will be rewarded "ten talents ["kingdoms], or "two talents" ["kingdoms], etc., "For to everyone who has, *more* will be given, and he will have abundance" [Matthew 25:29 REV]. The Lord's eleven original apostles (excluding Judas Iscariot)— Peter, Andrew, James, John (son of Zebedee), Philip, Nathanael, Thomas, Matthew, James (son of Alphaeus), Thaddaeus, Simon, plus Mathias added later—will minister out of New Jerusalem, primarily to the Jewish people. Their names will be inscribed on the wall of the city [Revelation 21:14] and also on the gates of the districts of land to be given to the twelve tribes at the onset of the Millennial Kingdom [Ezekiel 48:31].

Prophet

★ The ministry of a Prophet of God in the Millennial Kingdom will be both to the millions of Christians and the natural men and women being drawn to the Lord at that time. Old Testament prophets such as Elijah, Elisha, Daniel, Isaiah, Jeremiah, Ezekiel, and others will be raised from the dead in the resurrection of life and will serve the Lord directly out of Holy Jerusalem, primarily on behalf of the Jewish people. The tribes of Israel will inherit all the land promised by God to Abraham, an expanse of territory stretching from "the river of Egypt [according to scholars, not the Nile but a stream south of Gaza] to the great river, the River Euphrates" on the north [Genesis 15:18,19; also see Ezekiel 47 and 48]. These people, according to a prophecy of Jeremiah, will all be immortals: "But this *is* the covenant that I will make with the house of Israel after those days [the days of the Mosaic Law], says the Lord: I will put My law in their minds, and write it on their hearts; and I will be their God, and they shall be My people. No more shall every man teach his neighbor, and every man his brother, saying, 'Know the Lord,' for they all shall know Me, from the least of them to the greatest of them, says the Lord. For I will forgive their iniquity, and their sin I will remember no more" [Jeremiah 31:33,34 NKJV]. Thus one can only speculate on the precise purposes of the ministry of these Jewish prophets. However, they will serve in accordance with the priests, the Levites, and the King [Christ] and Prince [David] in the service of the new Temple and throughout the land that the Jewish people will inherit. The Christian Prophet will be supernaturally empowered to speak for the Lord to both Christians and the natural men and women being drawn to the Lord in terms of exhortation, reproof and admonition, comfort, instruction and guidance. In the Body of Christ today, and for nearly 2,000 years since the time of the First Century Church when a true Prophet was honored, the ministry of the Prophet has been sorely unappreciated. The leadership of many large congregations today are akin to those of Israel in the days of Elijah and Ezekiel, leaders who demanded that the prophets prophecy only "good news." "Thus says the Lord God: 'Woe to the foolish prophets, who follow their own spirit and have seen nothing!...who see visions of peace for her [Jerusalem] when there is no peace, says the Lord God" [Ezekiel 13:3,16 NKJV]. It's a sad commentary on how far modern Christianity has descended into apostasy. But God's Prophets in the Millennial Kingdom will surpass even Elijah, Elisha, Ezekiel and others in their spiritual authority and honor.

Evangelist

★ The gift ministry of the Evangelist during the Millennial Kingdom will be similar in purpose to evangelism in this present Age of God's Grace. Over the centuries of the Millennial Kingdom, natural men and women will repopulate the earth and, despite living in Paradise, will need to hear the saving good news of Jesus Christ as Lord. In this present age the Evangelist may have but a modicum of success in guiding hearers to a decision for Christ. In his or her everlasting life, however, he or she will enjoy supernatural ability in preaching and convincing the people to accept and appreciate Christ as Lord and Savior.

Pastor

★ The gift ministry of the Pastor in the Millennial Kingdom will be similar to pastoring in this present age. Natural men and women will repopulate the earth in a thousand years of Paradise restored. Evangelists will guide people to a decision for Christ. Teachers will teach them the word of God. And in their natural lives—or new Christian lives-- the people will have great need for pastoring—"tending to the flock"—shepherding and dealing with the sin nature of natural people and with individual failures in relationships. In this present age the Pastor may experience good success or possibly various degrees of frustration or even "burnout" in his or her pastoral duties. However, in the Millennial Kingdom the Pastor will be supernaturally gifted and guided via the spirit of Christ to shepherd the people and tend to the flock of God he or she is given. Like Christ Himself, they will be, in every sense of the name, the "Good Shepherd."

Teacher

* The gift ministry of the Teacher in the Millennial Kingdom will be very much like that of the Teacher of God's word in this present age. In this age the Teacher may experience times of good success in his or her ability to communicate the truths of the Bible to individuals or to groups of people, or he may experience frustration or disappointment from his inability to communicate effectively. In the Millennial Kingdom, however, the Teacher will be supernaturally enabled as an educator, a tutor, an instructor *par excellence* of the truths and the joy of God's word. The ministry of the Teacher will be both to Christians and to the many natural men and women—"students"--who will repopulate the earth over the centuries and who will need to be taught the life-changing principles and truths of the Bible. The Teacher in the Millennial Kingdom will be enabled to perceive clearly, to analyze and diagnose, via the spirit, the needs of the student and to adapt as required. He or she will be liberated from the self-doubt that sometimes limits the effectiveness of the Teacher in this present age. The Teacher will radiate the knowledge and the love of God's word to every student and will delight in the understanding and the joy he or she sees blossoming in their students' minds and lives.

Exhortation

* The gift of Exhortation will be commonplace in Paradise restored. For most Christians, Exhortation is not a primary gift

but is often a complimentary gift alongside the gift ministry of a Teacher, Evangelist, or Pastor, or as a secondary gift in Leadership or other ministries. For most inhabitants of Paradise restored, especially immortals, days on end will be days of delight—the lands fertile and blossoming, rivers and seas clean and teeming with fish and other sea creatures, an abundance of food for everyone, all animals plant eaters and docile, no crime, no war, and justice for all. For the billions of natural men and women, however, human nature will sometimes foster grievances or ingratitude, and they will need Exhortation—encouragement and guidance toward a more worthy endeavor in their lives, and especially as they are being drawn to the Lord. Sometimes in this present life the words of the Exhorter fall on "deaf ears" or are taken "with a grain of salt." In the Millennial Kingdom, however, the words of the Exhorter will be as the voice of Christ Himself in their spiritual impact on the hearer.

Mercy/Compassion

*   In the Millennial Kingdom, "the quality of mercy is not strained. It droppeth as the gentle rain from heaven," to quote Shakespeare. "I desire mercy and not sacrifice, and the knowledge of God more than burnt offerings," to quote God [Hosea 6:6 NKJV]. In the seven years of tribulation on the earth, billions of people will be annihilated. However, billions will survive the cataclysm and will enter the kingdom. Because many will have suffered trauma, endured sickness and disease, as well as mental and emotional torment because of the loss of family and friends, the gift of Mercy and Compassion will be needed in abundance, especially in the first century of the kingdom. Those who have the gift of Mercy/Compassion are especially sensitive to those who are hurting. They will be supernaturally empowered to reach out to the suffering with inspired knowledge via the spirit to uplift, soothe, and heal, and to radiate the extraordinary love of God in manifestation.

Giving

* The gift of Giving in the Millennial Kingdom will be valuable, as Apostles, Evangelists, and Teachers reach out to the billions of natural men and women who will repopulate the earth over the centuries. Many people will enter the kingdom essentially destitute following seven years of tribulation on the earth and will not have the means to provide for themselves or their families. Thus there will be great need for those with the gift of Giving to meet the needs of new Christian fellowships that will form. In accompaniment with other gifts such as Hospitality, Exhortation, and Helps/Service, those with the gift of Giving will be supernaturally blessed by God with resources and enablements to help others.

Helps/Service

* In the Millennial Kingdom those with the gift of Helps/ Service will have the servant's heart and will enjoy working "behind the scenes" in new Christian fellowships to get things done. The Lord will empower and enable them wonderfully to joyfully take responsibility off the shoulders of the Leader or Administrator, and they will have no problem sacrificing time and energy to "come alongside" leaders in the church or assembly in fostering growth. They will demonstrate the love of Christ beautifully by helping to meet the group's practical needs. Acts 6:1-3 (REV) informs us that in the early years of the First Century Church: "Now in those days, when the number of the disciples was multiplying, it came about that the Grecian *Jews* grumbled against the Hebrews, because their widows were neglected in the daily distribution *of food*. And the twelve [apostles] called the multitude of the disciples to them, and said, 'It is not fitting that we should forsake the word of God to serve tables. Therefore, brothers, pick out from among you seven men of *good* reputation, full of *the* spirit and wisdom, whom we can appoint over this business." No doubt these "seven men of *good*

reputation" had exhibited in their service in the church the gift of Helps/Service and even the gift of Administration. In the Millennial Kingdom such men and women will demonstrate the love of Christ beautifully by helping to meet the group's practical needs.

Hospitality

★ In the Millennial Kingdom those with the gift of Hospitality will enjoy a home or abode that is a special place and heart of Christian ministry. Christian immortals as well as natural men and women and families seeking fellowship will love to congregate there. Hebrews 13:1 and 2 (REV) says: "Let brotherly love continue. Do not forget to show love to strangers, for by *doing* this some have entertained angels without knowing it." In the home of the person with the gift of Hospitality in Paradise restored, angels may truly visit from time to time, as well as supernaturally gifted Teachers or Prophets in order to teach, exhort, comfort, and encourage those seeking the knowledge of God and loving fellowship. Christ will supernaturally enable those with the gift of Hospitality to make all visitors in their home feel welcome, comfortable, and loved, as well as having everyone's needs provided for.

Administration

★ In the Millennial Kingdom, as many new Christian fellowships spring up, guided by gifted Pastors, Teachers, and other Leaders, those who enjoy the gift of Administration will be necessary and exalted. These immortals will be strategic thinkers, supernaturally enabled by the Lord to manage people, projects, and finances without ever being overwhelmed by tasks, in order to help the local church or assembly meet objective goals. In the Greek text the word for Administration is *kubernesis*. Specifically it means "to rule," "govern," or "to steer." Thus the Administrator in the local church in the Millennial Kingdom will be complimentary to the Pastor or Leader in helping to organize, direct, and implement plans and details, and to engage others in the various needs and ministries of the church. Consider "the seven" in Acts 6.

Leadership

⋆ The gift of Leader is often complimentary to the gift ministry of an Apostle or Pastor. The Greek word for rule—*proistemi*—means "to lead," "to assist," "to protect," and thus to care for others. In the Millennial Kingdom, those with the gift of Leader, if they are not Pastors themselves, will free the Pastor or Apostle to be more people and relationship oriented, rather than task or detail oriented in practical application. Those with the gift of Leader in the church tend also to have the gift of Exhortation and to be visionary. They will love to exhort, guide, and help others to grow spiritually in their walk with the Lord. In Paradise restored the Leader will be supernaturally enabled to see the church exalted as he helps those with other gifts to watch over the flock.

Singers, Songwriters, Musicians, Artists

Let me ask you, did you ever dream a dream or imagine with intensity a situation where a song you sang or a melody you composed and performed was so beautiful, so divinely inspired, so supernaturally uplifting, that it imparted divine healing and solicited joyous cries of thanksgiving from the hearers? I have, many times over the course of my life, when I've heard a song or other music that absolutely thrilled my heart and lifted my soul. Such will be the supernatural quality and enablement in the joyous light of Paradise restored of certain Singers, Songwriters or Composers, and Musicians who have been blessed with the gift of Music. Perhaps, in certain situations, they may even facilitate the "Shekinah glory of God" in a fellowship of those for whom they perform. There is precedent. 2 Chronicles 5:11-14 (NKJV) informs us: "And it came to pass when the priests came out of the *Most* Holy Place...and the Levites *who* were the singers...with their sons and their brethren, stood at the east end of the altar, clothed in white linen, having cymbals, stringed instruments and harps, and with them one hundred and twenty priests sounding with trumpets—indeed it came to pass, when the trumpeters and singers *were* as one, to make one sound to be heard in praising and thanking the Lord, and when they lifted up their voice with the trumpets and cymbals and instruments of music, and praised the Lord, *saying*: '*For He is* good, for His mercy *endures* forever,' that the house, the house of the Lord, was filled with a cloud, so that the priests could not continue ministering because of the cloud; for the glory of the Lord filled the house of God."

In the Millennial Kingdom in Paradise restored, joyous praise and great delight will engulf the many gatherings and fellowships of Christians and Jews and natural men and women and families seeking the face of the Lord—thrilled and inspired by the music and song of the supernaturally gifted Singers, Musicians, and others. As well, gifted artists—painters, dancers, designers, and other craftsmen—will rise above their worldly limitations, frustrations or disappointments and will be enabled supernaturally to perform or produce beyond their natural expectations. For example, a gifted painter might discover, via the spirit, new qualities and combinations of colors and produce a landscape or abstract art so infused with light or so delightfully impressionistic that it thrills the hearts and souls of the viewers. For "God is light, and in him is no darkness at all" [1 John 1:5 REV]. Such will be the honor and blessing of supernaturally gifted artists in Paradise restored. After all, consider the sweep of the night sky even in our times unencumbered by city lights—yes, the sensational ocean of stars—galaxies upon stunning galaxies--scientists say two trillion galaxies and each with an average of 100 million stars twinkling and bursting with a variety of dazzling colors. Consider the incredible variety of flora and fauna all over this tiny blue planet—the brilliant variety and colors of beautiful birds and all amazing creatures great and small—more than 350 species of hummingbirds alone! Do you think for a moment that God is done with creation—that God is finished with His magnificent *divine design?* He's just getting started!—and you and I will behold *forever* wonder upon wonder in Paradise restored and, thereafter, in the Everlasting Kingdom where new wonders of the artistic hand of God are yet to be revealed.

"Now trust is firm confidence in *things* hoped for, a conviction regarding things not seen."

-Hebrews 11:1 (REV)

Paradise restored! All the earth, the skies, the seas and lakes and rivers pure and clean and thriving with new life! No hunger, no sickness or disease, no war, no injustice—all the animals docile and plant eaters so that a little child may gently lead about a lion, a bear, a wolf like a household pet!

Too good to be true? Is it all a pipedream—a delusion, a fantasy passed down to quixotic generations from ancient times? Not according to the Bible. According to the Bible in inspired prophecy after prophecy, it will all come to pass in God's timing. And anyone hoping to participate in God's brave new world must have trust in God's word. "Trust," Paul says in Hebrews 11:1,2 (REV) (the REV uses the word "trust" for "faith"), "is firm conviction [*hypostasis*—"foundation," "confidence"] regarding things hoped for, a conviction (the NKJV says "evidence") [*elegchos*—"proof"] of things not seen. For due to it the people of old obtained a *good* testimony *from God*." The Greek word for "trust" ("faith") is *pistis*, meaning "belief," "assurance," "conviction." "And without trust it is impossible to please *him*, for whoever comes to God must believe that he is, and *that* he rewards those who seek him" [verse 6]. Not only is this principle true and vital in this mortal life, it is an essential proposition for God's promise of the life to come and Paradise restored.

Genuine trust (faith) in the promises of God generates conviction. Hebrews 12:2 (REV) says we are "fixing our eyes on Jesus, the leader and finisher of our trust, who, for the joy that was set before him [consider His glorious transfiguration on the mountain] endured the cross, thinking nothing of *the* shame, and has sat down at *the* right hand of the throne of God." As we are "looking unto Jesus"--unto everything He said and did recorded in God's word--we are looking unto "the way, and the truth, and the life," and unto all of God's "exceeding great promises, so that by them you become partakers of the divine nature..." [2 Peter 1:4 REV].

Paul says in Romans 10:17 (REV): "So then trust (faith) comes by hearing, and hearing by the message of Christ." The student who reads and studies the Bible--thereby "renewing his mind" to the living word so as not to be conformed to the deceitful patterns of this world—builds trust in the promises of God. As we pursue this course for our lives, increasingly we find that we "walk by trust (faith), not by sight," as Paul says in 2 Corinthians 5:7 (REV). Indeed, our trust actually becomes a "shield"—"In addition to all this, taking up the shield of trust (faith), with which you will be able to quench all the flaming arrows of the Wicked *one*." This is an essential feature of our putting on "the whole armor of God" described in Ephesians 6 (REV). Thus we are building our trust over time—our trust is *increased* according to 2 Corinthians 10:15--for the hope that is set before us, just as it was set before Jesus Christ.

The story of Abraham is a remarkable example in God's word of a believer whose faith (trust in God) increased over time and trial as he faithfully looked to God for strength despite the improbability, even the hopelessness, of circumstances in his life. "And without being weak in *his* trust, he considered his own body as already having become dead (he being about 100 years old), and the deadness of Sarah's womb, yet, looking to the promise of God, he was not divided *in his mind* by unbelief, but he grew strong in his trust, giving glory to God, being fully convinced that what He had promised, He was also able to do. And therefore it was credited to him for righteousness" [Romans 4:19-22 REV]. This idea that Abraham became "fully convinced [some versions of the Bible read "fully persuaded"] suggests a progression *toward* being "fully convinced." The reality is, our trust in the promises of God grows, not only as we learn about Jesus at an early age, and eventually about the meaning of "Christ in you, the hope of glory," but it grows all along the course of our lives as we act upon the promises in the Bible until obedience becomes our lifestyle. For Jesus said: "...blessed rather are those who hear the word of God and keep it!" [Luke 11:28 REV]; and God says that "He is a rewarder of those who diligently seek Him." We believe Jesus and we believe God because the Bible says so, but especially when we "keep it" and find that it is true. Indeed, the quality of our Christian life is proportional to our trust in the teachings of Jesus Christ and the promises of God. As Jesus said, "It is the spirit that gives life; the flesh profits nothing. The words that I have spoken to you are spirit, and are life" [John 6:63 REV].

Hebrews chapter 11 is a great study about trust (faith). Despite overwhelming obstacles, these Old Testament believers, composing "the great cloud of witnesses" [Hebrews 12:1 REV], by trust undaunted obtained "a good testimony" in that, "through trust, [they] conquered kingdoms, enforced righteousness, obtained promises, shut the mouths of lions, quenched the power of fire, escaped the edge of the sword, from weakness were made strong, became strong in war, put to flight foreign armies. Women received back their dead by resurrection; but others were tortured, not accepting their release in order that they would obtain a better resurrection [the resurrection of life]. And others experienced mockings and floggings, and even chains and imprisonment. They were stoned, they were sawed in two, they were murdered with the sword. They went around in sheepskins, in goatskins; being destitute, afflicted, mistreated (of whom the world was not worthy), wandering in deserts and mountains, and *hiding in* caves and the holes in the ground. And all these, through having obtained a *good* testimony because of their trust, did not receive the promise [of inheriting the land in the Millennial Kingdom], God having provided something better for us, so that they would not be made perfect apart from us. Therefore, seeing we are surrounded by so great a cloud of witnesses, let us lay aside every weight, and the sin which so easily entangles us, and let us also run with endurance the race that is set before us, fixing our eyes on Jesus, the leader and finisher of our trust, who, for the joy that was set before him, endured the cross, thinking nothing of *the* shame, and has sat down at *the* right hand of the throne of God" [Hebrews 11:33-40;12:1,2 REV].

The question is: What is this "something better for us" that God has provided? The answer is: "Christ in you, the hope of glory!" These faithful Old Testament believers, however honored in the word of God, were not "born again" by the holy spirit of Christ in them. They will be exalted and blessed by God exceedingly abundantly in the resurrection of life when they inherit the land of Israel in the Millennial Kingdom, but God has planned and prepared "something better" for His Christian sons and daughters—"For as many as are led by the spirit of God, these are sons of God. For you did not receive a spirit of slavery to fall back into fear, but you received a spirit of adoption, in *connection with* which we cry out, 'Abba,' (Father). The Spirit himself bears witness together with our spirit, that we are children of God, and if children, then heirs, on the one hand, heirs of God, and on the other hand, co-heirs with Christ..." [Romans 8:14-17 REV]. And Ephesians 1:3 (REV) assures us: "Blessed *be* the God and Father of our Lord Jesus Christ, who has blessed us in Christ with every spiritual blessing in the heavenly *places....*" We are *heirs of God and co-heirs with Christ!* We have been blessed with *every spiritual blessing in the heavenly places in Christ!* "Thanks be to God for his indescribable gift!" [2 Corinthians 9:15 REV].

This "something better for us" that God has planned for and is already providing (for "we walk by faith and not by sight") includes the Rapture of the Church when we see Him "as He is" and receive our new bodies conformed to His glorious body, yes; it includes the glorious crowns and other rewards to be presented at the judgment seat of Christ, yes; it includes our everlasting lives in the Millennial Kingdom as we reign with Christ and judge the nations. And I have an inkling--in Paradise restored in my fabulous new body, *I can fly!* And maybe you can too! I can open the eyes of the blind! I can unstop the ears of the deaf! I can enjoy and function in my spiritual gifts "exceeding abundantly beyond all that we ask or think, according to the power that works in us" [Ephesians 3:20 REV]. "For who has come to know the mind of the Lord so as to instruct him? But *we have the mind of Christ!*" [1 Corinthians 2:16 REV, italics supplied]. And it is "the mind of Christ" *in us* that will become fully realized in our everlasting lives in Paradise restored, especially in those Christians who have remained faithful to the Lord throughout their lives. Indeed, my brothers and sisters—"Trust is the firm confidence in *things* hoped for, a conviction regarding things not seen."

"For the gifts and the calling of God are irrevocable."
-Romans 11:29 (REV)

Life is short. The psalmist says: "The days of our lives *are* seventy years; and if by reason of strength *they* are eighty years, yet their boast *is* only labor and sorrow; for it is soon cut off, and we fly away" [Psalm

90:10 NKJV]. James 4:14 (REV) puts it this way: "…you who do not know what tomorrow *will bring*. For what is your life? For you are a vapor that appears for a little while and then vanishes away." And 1 Peter 1:24,25 (REV) echo the same: "For, **All flesh is like grass, and all its glory is like the flower of grass. The grass withers, and the flower falls, but the word of the Lord remains forever.**"

This fragile mortal life, however full for some or brief for others, is a proving ground for our eternal destiny. For those who, at sometime in their lives, confess Jesus Christ as their Lord and Savior and believe in their hearts that God has raised Him from the dead, there is the "hope of glory" in Paradise restored, along with wonderful rewards: For "…each one's work will become plainly seen; for the Day will make it clear, because it will be revealed by [spiritual] fire, and the fire itself will test each one's work, *and show* of what kind it is. If anyone's work that he has built on it remains, he will receive a reward. If anyone's work is burned, he will suffer loss, but he himself will be saved, but it will be like escaping through fire" [1 Corinthians 3:13-15 REV]. And for those Christians who discover and learn to function effectively in their spiritual gifts, there will be great reward in Paradise restored in terms of exalted identity, spiritual authority and fulfilling missions for the Lord. Some will even enjoy a presence and personality infused with the likeness of Christ in His glory. Philippians 2:15 (REV) says that "we shine as lights in the world" in a figurative sense, but in the kingdom some faithful believers will literally shine with the likeness of Christ. A prophecy in Daniel 12:3 (NKJV) speaks to this reality: "Those who are wise shall shine like the brightness of the firmament, and those who turn many to righteousness like the stars forever and ever." Stars differ in their magnitude and luminosity. Likewise, even God's angels have varying degrees of authority and, one might surmise, brightness. Michael and Gabriel, the Bible says, are God's archangels, while other angels are subordinate. Lucifer [called "the king of Tyre" in Ezekiel 28] was "the seal of perfection, Full of wisdom and perfect in beauty. You were in Eden, the garden of God; Every precious stone *was* your covering…until iniquity was found in you" [Ezekiel 28:12b,13a,15b NKJV]. Is it possible that some saints of

God will shine even brighter and more beautifully than Lucifer in Paradise restored?

The probing question arises: How are we doing in our quest to be transformed in our character into the character of Christ? How are we doing progressively in the functioning of our spiritual gifts, whether as an exhorter, or helper, or giver, or in hospitality, or in mercy, or as an administrator, or leader, or intercessor, or teacher, or evangelist, or pastor, or as a singer, or composer, or artist? "For the gifts and the calling of God are irrevocable" [Romans 11:29 REV]. Other versions of the Bible say: "For God's gifts and His call can never be withdrawn," and "unrepentant of are the gifts and the call of God," and "He does not withdraw what He has given," and "the gifts and the calling of God are not subject to repentance." In other words, for the Christian, the gifts and the calling of God go with us into eternity and *characterize* who we will be and what we will be doing forever.

Alas, for those Christians who squander many of the days of their lives in the pursuit of the self-centered cares of this world, "he himself will be saved" [1 Corinthians 3:15] and will appreciate everlasting life in Paradise restored, and yet, perhaps, will, even in the midst of the joy and thanksgiving of salvation, may, for a long, long time, endure a haunting regret that he could have and should have done much better in his brief mortal life. And he may be reminded of this time and again when he meets believers whose rewards and glorious presence outshine his own. And, again I say, this is *forever.*

For the unbeliever and the God-rejecter throughout the centuries of human history—"everlasting destruction from the presence of the Lord." For it is "a clear indication of the righteous judgment of God, that you [Christians] are counted worthy of the Kingdom of God, for which you also are suffering. For indeed, it is a righteous thing with God to repay with affliction those who are afflicting you, and to *give* relief to you who are being afflicted, as well as to us, when the Lord Jesus is revealed from heaven with his powerful angels, in flaming fire inflicting vengeance on those who do not know God and on those who do not obey the Good News of our Lord Jesus. These will pay the penalty: cut off forever from the face of the Lord and from the glory of His strength, when he comes to be glorified in his holy *ones* [all believers] and to be marveled at by all those who believe (*this includes you* because our testimony to you was believed in that day" [2 Thessalonians 1:5-10 REV]. Indeed, this "cut off forever from the face of the Lord" (the NKJV reads "everlasting destruction") is what Revelation 20:14 calls "the second death."

Christianity is "the way, and the truth, and the life."

Consider this: Christianity is not merely one of the religions competing with the religions of the world; Christianity, in essence, is "the way, and the truth, and the life." All other religions are counterfeits of the truth, notwithstanding that some of their values may be similar to Christian values. Because, as my old Bible teacher used to say, "the closer the counterfeit is to the truth, the more effective is the counterfeit." Satan is the author of all counterfeit religions. In Deuteronomy 6:4 (NKJV) God, via Moses, declares: "Hear, O Israel: the Lord our God, the Lord is one!" And in chapter 5:7-9 (NKJV): "You shall have no other gods before Me. You shall not make for yourself a carved image—any likeness of anything that is in heaven above, or that is in the earth beneath, or that is in the water under the earth; you shall not bow down to them, nor serve them. For I, the Lord your God, am a jealous God…." And in Deuteronomy 12:2 and 3 (NKJV), God tells Israel: "You shall utterly destroy all the places where the nations which you shall dispossess served their gods, on the high mountains and on the hills and under every green tree. And you shall destroy their altars, break their sacred pillars, and burn their wooden images with fire; you shall cut down the carved images of their gods and destroy their names from that place. You shall not worship the Lord your God with such images." God explains it all in 21:18: "lest they teach you to do according to all their abominations which they have done for their gods, and you sin against the Lord your God." And the record shows that the Children of Israel did precisely that: "They did not destroy the peoples, concerning whom the Lord had commanded them, but they mingled with the Gentiles and learned their works; They served their idols, which became a snare to them. They even sacrificed their sons and their daughters to demons, and shed innocent blood, the blood of their sons and daughters, whom they sacrificed to the idols of Canaan; And the land was polluted with blood. Thus they were defiled by their own works, and played the harlot by their own deeds" [Psalm 106:34-39 NKJV].The psalmist says: "Their idols *are* silver and gold, the works of men's hands. They have mouths, but they do not speak; eyes they have, but they do not see; they have ears but they do not hear; noses they have, but they do not smell; they have hands, but they do not handle; feet they have, but they do not walk; nor do they mutter through their throat. Those who make them are like them; *so is* everyone who trusts in them" [Psalm 115:4-8 NKJV]. In our day and time God has not changed His mind regarding satanic counterfeit religions. His original principle stands firm—"lest they teach you to do according to all their abominations ...." Little has changed in human societies since God's commandments to the Children of Israel to abhor and destroy all vestiges of counterfeit religions— except for the coming of the Son of God, mankind's Redeemer. All counterfeit religions of the world *reject* Jesus Christ as the Son of God. Their rejection of Christ is the foundation of God's condemnation. Paul writes: ("But even if our Good News is veiled, it is veiled to those who are perishing, in whom the god of this world [Satan] has blinded the minds of those who do not believe, to keep them from seeing *and shining forth* the light of the Good News of the glory of Christ, who is the image of God) [2 Corinthians 4:3,4 REV]. And 1 Peter 4:5 (REV): "They [unbelievers] will give account to him who is ready to judge the living and the dead!" The reality is, every counterfeit religion is a satanic seduction that leads its adherents away from the truth that is Jesus Christ. No one who is a follower of a counterfeit religion gets "born again," and "flesh and blood is not able to inherit the Kingdom of God; neither does corruption inherit incorruption" [1 Corinthians 15:50 REV]. During the Great Tribulation on the earth, I believe God will utterly lay waste to all the altars, the sacred pillars, the manmade images, statues, temples, mosques, and edifices of all satanic religions that represent a fundamental contradiction to the life, teaching, and truth of Jesus Christ. This will culminate in the capture and destruction of the beast [Antichrist] and the false prophet who will have deceived the whole world [with oppressive counterfeit religion] and perpetrated "the abomination of desolation" [Matthew 24:15,16; Daniel 9:27;11:31; Revelation 19:20] in the temple in Jerusalem. Let it be noted, however, that there remains the promise of the Sheep and Goats Judgment at the onset of the Millennial Kingdom in which some individuals who survived the carnage of the Great Tribulation will be judged "worthy" to enter the kingdom based on the attitude of their minds and hearts in helping others over the course of their lives.

"Knowing this first, that in the last days mockers will come..."
2 Peter 3:3 (REV)

"Knowing this first, that in the last days mockers will come with mockery," the Apostle Peter warns in his second letter to the Church, "walking after their own lusts, and saying, 'Where is the promise of his coming? For, from the day that the Fathers fell asleep, all things continue as they were from the beginning of the creation.' For this they willingly forget: that by the word of God *the* heavens existed long ago, and *the* earth was formed out of the water and by water, by which means the world that was *back* then, having been inundated with water, perished. But the heavens that are, and the earth, by the same word have been reserved for fire, being kept for the day of judgment and destruction of ungodly people. But do not forget this one thing, beloved, that with the Lord one day is as 1,000 years, and 1,000 years are as one day. The Lord is not slack concerning his promise, as some count slackness, but is longsuffering toward you, not wishing that any should perish, but that all should come to repentance. But the Day of the Lord will come as a thief, in which the heavens will pass away with a great noise, and the elements will be dissolved with fervent heat, and the earth and the works that are in it will be burned up. Seeing that all these things are to be destroyed in this way, what sort of people do you need to be in your holy manner of life and godliness as you wait for and earnestly desire the coming of the Day of God, because of which the heavens, being on fire, will be destroyed, and the elements will melt with the intense heat? But, according to his promise, we look for new heavens and a new earth [Revelation 21] in which dwells righteousness" [2 Peter 3:3-13 REV].

Peter's prophecy of the final events of the Day of the Lord, "in which the heavens will pass away with a great noise, and the elements will be dissolved with fervent heat, and the earth and the works that are in it will be burned up," perplexed me for years. This is the cataclysmic event or series of events phasing out the Millennial Kingdom and ushering in the Everlasting Kingdom with "a new heaven and a new earth." Why, I wondered, would God feel a need to destroy Paradise restored in order to bring about a new era? For the purposes of this study, I looked into what some of the most insightful Bible commentators had to say about this. First, some background. Isaiah prophesied: "For behold, I create new heavens and a new earth; and the former shall not be remembered or come to mind" [Isaiah 65:17 NKJV]. And Isaiah 66:22 (NKJV): "For as the new heavens and the new earth which I will make shall remain before Me," says the Lord, "so shall your descendants and your name remain." "But, according to his promise," Peter says, "we look for new heavens and a new earth in which dwells righteousness." The question arises: Will righteousness not dwell in the Millennial Kingdom? The answer is, yes, of course it will, but also iniquity will be found increasingly in the latter years of the kingdom. Many natural men and women living in the kingdom will turn to the Lord in time and be granted everlasting life, but many will not. They will continue to live according to their sin nature. Finally, "and when the 1,000 years are finished, the Adversary will be loosed out of his prison and will come out to deceive the nations that are in the four corners of the earth, Gog and Magog, to gather them together to the war, the number of whom is as the sand of the sea. And they went up over the breadth of the earth and surrounded the camp of the holy *ones* and the beloved city, and fire came down out of heaven and devoured them" [Revelation 20:7-9 REV]. Even in Paradise restored, when Satan is released, he and his millions of demons will deceive the nations into total rebellion against God and His Son. God will utterly destroy them—and that will be the end of all natural men and women in the kingdom. Only immortals, both Jews and Christians, will inhabit the Everlasting Kingdom. And because iniquity—unrighteousness—will have polluted the Millennial Kingdom in the end, "both the earth and the works that are in it will be burned up." Just as the flood was the first baptism of the earth [Genesis

1:2 NKJV]: "The earth was without form, and void; and darkness was on the face of the deep. And the Spirit of God was hovering over the face of the waters"], even so God's baptism of the earth by fire will purify the earth and cleanse it wholly from Adam's curse described in Genesis 3. Peter states it succinctly: "For this they willingly forget, that by the word of God *the* heavens existed long ago, and *the* earth was formed out of water and by water, by which means the world that was *back* then, having been inundated with water, perished [the initial baptism, as the result of the cataclysm which occurred between Genesis 1:1 and 1:2; see chapter 2, subhead: The Bible and Science]. If one considers Noah's flood to be a second baptism which only partially cleansed the earth of human iniquity [Genesis 6:9 (NKJV) tells us that "Noah was a just man, perfect in his generations. Noah walked with God"], but Noah was a man under the curse of Adam, and he and his family repopulated the earth, perpetuating the curse. "But the heavens that now are, and the earth, by the same word have been *reserved for fire* [italics supplied—a third and final baptism], being kept for the day of judgment and destruction of ungodly people" [2 Peter 3:5,6 REV].

Peter says that "we look for new heavens and a new earth in which dwells righteousness" [2 Peter 3:13 REV]. This is because all pollutions will have been removed by God's baptism by fire. There will never be a hint of unrighteousness in the Everlasting Kingdom. Moreover, some commentators state that the earth as it will exist in the Millennial Kingdom, although it is destined to be burned up, will not be destroyed in the sense of being annihilated; rather, in the end it will actually be renewed and refined and purged by fire from all immoral and natural imperfection. Thus the ultimate purpose of the Millennial Kingdom is to prepare the earth for the coming of Almighty God in the fullness of His glory *to the earth* and to reign in the Everlasting Kingdom in the very presence of His people forever and ever. As Paul points out: "Then *comes* the end, when He [Christ] delivers the kingdom to God, even the Father, after he [Christ] brings to an end all rule and all authority and power. For it is necessary for him to reign until he has put all his enemies under his feet. *The* last enemy *that will be* brought to an end *is* death [at the Great White Throne Judgment]. For he [God] has put all things in subjection under his [Christ's] feet. But when it says, 'All things have been put in subjection,' it is clear that the one [God] who subjected all things to him [Christ] is not included. And when all things have been subjected to him [Christ], then the Son will subject himself to him [God] who subjected all things to him [Christ], so that God is all in all" [1 Corinthians 15:24-28 REV]. "O the depth of the riches of both the wisdom and knowledge of God! How unsearchable are his judgments and untraceable his ways!" [Romans 11:33 REV]. Indeed, it is impossible in our finite human thinking to even imagine the awesomeness of God's authority and His plans for the future of His faithful people.

Perhaps like many faithful believers, I have wondered exactly what Peter meant when he prophesied that "we look for new heavens and a new earth in which dwells righteousness," and also what it will be like on the earth when, according to John's prophecy: "Look! The tabernacle of God is with man, and he will dwell with them, and they will be his people, and God himself will be with them, *and be* their God" [Rev. 21:3 REV]. In the garden of Eden, before the fall, God was personally present with the first man and woman. And because 1 John 1:5 (REV) informs us that "God is light, and in him there is no darkness at all," it must have been a beautiful time in that garden; in fact, there must have existed a *different dimension* altogether from what we perceive and are conscious of today. In the Greek text, the word "dwell" is the word *katoikei*. It means "settle in," "inhabit," "to house permanently." In the Everlasting Kingdom, when God *dwells with us,* it will be a *wonderful new dimension* of righteousness which we will enjoy—it will be the physical existence of the transfiguring light of God's presence that we will perceive. It will be even more beautiful, more inspiring, more healing, more delightful than the soft morning light of a spring morning we might enjoy today. It will be heaven on earth.

"KING OF KINGS, AND LORD OF LORDS"
-Revelation 19:16 (REV)

In the Millennial Kingdom Christ will reign as King of Kings and Lord of Lords from the magnificent new temple in Holy Jerusalem. "Many nations shall come and say, 'Come, and let us go up to the mountain of the Lord, to the house of the God of Jacob; He will teach us His ways, and we shall walk in His paths" [Micah 4:2 NKJV]. All Christian saints in the kingdom will also enjoy the privilege of making a pilgrimage to Holy Jerusalem from time to time. We will "enter into His gates with thanksgiving, *and* into His courts with praise" [Psalm 100:4 NKJV]. And at that time the Lord may put a new song of praise and joy and thanksgiving in the mouths and on the lips of His people as we worship Him in the temple—"Oh, sing to the Lord a new song! For He has done marvelous things; His right hand and His holy arm have gained Him the victory!" [Psalm 98:1 NKJV]. What a time of incomparable joy and fellowship that will be—"Praise the Lord! Praise God in His sanctuary; Praise Him in His mighty firmament! Praise Him for His mighty acts; Praise Him according to His excellent greatness! Praise Him with the sound of the trumpet; Praise Him with the lute and harp! Praise Him with the timbrel and dance; Praise Him with stringed instruments and flutes! Praise Him with loud cymbals; Praise Him with clashing cymbals! Let everything that has breath praise the Lord! Praise the Lord!" [Psalm 150:1-6 NKJV]. However, in the Everlasting Kingdom, there will be no need of a temple in the great city, the holy Jerusalem, "for the Lord God Almighty and the Lamb are its temple. And the city [will have] no need of the sun or of the moon to shine in it, for the glory of God [will] illuminate it. The Lamb *is* its light" [Rev. 21:22,23 NKJV].

When Jesus began His earthly ministry in Galilee and "manifested His glory" so that "his disciples believed in Him" [John 2:11 REV], He enjoyed the fellowship of a wedding feast in the village of Cana. Surely at that feast He partook of a glass of the "good wine" [verse 10] that He produced from the water in the waterpots of stone. Won't it be delightful when we all—yes, you and I--and perhaps in the company of our families and many other immortal brothers and sisters, join the Lord Jesus Christ in sharing a glass of the "good wine" at a wedding feast or at many other festive occasions? What marvelous times they will be!

As well, when Jesus revealed Himself to His disciples at the Sea of Tiberias [Sea of Galilee] after His resurrection [John 21], He prepared a breakfast of fried fish and bread for Peter and the disciples after they

182

had gone fishing. "When they had finished breakfast, Jesus says to Simon Peter, 'Simon *son* of John, do you love me?'" [John 21:16 REV]. Peter replied nervously, "Yes, Lord, you know that I am your friend." This occurred three times and each time Jesus said to Peter, "Feed my lambs...Tend my sheep...Feed my sheep." This was a prescient hour when the Lord commissioned Peter to take the gospel of Jesus Christ to the Jewish nation and, in league with Paul and many others, to the whole world—"But you will receive power when the holy spirit has come upon you, and you will be my witnesses both in Jerusalem, and in all Judea and Samaria, and to the uttermost part of the earth" [Acts 1: 8 REV]. In a general sense, this occasion marked the dawn of Christianity—a movement that eventually enraptured billions of people all over the earth in every tribe and nation and generation—including you and I—so that we might enjoy everlasting life in Paradise! And so I say, Come! Yes, come with me, my brothers and sisters, come to the pristine beach along the shores of the Sea of Galilee in Paradise restored. We are invited to join the Lord Jesus Christ Himself as He prepares a fish fry for all of us! And Simon Peter will be there! Yes, it will be a marvelous reunion of Peter, and Thomas, and Nathanael, and the sons of Zebedee, and many other disciples. And Mary Magdalene will be there! And Mary the mother of Jesus! And the beloved disciple! And Lazarus! And we will rejoice together as the family of God in a heavenly Paradise!

Moreover, from time to time, just as described in the Beatitudes, the Lord Himself may visit His people in the valleys, in the hills, on the plains, by the lakes and rivers, and we--His glorified, beloved friends--will bring to Him the little children so that He may hug and bless them,--"for of such is the Kingdom of God." And in speaking to us with words of encouragement and dedication, the Lord might even say: "Blessed are you who have hungered and thirsted for righteousness, for you have now been filled! Blessed are you who mourned and were poor in spirit, for yours--now and forever--is the Kingdom of Heaven! And blessed are you—the merciful—for you have now obtained mercy. And blessed are you—the peacemakers—for you are now the sons of God. And blessed are you who were

persecuted for righteousness' sake, for, behold!—now and forever--
yours is the Kingdom of Heaven!"

**"Look!, I am coming quickly, and
my reward is with me, to render to
each one according to his work."**
-Revelation 22:12 (REV}

ABOUT THE AUTHOR

When I was twelve years old, I loved to listen to a Sunday evening radio broadcast entitled *The Master Speaks*. I'd lay in bed thinking about school the next day, and then I'd hear the narrator say: "Come with us to the hillsides of Galilee. The people have gathered there to hear the Master." Then the narrator would say: "Listen! The Master speaks." And I'd picture Jesus standing in the sun by the seaside. And in a deep reassuring voice He'd begin to speak intriguing words that always touched my heart: "I am the way, and the truth, and the life. No one comes to the Father except through Me." And: "I am the light of the world. He who follows Me shall not walk in darkness, but have the light of life." Sometimes it seemed like He was speaking to me face to face. It was during one of those Sunday evenings listening to the Master speak that I gave my heart to Jesus and confessed Him as my Lord and Savior. I believe I was baptized in holy spirit at that time but, of course, I did not even realize it.

Throughout high school and college, occasionally I would seek out Bible study groups, but mostly I was out of touch with Jesus until many years later. Those years of wandering and how I kept searching for the "light" in all the wrong places—including hallucinogenic drugs and Eastern religions—are revealed in my first book--*The Hope of Glory: In Search of the Light*-- published in 1979. The truth is, I had become a drug addict at that time in my life—obsessed with seeking a return to the hallucinogenic ecstasy of the "Clear Light of the Void" and the Buddha state of mind that the "sacrament" of mescaline powder induced for me. In time I became borderline schizophrenic—longing for the enchanting

185

experience of the counterfeit "light" of drug-induced Nirvana and yet having to make a living in an uncaring world. After months of sorrow and yearning for the experience of the "light," which over time seemed to have faded into some distant imperial realm despite my stronger doses of the "sacrament," I was at the end of my rope and even considered running off to the desert to join Timothy Leary who had earlier encouraged me to "turn on, tune in, and drop out." Until one night I met a remarkable new friend with whom I had a compelling discussion about it all. His name was Daniel. In our discussion about the "light," and when I finally complained to him—"Daniel, how do I get back to the 'light?' I can't seem to get to the 'light' anymore, no matter how much mescaline I snort"--I will never forget what Daniel replied on that transformative night of my life. He said: "Don't you remember the One who said: 'I am the light of the world. He who follows Me shall not walk in darkness, but have the light of life?'" And that evening in a dimly lighted cubicle of a bath house on the south-side of San Francisco, I came back home to the loving presence of my Lord and Savior Jesus Christ.

A week or so later Daniel introduced me to friends involved in a sweet fellowship of Christian believers where I began to learn simple Bible principles of "power for abundant living." I was hungry to learn and signed up for an intensive 30-hour film class all about keys to understanding the Bible. As the hours of the class unfolded over several evenings, I felt ushered into the presence of the Lord by the gracious words that the teacher spoke. "The word of God is living," the teacher would say, "and powerful, and sharper than any two-edged sword, piercing even to the division of soul and spirit, and of joints and marrow, and is a discerner of the thoughts and intents of the heart." It was about halfway through the class when the teacher in the film stood up from his desk and, walking toward the camera, and seeming to point directly at me, said: "To you God willed to make known what are the riches of the glory of this mystery among the Gentiles: which is *Christ in you, Christ in you, Christ in YOU*—the hope of glory!" At that moment it was as if the holy spirit in me leaped for joy as my heart burned with a hunger to understand, and I knew at that moment that I had made a silent vow to search and to discover just what "Christ in you!" was all about.

Even before completing that Bible class, I asked my friend Daniel about the baptism in the holy spirit and the manifestations of the spirit of speaking in tongues, interpretation of tongues and prophecy that I saw and heard being practiced during the fellowship meetings. As Daniel demonstrated speaking in tongues for me, I asked him: "Can I do it?" He said: "Sure, if you want to. You're born again of the spirit." As he taught me the simple principles of how to speak in tongues and its amazing benefits, I too began speaking "the wonderful works of God" that very evening. Over the next days and weeks I would go out to the cliffs overlooking the Pacific Ocean and, high above the rolling waves of the ocean and beneath the dazzling blue sky, I would speak in tongues much so that soon my words were like "rivers of living water" flowing up and out of my belly toward heaven.

It's been more than fifty years since I began that hallowed quest to discover the meaning of "Christ in you, the hope of glory." A few months after graduating from that life-changing Bible class, I left San Francisco to participate in the summer school classes and activities of a four-campus international biblical research and teaching center headquartered in west-central Ohio. In my hunger to learn and my zeal for the word of God, at the conclusion of the summer school program I was invited to join the staff of that ministry. As God provided over time, I spent nearly fifteen years on staff (and afterwards with my own publishing business in association with the ministry), rising to the level of managing editor of publications, a member of the faculty, and a member of the President's Cabinet of directors. I confess—it was all a labor of love.

In 2011 I finally published my second book which I had been working on for years—*The Secret to Holy Spirit Authority: In the Power of the Spirit*. And in 2014 came *The Voice of My Brother's Blood: A Love Story,* a memoir of my years in that evangelical ministry.

Indeed, in my more than 78 years of living and loving life, I have "tasted that the Lord is gracious." *Your Everlasting Life: Who Will You Be in Paradise?* is the culmination of my years of study and teaching. I consider it the crowning achievement of my life's work. Certain revelations in the book may be shocking to some readers but, I'm sure, a joy and encouragement to others. My hope and prayer is that it will inspire all who read it toward a more worthy endeavor in the upward call of God in Christ Jesus.

David Charles Craley
Spring 2022

BIBLIOGRAPHY

Custance, Arthur C., *Without Form And Void, A Study of the Meaning of Genesis 1:2,* © 1970, Arthur C. Custance, Classic Reprint Press, Windber PA, 2008.

Delumeau, Jean, *History Of Paradise, The Garden of Eden in Myth and Tradition,* © 1995 by The Continuum Publishing Company, New York.

Howard, Rick; Lash, Jamie, *This Was Your Life!, Preparing to Meet God Face to Face,* © 1998, Published by Chosen Books, Grand Rapids MI.

Fortune, Don & Katie, *Discover Your God-Given Gifts,* © 1987, 2009, Published by Chosen Books, Grand Rapids MI.

Boyd, Gregory, *God of the Possible, A Biblical Introduction to the Open View of God,* © 2000, Published by Baker Books, Grand Rapids MI, 2004.

Gill, John, 1697-1771, *Exposition of the Bible,* © 2021 *John Gill's Exposition of the Bible,* Christianity.com.

Schoenheit, John W., *The Bible, You Can Believe It,* © 2002, 2005, Christian Educational Services, Indianapolis IN.

Schoenheit, John W., *The Christian's Hope, The Anchor of the Soul,* © 2001 Christian Educational Services, Indianapolis IN.

Wierwille, Victor Paul, *Are the Dead Alive Now?* © 1971 by The Devin-Adair Company, Old Greenwich CT.

BIBLIOGRAPHY